T0301028

Mapping China's Growth and Development in the Long Run

221 BC to 2020

Mapping China's Growth and Development in the Long Run

221 BC to 2020

Kent Deng

The London School of Economics and Political Science

World Scientific

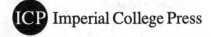
ICP Imperial College Press

Published by

World Scientific Publishing Co. Pte. Ltd.

5 Toh Tuck Link, Singapore 596224

USA office: 27 Warren Street, Suite 401-402, Hackensack, NJ 07601

UK office: 57 Shelton Street, Covent Garden, London WC2H 9HE

Library of Congress Cataloging-in-Publication Data
Deng, Kent G.
    Mapping China's growth and development in the long run, 221 BC to 2020 / Kent G. Deng.
      pages cm
    Includes bibliographical references and index.
    ISBN 978-9814667555 (alk. paper)
    1. Economic development--China--History. 2. China--Economic conditions. 3. China--Social
conditions. 4. China--History. I. Title.
    HC427.6.D465 2015
    338.951--dc23

                        2015015329

British Library Cataloguing-in-Publication Data
A catalogue record for this book is available from the British Library.

In-house Editor: Dong Lixi

Typeset by Stallion Press
Email: enquiries@stallionpress.com

Printed in Singapore

Contents

About the Author

Dr. Kent G. Deng has a PhD in Economics. He joined London School of Economics and Political Science (LSE) in 1995. He is now Reader in Economic History at the LSE and Fellow of the Royal Historical Society. At LSE, he teaches a number of courses on shipping and sea power in Asian waters, economic growth and development in China, economic growth and development in East Asia, the state and the market in the developing world, and comparisons between Europe and Asia in history.

Dr. Deng is specialized in economic history of China over the long run, including both premodern (pre-1800) and modern (post-1800) periods. He has published six monographs, fifteen journal articles, and eleven book chapters. His publications cover a wide range of areas including growth and development in maritime activities, agriculture, state-building and governance, modernization, economic reforms and globalization. He is also active in the media with regular interviews with the BBC and other news providers.

Preface

This book is based on my MSc course 'Economic Development in East and Southeast Asia' (EH446) which I have been teaching over the past two decades at the London School of Economics and Political Science. In that guided reading course, China counts for about a quarter of the total weight.

Incidentally, when I first joint the LSE in the mid-1990s, teaching China was not yet in high demand. I taught specific country cases of Russia, India, and Japan. China was 'buried' in the 'developing world of Asia, Africa and Latin America'. In the recent decade, though, China has quickly become one of the key subject areas at the LSE across just about all departments. It is my hope that this book can make some contribution to our collective understanding of China and its growth and development over the very long run.

I wish to thank my departmental colleagues Professors Patrick O'Brien, Colin Lewis, Janet Hunter, Gareth Austin, Peter Howlett, and Larry Epstein with whom I have enjoyed teaching for two decades.

Kent G. Deng
London
2015

Chapter One

Introduction

1. General Focus of the Book

China has long been recognised in the field of world history as a sophisticated civilisation during the pre-modern or pre-industrial era. Her remarkable advancement ranged widely from governance, technology, education, production, consumption, distribution to commercial activities. China remained the leader in East Asia in just about all aspects of socio-political and economic life.

But that view applies to the history prior to 1800: many were convinced that China's glory on the world stage was finally over thereafter, judging from her turbulent and often extremely violent history from the late nineteenth to late twentieth centuries. Until recently, China still bore the demeaning nickname of the 'Sick Man of Asia'. Against this backdrop, China has taken the world by surprise in the past three decades or so with her new growth and development on a record scale and scope, as well as the incredible speed at which it took place. So much so, 'when China takes over the United States', is no longer pure speculation.

China's bouncing back is probably the most sensational turn-around in the past 200 years of world history. This book aims to show why and how China has been the civilisation as it is. In particular, this book will take the reader through China's history in terms of growth conditions and patterns, key factors, and main landmarks over the very long run so that the country and its history can be better understood. The narrative of China's history in this book is 'theme-led' rather than conventionally chronicle-based.

1

2. General Debates on China's Growth Performance

There is a division between China as a cultural/civilisational entity and China as a body of polity. The former began much earlier than the latter, although both were interconnected. From the viewpoint of a relatively stable ideological, political, economic and record-keeping system within a relatively stable territory, China began with the Qin Empire (221–207 BC). China has continued in such a manner to become the longest lasting empire in the world. This is where the present narrative begins.

So far, one debating point on China has been about how distinctive the empire has been in world history. Accounts by early travellers, such as the ninth century merchant Sulaiman al-Tajir, Marco Polo (1254–1324), Mateo Ricci (1552–1610), Sir George Staunton (1781–1859), and Évariste Régis Huc (or the Abbé Huc, 1813–1860), all showed the uniqueness of China in numerous ways. It was such uniqueness that inspired European thinkers including René Descartes (1596–1650) and Francois Quesnay (1694–1772) to consciously learn from China in various ways. The same uniqueness also forced Karl Marx to treat Asia differently in the form of the 'Asiatic Mode of Production',[1] leaving Asia out of his universal developmental mainstream.

In post-1949 Mainland China, however, there has been a dogmatic view that China's history was subject to a universal iron law advocated by the Marxists. China has been re-interpreted as more or less another Europe, only developing more slowly. To align with that view, post-221 BC China has been relabelled as a 'feudal' society and a 'sprouting capitalism' headed for its full potential if without external interferences.[2] The evidence cited has been (1) the alleged 'all land under the sky belonging to the King' cited in a lone and romantic classic composed four centuries prior to the formation of the Qin Empire,[3] and (2) profit-making activities recorded throughout China's historical records. The problem is that if

---

[1] F. L. Pryor, 'The Asian Mode of Production as an Economic System', *Journal of Comparative Economics*, 4/4 (1980), pp. 420–442. Its spin-off was K. A. Wittfogel, *Oriental Despotism — A Comparative Study of Total Power* (New Haven: Yale University Press, 1957).

[2] Xu Dixin and Wu Chengming (eds.), *Zhongguo Ziben Zhuyide Mengya* (*Sprouting Capitalism in China*) (Beijing: People's Press, 1985).

[3] Anon., *Shi Jing* (*Book of Odes*), ch. 'Xiaoya'.

traditional China did not have private property rights for the ordinary producers. Where did China's active market and economic freedom come from? Another point is the assertion of classes and class struggle between feudal masters and feudal serfs in China's countryside, and between the bourgeoisie and the proletariat in China's cities that seems to justify the alleged inevitable phase of communism in the wake of capitalism. Dogmatists often forget the Marxian 'Asiatic Mode of Production', which excluded China from feudalism or rudimentarily capitalism altogether. According to Marx's own logic, therefore, a society under the Asiatic Mode of Production is remote to communism.

Marxism aside, there has been a lively debate on why and how China slowed down after its glory achieved during the Song Period (960–1279). A repertoire explanation is that a Malthusian crisis emerged due to a declining man-to-land ratio in the country after c.1500.[4] This explanation is valid if China developed or adopted no new technology in food production during this period. Given that the 'New-World crops' — white potatoes, sweet potatoes and maize — as well as the practice of rice double-cropping were all introduced to China during this time, and given that vast farming regions in Mongolia, Manchuria, and Sichuan Basin were opened up for internal migration, the man-to-land ratio explanation becomes questionable.

Another explanation is the bureaucracy that lacked interest in allocating resources for technical learning and development. Therefore, China did not have a scientific revolution and/or industrial revolution.[5] However, the actual number of literati members who managed to get into officialdom during any given period in China's history was tiny. If so, it was almost certain that a large proportion of the literati joined other strata to make a living. Besides, during the Song Period, when bureaucrat recruitment examinations really took off, China's technology thrived. There was no particular reason for such symbiosis to stop in the post-Song era.

The third popular explanation attributes China's problem to endogenous factors or external forces. The Song growth ended with the Mongol

---

[4]Kang Chao, *Man and Land in Chinese History: An Economic Analysis* (Stanford: Stanford University Press, 1986).
[5]Mark Elvin, *The Pattern of the Chinese Past* (Stanford: Stanford University Press, 1973), ch. 17.

invasion and conquest of China. Mongol discrimination against the Han Chinese followed. During the late Qing, there were the rise in opium trade, the outbreak of the opium wars (1839–42 and 1856–60), the Sino-French War (1884–5), the Sino-Japanese Wars (1894–5, 1931–45) and consequential unequal treaties imposed on China. Without a doubt, these interferences slowed China down and changed China's growth trajectory. But, the conventional wisdom often views the Mongol Period (1279–1368) as a period of continuation of the Song growth; ignoring the heavy losses of human lives, economic assets, and freedom among the Han Chinese. Modern imperialism is condemned without noticing that China as a whole was not colonised by the West or by Japan, and that the loss of lives and ordinary people's assets by 1900 was not nearly as heavy as during the Mongol invasion and conquest. More importantly, the Mongols did not represent more advanced institutions or technology but the capitalist West did. Why then should modern imperialism be viewed so negatively?

The latest debate is that of the 'Great Divergence' launched by the 'California School'. The essence of the new thinking is that the economic growth pattern (called 'Smithian growth') and the consumption pattern remained similar between Western Europe and China until the eighteenth century. What separated Western Europe from China were 'coal and colonies' after the eighteenth century.[6] The most significant contribution of the California School is to use the 'consumption function', and hence living standards, as the alternative benchmark to measure economic performance. This, however, has been challenged by neo-classic economics, which tries to reinstate the European supremacy in 'production function' (including labour productivity or the 'real wage') that dictates living standards.

On China's modern economic growth, the main debate has been the 'pluses' and 'minuses' of 'Westernisation' and/or 'Sovietisation' of the state and the economy after 1840. The late Qing elite, such as Zeng Guofan (1811–72), Zuo Zongtang (1812–85), Li Hongzhang (1823–1901), and Zhang Zhidong (1837–1909), spearheaded top-down Westernisation with a wholesale introduction of new technology, new institutions and new diplomacy, compatible with the West of the time.[7] However, this new

---

[6] Kenneth Pomeranz, *The Great Divergence: Europe, China and the Making of the Modern World Economy* (Princeton: Princeton University Press, 2000).

[7] Xia Dongyuan, *Yangwu Yundong Shi* (*A History of the Westernisation Movement*) (Shanghai: East China Normal University Press, 1992).

development ended with the fall of the Qing regime in 1911 and political instability that ensued. The country's period of Sovietisation, coming with the Communist military victory over the Republicans in 1949, was marked by state ownership and allocation of all key resources (land, capital, labour, and technology). The economy was systematically distorted to hasten a growth in heavy industry. This Sovietisation ended with 'production for the sake of it'. Its track record includes tens of millions dying during a man-made famine in 1959–62, the closure of all universities and high schools, and wrecking of the state apparatus and urban modern production in the 1960s.[8] Legacies of Westernisation and Sovietisation have been widely divided with no consensus.

Deng Xiaoping's de-Sovietisation reforms after 1978 have been hailed as the saviour of the Chinese economy. The main debate is whether Deng's reforms rescued China's ailing economy or merely made Mao's Sovietisation a bit more efficient. Side effects of Dengist reforms, known as 'high production inputs, high environmental pollution, high official corruption, and high social inequality', have received increasing attention. The key question is whether the combination of a party-state and bureaucratic capitalism is capable of producing a balanced and sustainable growth to benefit the general population in China. Only time will tell.

3. General Narrative Style of This Book

Instead of following the commonly shared chronology in works on China's history, the narrative adopted in this book is based on facts and factors (such as resource endowments, institutions, and technology) and themes (such as economic patterns and path dependence) in order to disentangle the complicity of China's long history. Estimates are to be used at the minimum, as they can be misleading.[9]

---

[8] Yang Jisheng, *Mubei — Zhongguo Liushi Niandai Dajihuang Jishi* (*Gravestone for the Great Leap Famine Victims, Evidence from History*) (HK: Tiandi, 2008); Frank Dikötter, *Mao's Great Famine* (London: Bloomsbury, 2010); A. G. Walder, J. W. Esherick, and P. G. Pickowicz (eds.), *China's Cultural Revolution as History* (Stanford: Stanford University Press, 2006).

[9] For example, see Angus Maddison, *Chinese Economic Performance in the Long Run* (Paris: OECD, 1998).

4. How to Define China and China's Historical Periods

It has been debated whether China has been a civilisation (a mono-cultural territory),[10] nation (mono-ethnic territory), or an empire (a multi-cultural and multi-ethnic territory). A final judgement often comes down to ethnicity and hence the dominance of the Han population. Modern genetics has revealed, however, that the 'ethnic Han Chinese' is a sheer myth. In reality the Han have been a genetic mix with multiple strains from various donors in East Asia.[11] In addition, China was ruled several times by non-Han groups during the Tang,[12] Yuan and Qing Periods. In this book, China is thus defined as a multi-cultural and multi-ethnic land-based empire. To avoid controversy, the terms of 'Empire of China' (instead of the 'Chinese Empire'), 'China's history' (instead of 'Chinese history'), 'China's state' (instead of the 'Chinese state'), 'China's population' (instead of 'the Chinese population'), and so forth are used simply because China has never been a mono-ethnic and mono-cultural unit.

China has had 17 historical periods of which four periods are marked by internal disintegration for an aggregate of over four centuries (marked by an asterisk) with multiple states. Even so, China is justifiably to be seen as a single political unit over the last two millennia:

Pre-Modern Era
Qin: 221–207 BC
Western Han: 206 BC–24 AD
Eastern Han: 25–220
Three Kingdoms: *220–265/280
Western Jin: 265–316
Eastern Jin: 317–420
Northern and Southern Dynasties: *420–581

---

[10] If the framework of 'Islamdom' applies to East Asia, one may think of a virtual cultural territory of 'Confucianism-dom', 'Taoism-dom', 'kanji-dom', 'lunar calendar-dom', 'chopstick-dom', all going beyond China's political boundaries.

[11] Tong Zhuchen, 'Zhongguo Xinshiqi Shidai Wenhuade Duozhong Xi Fazhan Lu He Fazhan Bu Pingheng Lun' (On the Multi-centre Nature and Heterogeneity of the Chinese Neolithic Age), *Wenwu* (*Cultural Relics*), 2(1986), pp. 16–39.

[12] The Tang ruling house was ethnically of the non-Han.

Sui: 581–618
Tang: 618–907
Five Dynasties: *907–960
Northern Song: 960–1127
Southern Song: *1127–1279
Yuan: 1279–1368
Ming: 1368–1644
Qing: 1644–1800

Modern Era
Qing (Continued): 1800–1911
Republic:* 1911–1949
People's Republic: 1949–present day

5. Structure and Thrust of This Book

For the convenience of narrative, this book has two parts. The first part, from Chapters Two to Six, deals with China's pre-modern period prior to 1800; and the second part, Chapter Seven, covers China's modern era. The distribution of chapters between pre-modern and modern eras (5 to 1) is justifiable because the actual duration ratio between these two eras is 21 to 1 in history.

The main thrust of this book lies in its quantitative evidence from historical data mainly from Chinese sources which are not always available in non-Chinese texts. The reader will thus obtain a picture of China closer to historical reality. Moreover, for the benefit of the reader, the length of the book is kept short.

Chapter Two

Size and Longevity of the Empire

China has conventionally been portrayed as an old civilisation as well as an empire: It is a civilisation whose origin can be traced back four millennia in written records. However, the history of China as a civilisation was related to, but not identical with China as an empire. China was not the earliest or oldest empire — but it has been the longest lasting. Moreover, the territory and population of the empire fluctuated over time. So, size and longevity is our first point of observation.

1. Size of the Empire

As an empire, China grew in size over time as illustrated by Figure 1. By the 1890s, the core had claimed about 80 percent of China's total population.[1] A similar percentage (79 percent) remained according to China's 2010 official census.[2]

(1) A Stable Core and Moving Frontiers

Apart from the era dominated by the Mongol Yuan (1279–1368), China's territory before 1800 was 13 million km^2 maximum. China's frontiers moved in the north, northeast, northwest, and southwest directions

---

[1] Cao Shui, *Zhongguo Renkoushi* (*A Demographic History of China*) (Shanghai: Fudan University Press, 2001), Vol. 4, pp. 828–9.

[2] See on line at: http://wenku.baidu.com/view/45a739a9284ac850ad02426d.html.

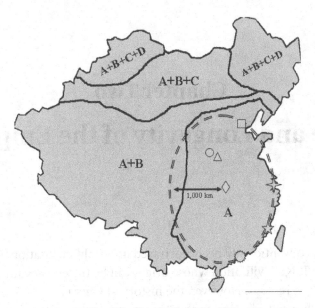

Figure 1. China's Changing Size.

Source: Based on Tan Qixiang, *Jianming Zhongguo Lishi Dituji* (*Concise Maps of Chinese History*) (Beijing: China's Map Press, 1991), pp. 15–18, 39–40, 57–8, 67–8.

Note: The Qing boundaries are used as a template. A = the Qin territory; A + B = the Western Han territory overlapping with the Qing; A + B + C = the Tang territory overlapping with the Qing; A + B + C + D = the Yuan overlapping with the Qing territory. Above the 40° latitude = sub-arctic; the 30–40° latitudes = the temperate zone; below the 30° Latitude = subtropical.

Symbols: circle = the Qin capital Xianyang; triangle = the Western Han and Tang capital Chang-an; square = the Yuan, Ming and Qing capital Beijing; diamond = Wuhan, the centre of the circle to mark China's core with a radius of 1,000 km; cross = Shanghai; five-pointed star = Quanzhou; sun = Canton; dash line circle = China's economic and demographic core.

during the Tang, Song and Ming Dynasties, for example. What this meant, first of all, was that there was a general trend that the supply of land for farming was elastic until as late as the Qing Dynasty (1644–1911), a factor vital for the survival and sustainability of the empire's economy. What remained stable was China's interior core of about 3 million km²,[3] made of mature farming zones in the middle and lower reaches of three rivers: the Yellow River, Yangzi River and Pearl River (Zone A in Figure 1).

Secondly, a general pattern of territorial expansion was dictated by isohyets, isotherms and soil types that ultimately determined farming

---

[3]Measured by a circle with a radius of 1,000 km centred in Wuhan near the 30° latitude.

productivity. As a rule of thumb, above the 40° latitude to which the empire expanded, the frost-free period was about 120 days per annum, an annual rainfall was about 100 mm (in the west) and 500 mm (in the east), and the main soil type was chernozem (black soil) — conditions which were suited only for dry farming. China's interior core, situated, between the 40° and 30° latitudes, has a frost-free period of about 200 days with an annual rainfall of 500–1,000 mm. The main soil types include yellow loam and loess. Regions below the 30° latitude has a frost-free period of 300 days a year, an annual rainfall of 1,500–2,000 mm, and the main soil type of red loam with high permeability. Although the temperature below the 40° latitude favours rice cultivation, rain-fed rice farming has been rare in China: about 5 percent, compared with 40 percent in South and Southeast Asia and 29 percent on average worldwide.[4] In the region below the 30° latitude, for sample, annual rainfall supports rice-growing for mere a week (see Table 15).[5] Therefore, irrigation is always the *sine qua non* for rice-farming in China which implies huge capital investment in channels, ditches, dykes, and pumps.

Thirdly, the 40° latitude in the west (current-day Xinjiang), where expansion took place from the period of the Western Han (206 BC–24 AD) until the Tang Dynasty (618–907), was also where China's inland trade corridor to the outside world, including the Silk Road, lay and where China's annual tea-for-horse trade with local nomads perpetuated. External trade created the incentives for the empire to control that region.

(2) Demography and Migration

Despite popular perceptions, population growth in China remained modest prior to 1500 AD (see Figure 2).

The main debate is whether China's population **continued** to grow after 1400 or stagnated until *c.* 1700. The real pattern was that by *c.* 1000 AD, China's standing population was around 60 million. It suddenly doubled in 1000–1100 during the Northern Song Dynasty (960–1127). A similar

---

[4]Neue, Heinz-Ulrich, 'Methane Emission from Rice Fields', *BioScience*, 43/7 (1993), p. 467, Table 4.
[5]Zhao Gesheng, Lai Laizhan and Zheng Jingui, *Zhongguo Tezhong Dao* (*Sorted Rice Types in China*) (Shanghai, 1995), p. 100.

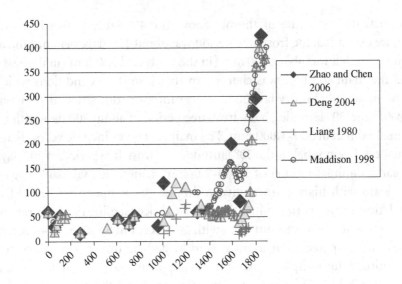

Figure 2.   China's Long-term Demographic Pattern (in Million), 1–1900 AD.*

Source: (1) Official censuses based on Liang Fangzhong, *Zhongguo Lidai Hukou Tiandi Tianfu Tongji* (*Dynastic Data for China's Households, Cultivated Land and Land Taxation*) (Shanghai: Shanghai People's Press, 1980), pp. 4–11; adjusted official population data are based on Kent Deng, 'Unveiling China's True Population Statistics for the Pre-Modern Era with Official Census Data', *Population Review*, 43/2 (2004), pp. 1–38. (2) Estimates: Angus Maddison, *Chinese Economic Performance in the Long Run* (Paris: OECD, 1998), p. 267; Zhao Gang and Chen Zhongyi, *Zhongguo Tudi Zhidu Shi* (*A History of Land Ownership in China*) (Beijing: New Star Press, 2006), p. 110.[6]
Note: *The actual size of China's population has been subject to debate in the past 50 years.

pattern occurred after 1900: China's population stagnated from 1900 to 1950 before taking off again (see Figure 3). In this regard, strong population growth in post-Song China occurred only twice: From 1700 to 1900, and from 1950 to 2010.

It is worth noting that before modern GDP accounting was available, population size was conventionally used as a proxy for the size of the

---

[6] There are other estimates, such as J. D. Durand, 'The Population Statistics of China, AD 2–1953', *Population Studies*, 13 (1960), pp. 209–57; Colin McEvedy and Richard Jones (eds.), *Atlas of World Population History* (Harmondsworth: Penguin Books, 1978), pp. 166–74; Kang Chao, *Man and Land in Chinese History: An Economic Analysis* (Stanford: Stanford University Press, 1986), p. 41; Jiang Tao, *Lishi Yu Renkou — Zhongguo Chuantong Renkou Jieguo Yanjiu* (*History and Demography — China's Traditional Demographic Pattern*) (Beijing: People's Press, 1998), p. 84; Ge Jianxiong, *Zhongguo Renkou Shi — Qing Shiqi* (*A Demographic History of China, Vol. 5, The Qing Period*) (Shanghai: Fudan University Press, 2000), pp. 831–2.

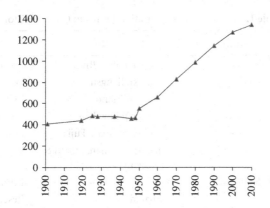

Figure 3.   China's Modern Demographic Pattern, 1910–2010.

Source: Data prior to 1950, see Hou Yangfang, *Zhongguo Renkoushi* (Shanghai: Fudan Press, 2001), Vol. 6, pp. 233, 235–8, 257, 266, 274, 278. For post-1950 data, see National Statistical Bureau, *Zhongguo Renkou He Jiuye Tongji Nianjian, 2013* (*China's Statistical Yearbook of Population and Employment*) (Beijing: China's Statistical Press, 2013).

Note: Numbers are in million.

economy. The problem is that any such estimate is likely to be a minimum GDP. They therefore represent a rather bare-bone picture of China's economy. This is because one does not know how much surplus was produced, how many luxuries were consumed, or how much saving and investment were made in the economy. In addition, the error of margin, 100 million people at some points,[7] is simply too large to make estimates reliable.

What supported China's population growth included internal migration, which was often tolerated and assisted by the state. Under the Qing policy of 'farming by invitation' (*quannong*), the state provided migrants with property rights, free passage, working capital, and tax holidays. In the case of Sichuan in the upper reaches of the Yangzi River, a surge of immigration began in 1713 under Emperor Kangxi's edict.[8] In 1743–8

---

[7] See D. H. Perkins, *Agricultural Development in China, 1368–1968* (Edinburgh: Edinburgh University Press, 1969); Maddison, *Chinese Economic Performance*.

[8] Commonly known as 'filling up Sichuan with the population from Hubei' (*huguang tian sichuan*); see Tian Fang and Chen Yijun, *Zhongguo Yimin Shilue* (*Brief History of Migration in China*) (Beijing: Knowledge Press, 1986), pp. 113–4; Chen Hua, *Qingdai Quyu Shehui Jingji Yanjiu* (*Regional Socio-Economic Conditions during the Qing Period*) (Beijing: People's University Press, 1996), ch. 8; Jiang Tao, *Renko Yu Lishi: Zhongguo Chuantong Renko Jiego Yanjiu* (*Population and History: A Study of Chinese Traditional Demographic Structure*) (Beijing: People's Press, 1998), p. 96.

Table 1.   Main Internal Migration Events in China's History.

Period	From	To	Type
W. Han	—	Upper Yellow River	Economic migrants
E. Han	Shaanxi	Shanxi, Jiangsu	War refugees
Sui	—	Hainan Island	Exile
Tang	—	Upper Yellow River	Economic migrants
	—	Hubei, Yunnan, Fujian	Resettlement
	—	Jiangsu, Hunan, Fujian & Sichuan	War refugees
N. Song	Fujian, Sichuan	—	Economic migrants
	—	Shanxi	Resettlement
	—	Guangdong	Economic migrants
S. Song	Henan	Hunan	War refugees
	Jiangxi	Hunan	Economic migrants
Ming	Hunan	Anhui	Economic migrants
	Hubei	Sichuan	Economic migrants
	Jiangsu	Anhui	Economic migrants
	Jiangxi	Anhui, Hunan	Economic migrants
	Shanxi	Jiangsu, Henan, Beijing	Economic migrants
	—	Fujian	Exile
	Henan, Shanxi	Shaanxi	Economic migrants
	Fujian	Zhejiang, Taiwan	Economic migrants
Qing	Shanxi	Sichuan	Economic migrants
	Hunan	Guangdong, Fujian	Economic migrants
	Anhui, Hubei, Henan & Jiangxi	Shanxi	Economic migrants
	Hunan, Guangdong	Sichuan	Economic migrants
	Jiangxi	Fujian	Economic migrants
	Fujian, Guangdong	Hunan	Economic migrants
	Fujian	Zhejiang, Taiwan	Economic migrants
	Shandong	Manchuria	Economic migrants
	Shanxi	Mongolia	Economic migrants

Source: Ge Jianxiong (ed.), *Zhongguo Yimin Shi* (*A History of Migration in China*) (Fuzhou: Fujian People's Press, 1997), Vol. 1, pp. 169–402.

Note: The actual numbers of migrants are often unavailable. Often, only a vague amount was mentioned in a migration scheme such as 'several tens thousand persons/households', or '60 to 70 percent of the locals left'.

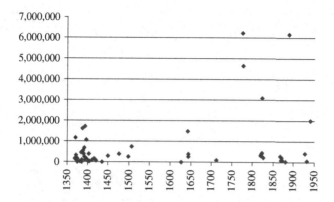

Figure 4. Internal Migrants during the Ming-Qing Period (Persons).
Source: Ge, *History of Migration in China*, Vol. 1, pp. 342–402.
Note: Y Axis = number of migrants.

alone, a quarter of a million migrants re-settled there.[9] Table 1 lists the main migration events recorded by the state.

Figure 4 shows the growth momentum in internal migration during the Ming-Qing Period.

Geographic movements of migrants can be highlighted in Figure 5. Counting the arrows, the highest recipient regions were Shaanxi (× 6), Hunan (× 5), Sichuan (× 4), and Anhui (× 3). The main donors were Shanxi (× 5), Jiangxi (× 5), Fujian (× 5), and Hunan (× 4). The majority migration was carried out to neighbouring provinces (22 events) compared to more remote regions (10 events). Migrants were after farmland and market opportunities. During the eighteenth century, over 50 percent of them migrated for new land to farm and about 26 percent sought after a market for services (commerce).[10]

A new trend emerged during the Qing Period for migrants to move from the core (such as Hebei, Henan, Shandong, Shanxi, and Shaanxi) to frontier areas.[11] By the 1660s, just one generation after the establishment

---

[9]Anon., *Qing Gaozong Shilu* (*Veritable Records of Emperor Gaozong of the Qing Dynasty*) (Originally published in 1799. Reprint. Taipei: Hualian Press, 1964), Vol. 311, Entry 'Shisannian Sanyue' (The Third Month of the Thirteenth Year under the Gaozong Reign).
[10]Yu Xinzhong, *Zhongguo Jiating Shi, Disan Juan* (*A History of Families in China*) (Guangzhou: Guangdong People's Press, 2007), Vol. 3, p. 49.
[11]For the eighteenth century, see Pierre-Etienne Will, *Bureaucracy and Famine in Eighteenth-Century China* (Stanford: Stanford University Press, 1990), Part 2.

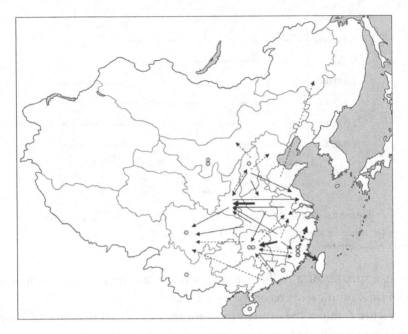

Figure 5. Main Internal Migrants' Movements in the Long Run.

Source: Ge, *A History of Migration in China*, pp. 169–402.

Note: The actual numbers of migrants during this time period are often unavailable; these recorded events are hence mere indications. Solid lines = southward migration; broken lines = northward migration; thick lines = repeated twice over different periods; circles = new communities whose original places were unclear.

of the Qing, Manchuria absorbed a staggering total of 14 million immigrants from China proper, or the core.[12] In the nineteenth century, the annual Manchuria-bound immigrants were 600,000. The number had increased to two million by 1907 for Heilongjiang alone (see Table 2).[13]

Large-scale immigration also took place in Mongolia. In 1712, the number of immigrants from the Shandong counted for over 100,000 despite an alleged ban.[14] Migrants moved to China's southern frontiers, too.[15]

---

[12] Zhang Limin, 'Chuang Guandong Yiminchao Jianxi' (Advancing to Manchuria), *Zhongguo Shehui Jingjishi Yanjiu* (*Study of Chinese Socio-Economic History*), 2 (1998), pp. 57–64.

[13] Tian and Chen, *Brief History of Migration in China*, pp. 110–12.

[14] Zhao Erxun, *Qingshi Gao* (*Draft of the History of the Qing Dynasty*) (Originally published in 1927. Reprint. Beijing: Zhonghua Books, 1977), Vol. 120, Entry 'Shihuo Zhi' (Economy); see also Jiang, *Population and History*, p. 96.

[15] James Lee, 'Population Growth in Southwest China, 1250–1850', *Journal of Asian Studies*, 41/4 (1982), pp. 711–46.

Table 2. Migration and Farming Expansion in Manchuria, 1661–1908.

Year	Farmland *(mu)*	Persons
1683/5	312,859(100)	26,227(100)
1864	2,080,000(665)	2,187,286(8,340)
1898	10,616,524(3,393)	5,413,000(20,639)
1908	109,839,014(35,108)	14,457,087(55,123)

Source: Lin Shixuan, *Qingji Dongbei Yimin Shibian Zhengcezhi Yanjiu* (*Qing Policy of Manchurian-bound Migration to Strengthen Frontiers*) (Taipei: National Cheng-Chi University, 2001), p. 311.

Between 1743 and 1748, a quarter of a million migrants moved under the scheme of 'filling up Sichuan with immigrants'. Elsewhere, migration also occurred.[16] Table 3 highlights the gain in new farmland during the Qing.

A recent path-breaking study shows that in modern-day Manchuria, Mongolia, and Sichuan there are the lineage extensions of Shandong-Hebei and Hubei-Hunan.[17] To a great extent, Manchuria, Mongolia, and Sichuan functioned as 'China's New World'.

2. Running Costs

From an economic perspective of running a country, a larger territorial unit is more likely to benefit from the economies of scale, or social savings. This seems to have been the case for China, where state officials and the literati members per capita were extremely small (*c.* 1850):[18]

Population-to-county magistrate	214,710:1
Population-to-officials	15,136:1
Population-to-gentry	266:1
Gentry-to-officials	57:1

[16] *Ibid.*

[17] Yuan Yida and Zhang Cheng, *Zhongguo Xingshi Qunti Yichuan He Renko Fenbu* (*Chinese Surnames, Group Genetics and Demographic Distribution*) (Shanghai: East China Normal University Press, 2002), pp. 6–57.

[18] Based on the facts that 90 percent of the Qing population (359 million in 1,672 counties in 1833) were rural. The long-term ratio between degree-holders and official openings was 30:1 and 100:1; see Gang Deng, *Development versus Stagnation: Technological Continuity and Agricultural Progress in Premodern China* (New York and London, 1993), p. 102; Chung-li Chang,

Table 3. Supplies of New Farmland (Km^2), *c.* 1640 vs. 1887.

	Land mass	Privately farmed land*
1. Total territory		
Qing	11,604,000	607,984
Ming (I)	5,964,000	467,598
Gain under the Qing (II)	5,640,000	140,386
II/I	94.6	30.0
2. Interior redevelopment		
Sichuan Basin	560,000	—
Yangzi–Han Plain	400,000	—
Total (III)	960,000	—
III/I	16.1	—
3. Total gain (IV = II + III)	6,600,000	
IV/I	110.7	

Source: Based on Liang, *Dynastic Data*, pp. 346, 380.

Note: Data for the Ming territory are based on the year 1644; and 1812 data for the Qing territory. Conversion of *mu* to square kilometre with the ratio of 1,500:1. * Privately farmed land was about 90–95 percent of the Ming-Qing total farmland.

In other words, the Qing officials formed a tiny 0.007 percent of China's total population; the Qing armed forces, 0.2 percent; and the Qing gentry, 1.5 percent (if one includes their families). The Qing state-cum-population amounted to just two percent of China's total. It is important to note

---

The Chinese Gentry: Studies on Their Role in Nineteenth-Century Chinese Society (Seattle: University of Washington Press, 1955), pp. 83–92; J. K. Fairbank, (ed.) *Chinese Thought and Institutions* (Chicago: University of Chicago Press, 1957), pp. 251–68; Ping-ti Ho, *The Ladder of Success in Imperial China; Aspects of Social Mobility, 1368–1911* (New York: Columbia University Press, 1962), p. 262; Deng Ciyu, *Zhongguo Kaoshi Zhidu Shi* (*History of the Chinese Imperial Examination System*) (Taipei: Xuesheng Books, 1967), pp. 163–4; Wang Dezhao, *Qingdai Keju Zhidu Yanjiu* (*A Study of the Civil Examinations of the Qing Dynasty*) (Hong Kong: The Chinese University Press, 1982), pp. 65–6. The Qing military included 120,000 Eight Banners (*baqi*) and 660,000 Green Standards (*lüying*, literarily 'Green Corps'); see Zhao, *History of the Qing Dynasty*, Vol. 131, Entry 'Military', in *TFOH*, Vol. 11, pp. 9305, 9307.

that although the Qing population multiplied, the number of officials remained stagnant. Between 1700 and 1850, officials increased by less than 10 percent (from 24,150 to 26,355) with an annual average of just 0.06 percent. Meanwhile, the Qing population increased at a speed of 1.5 percent annually, 25 times that of the growth in the number of officials.[19] With the introduction of the party-state by the Soviet Union, Mao's China was ruled during the 1960s by 12 million cadres,[20] or 15 percent of China's population — and this does not count his army officers. The civilian-to-official ratio was 5:1, over 50 times that of the Qing level. As of 2012, China is run by over 60 million government employees, a ratio that is more or less the same as during Mao's time.[21]

As a result, the Qing state only controlled about five percent of China's total GDP (see Table 4). Comparatively, in Tokugawa Japan, the *bakufu* imposed a tax rate of 40 percent; while individual *daimyo* usually taxed away 50–70 percent of the peasants' annual total output.[22] Later, the Meiji state taxed away 30–50 percent of all agricultural income, which was worth about 20 percent of Japan's total GDP.[23] In Western Europe, the French government commanded 19 percent of the country's GDP (as of 1840); Austria, 27 percent (1790); Prussia, 35 percent (1760); and Britain, 43 percent (1810).[24]

All the Qing ratios mean that society had to be to a great extent self-governed, unless the traditional bureaucracy of China was extremely efficient. In other words, if anything, the Qing state was not totalitarian.

---

[19] For the Chinese population, see K. G. Deng, 'Unveiling China's True Population Statistics for the Pre-Modern Era with Official Census Data', *Population Review*, 43/2 (2004), Appendix 2.

[20] Mikiso Hane, *Modern Japan: A Historical Survey* (New York: Westview Press, 2001), p. 50; see also, E. H. Norman, *Japan's Emergence as a Modern State* (Westport: Greenwood Press, 1973), p. 23.

[21] Li Yi, *The Structure and Evolution of Chinese Social Stratification* (Lanham [Maryland]: University Press of America, 2005), p. 83.

[22] Data avalaible on line at: http://blog.sina.com.cn/s/blog_4b8bd1450102edb0.html.

[23] Penelope Francks, *Japanese Economic Development, Theory and Practice* (London: Routledge, 1992), pp. 30, 103.

[24] Michael Mann, *The Sources of Social Power, The Rise of Classes and Nation States, 1760–1914* (Cambridge: Cambridge University Press, 1993), Vol. 2, p. 366. The British data are the maximum including its national debt payments.

Table 4. China's GDP and Tax Revenue in the 1880s.

Estimates	Change	Feuerwerker	Liu *et al.*	Average
Total GDP*(I)	104,300	125,200	131,600	120,370
State total revenue (II)				5,801
II/I (%)				4.8

Source: Chung-li Chang, *The Income of the Chinese Gentry* (Seattle: University of Washington Press, 1962), p. 296; Albert Feuerwerker, *The Chinese Economy, 1870–1949* (Ann Arbor: Center for Chinese Studies of the University of Michigan, 1995), p. 16; Liu Foding, Wang Yuru and Zhao Jin, *Zhongguo Jindai Jingji Fazhanshi* (*A History of Economic Development in Early Modern China*) (Beijing: Tertiary Education Press, 1999), p. 66.
Note: *In metric tons of pure silver, converted from silver *taels*.

Table 5. Empire Life Spans throughout History.

Country/Region	Life Span	Years	% Index (China = 100)
China	221 BC–1911	2132	100
Global average	—	540	25
Africa empires			
Egyptian	*c.* 1600 BC–*c.* 1200 BC	400	19
Ghanaian	300 AD–1000	700	33
Ethiopian	1137–1975	838	39
Mali	1235–1600	365	17
Ashanti	1700–1957	257	12
America's empire			
Inca	*c.* 1200 AD–1572	372	17
Eurasian empires			
Persian (I)	550–330 BC	220	10
Hellenistic	323–31 BC	292	14
Persian (II)	247 BC–651 AD	898	42
W. Roman	27 BC–476 AD	503	24
Byzantium	330 AD–1453	1123	53
Carolingian	800–888	88	4
Ottoman	1301–1922	621	29
Iranian	1501–1979	478	22
Mughal	1526–1707	181	8
Russian	1721–1917	196	9

(*Continued*)

Table 5.   (*Continued*)

Country/Region	Life Span	Years	% Index (China = 100)
Modern colonial empires			
Portuguese	1415–2002	587	28
Spanish	1492–1892	400	19
French	1534–1977	443	21
British	1583–1997	414	19
Dutch	1602–1975	373	17

Source: Nicholas Ostler, *Empires of the World* (London, HarperCollins, 2005).

The notion that the Empire of China had a small and 'doing-little' state is again best illustrated by the government tax revenue collected in the early modern and modern periods. Towards the end of the Qing Period (1644–1911), in the 1880s, the state controlled insignificant amount of the empire's total wealth (see Table 4).[25]

3. Longevity of the Empire

To understand how China performed, a global comparison is presented in Table 5 where the life span of the Empire of China was four times that of the global average. The Byzantium Empire and the Persian Empire were remotely close to the second and third places, respectively.

There is a notion that China's longevity was a result of the empire's isolation, a point that we will come back to later.

---

[25] At this stage, the current study does not want to re-work China's GDP but to take the average amongst the available estimates.

Chapter Three

Empire-building and Empire Maintenance

China was not an empire until 221 BC when the Qin Kingdom succeeded in achieving two things for the first time in China's history: (1) It unified China through war and conquest, and (2) it implemented a centralised administration known as the 'prefecture-county system' (*junxian zhi*). This was a vital turning point in China's history and put China on a different trajectory — socially, politically, and economically.

1. From Zhou Feudalism to the Anti-feudal Qin Empire

Three 'dynasties' had passed before the empire first emerged in China's history: The Xia (*c.* 21st–16th centuries BC), Shang (16th–11th centuries BC), and Zhou (11th century–221 BC). Of the three, the best recorded was the Zhou Dynasty. Based on available information, the Zhou ran a highly decentralised feudal system (yes, feudal). On the top of society sat the head of the state, the 'Son of Heaven' (*zhou tianzi*), under whom there were five layers of hereditary landed lords who ran their own fiefs and kingdoms (*gong, hou, bo, zi, nan*). There was no uniform judiciary, taxation, or administration across China. A nominal universal order was maintained through carefully choreographed hierarchical rituals (*zhou li*) between territorial aristocrats. No private ownership was legally allowed for the tillers. Feudal tenants were obliged to work collectively on their

23

lord's plot before looking after their allotments for their own subsistence, a system called 'chessboard fields' (*jingtian*).[1]

This system began to crumble during the Late Zhou (Eastern Zhou) Period from 770 BC onwards. In the following five centuries, the once well-maintained Zhou system disintegrated. The first to go was the Zhou rituals during the 'Spring and Autumn Period' (769–476 BC) when feudal lords openly committed transgression, commonly known as 'the collapse of the Zhou rites and the corruption of the Zhou music' (*libeng yuehuai*). Even worse, wars frequently broke out: 384 military clashes during the Spring and Autumn Period, or 1.3 each year, compared with only 43 recorded military clashes for the previous 1,430 years prior to 770 BC or 230 battles during the following Warring States Period (0.9 per year).[2]

Meanwhile, competition among feudal fiefs and *de facto* China-wide political freedom ushered in an era of 'one hundred flowers' in art, technology, philosophy, and politics. Among the prominent schools of thought were Legalism, Taoism, and Confucianism. Legalism promoted a strong state and universal rule of law in order to replace the old dysfunctional Zhou social order. Taoism preferred a laissez-faire system with no government, given that the Zhou state failed. Confucianism promoted the idea of a small state governing a large population via a code of good conduct — not only between the upper classes, but also within and across all strata. Legalism often delivered quick results; Taoism went nowhere; and Confucianism was a slow burner, taking a long time to produce any impact, and hence remained academic most of that time. Geographically speaking, Legalism was more popular in the less affluent and less cultured west (e.g. Shaanxi) where life was harsh; and Confucianism, in the wealthier and more cultivated east (e.g. Shandong) where life was more manageable. The sphere of influence that Taoism had was unclear.

While Confucians remained armchair revolutionaries, Legalists pressed hard for reforms against the Zhou feudal system. Such reforms began with Guan Zhong (725–645 BC) who proposed a set of principles for a new centralised state. His idea attracted Duke Huan (? – 643 BC) of the

---

[1]The Chinese characters of *jing* and *tian* both look like a chessboard with evenly divided squares, representing feudal farming plots.

[2]Fu Zhongxia, Tian Zhaolin, Zhang Xing, and Yang Boshi, *Zhongguo Junshi Shi* (*A Military History of China*) (Beijing: PLA Press, 1985), Vol. 1, p. 3.

Qi Dukedom. However, it was not until about three centuries later in 356 BC during the Warring States (475–221 BC), when wars of annexation between feudal units became common,[3] that Shang Yang (390–338 BC) found his audience in the Qin Dukedom, a marginal player of the time, and led a full-fledged and offensive Legalist reform.[4]

Shang Yang's radical reform systematically abolished feudalism within the Qin domain. Firstly, the hereditary feudal rights were scratched, and aristocrats were replaced by centrally appointed non-hereditary merito-crats who administrated the territory in a vertical system consisted of prefectures and counties under one government. Members of the royal family were not to have titles unless they had military exploits. Secondly, farmland under the Zhou 'chessboard field system' was privatised to create a new class of owner-tillers who now paid taxes directly to a central coffer instead of aristocrat masters. A land property market emerged among small private landholders.[5] Thirdly, 'nuclear families' were promoted as the basic taxation unit. Upon marriage, sons were obligated to establish their own independent households (*fengjia*) for taxation purposes under a new household registration. The old extensive families were penalised with a doubled tax rate. Fourthly, all citizens were organised in a mutual respon-sibility system (*lijia*) against crimes and social unrest. Finally, a new army was established under the command of the central government and financed by centralised revenues.[6] In the following 135 years, the Qin forcefully expanded its territory until the same system was implemented across East Asian Mainland.

By definition, the Zhou and Qin systems were mutually exclusive. To call the Qin political superstructure a 'feudal empire', as most Chinese

[3] *Ibid.*, p. 3.
[4] Shang Yang was described as 'a mean person' (*tianzi kebo*). He was found guilty of treason and died a violent death after clashing with the vested interest group in the Qin system. See Sima Qian, *Shi Ji* (*The Book of History*) (Originally published in 91 BC. Reprint), Vol. 68, Entry 'Shangjun Liezhuan', in *Er-shi-wu Shi* (*Twenty-Five Official Histories, or TFOH*) (Shanghai: Shanghai Classics Press, 1986), Vol. 1, p. 255.
[5] Ban Gu, *Han Shu* (*History of the Han Dynasty*) Vol. 24, ch. 'Shihuo 4' (Originally published in 82 AD. Reprint) in *Er-shi-wu Shi* (*Twenty-Five Official Histories, or TFOH*) (Shanghai: Shanghai Classics Press, 1986), Vol. 1, p. 477.
[6] Sima, *Book of History*, Vol. 68, Entry 'Shangjun Liezhuan', in *TFOH*, Vol. 1, pp. 254–6.

Marxian historians do, is a gross misreading of China's imperial past.[7] These Marxian historians mistake China for another Europe, not knowing that Karl Marx deliberately separated Asia from Europe as seen from his reference to 'Asiatic Mode of Production'.[8]

2. Bureaucratic Monarchy: Its Structure and Daily Function

Unlike the European absolute monarchy or constitutional monarch, post-Qing China ran a bureaucratic monarch (Figure 6) in which the monarch depended on the bureaucracy to exist, but not *vice versa*, due to asymmetric information.

(1) Fine-Tuning of the Empire System: Confucianisation of the Ruler and State-Peasant Alliance

The Legalist approach worked effectively in destroying Zhou feudalism and building up an empire, but it was far from stable. Political centralisation opened the door for power abuse and rent-seeking. The best examples were the unprecedented public works known to society: The Great Wall, the Qin Palace (*erfanggong*), and the Qin mausoleum, all built in a short space of time between 221 BC and 210 BC. Despite the notion of 'farming-and-weaving being the essential occupation of the country',[9] the Qin state squeezed the population to the very last drop for revenues 20 times more than past levels, and for corvée services, 30 times more.[10] To silence criticism, the Qin state 'burned books and executed intellectuals' (*fenshu kengru*). The public resentment eventually resulted in an empire-wide rebellion in 209 BC. Now, a counter-balance of a centralised state was created in a bi-polar society made up of ordinary citizens *vis-à-vis* a

---

[7]Eurocentric and dogmatic Marxists have long mislabelled the post-Qin system as a 'feudal empire' (*fengjian diguo*), 'centralised feudalism' (*fengjian jiquan*), 'feudal totalitarianism' (*fengjian zhuanzhi*), 'feudal emperor' (*fengjian huangdi*), and 'feudal bureaucracy' (*fengjian guanliao*).

[8]Pryor, 'The Asian Mode of Production'.

[9]Sima, *Book of History*, Vol. 68, Entry 'Shangjun Liezhuan', in *TFOH*, Vol. 1, p. 255.

[10]Ban, *History of the Han Dynasty*, Vol. 24, 'Shihuo 4', in *TFOH*, Vol. 1, p. 477.

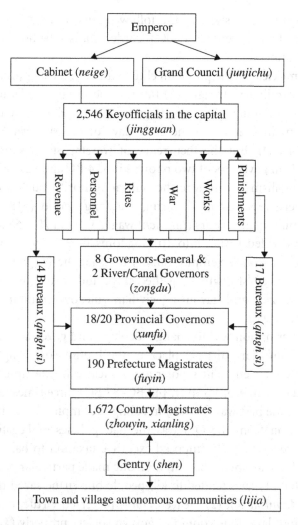

Figure 6.   Late Qing Administrative Framework, *c.* 1800.

Source: Based on Zhao Erxun, *Qingshi Gao* (*Draft of the History of the Qing Dynasty*) (Originally published in 1927. Reprint. Beijing: Zhonghua Books, 1977), Vols. 54–81 'Administrative Geography'; Tang Jing and Zheng Chuanshui, *Zhongguo Guojia Jigoushi* (*A History of Administrative Structures in China*) (Shenyang: Liaoning People's Press, 1993), pp. 424–8; Zhang Deze, *Qingdai Guojia Jiguan Kaolue* (*The State Apparatus of the Qing Period*) (Beijing: Xueyuan, 2001); Yuan Gang, *Zhongguo Gudai Zhengfu Jigou Shezhi Yange* (*Evolution of the State Apparatus in Premodern China*) (Harbin: Heilongjiang People's Press, 2003), pp. 629–64; Roland Mousnier, *Peasant Uprisings in Seventeenth-Century France, Russia and China* (London: George AU, 1971), p. 256; Yang Zhimei, *Zhongguo Gudai Guanzhi Jiangzuo* (*Bureaucracy of Premodern China*) (Beijing: Zhonghua Books, 1992), pp. 420–1; and Zhang, *State Apparatus of the Qing Period*, pp. 6, 39, 43, 57, 79, 106, 127.

centralised autocratic state. In the following two-millennium history of the empire, there were over 2,000 recorded mass rebellions against the tyranny of autocracy.[11]

It became clear to the post-Qin elite that the Legalist approach created political and military strength (*li*) but not moral virtue (*de*) to maintain social harmony.[12] One option was to go back to the Zhou feudalist system. This was put in practice in the early days of the Western Han Period (206 BC–24 AD). But the recurrence of warring states soon followed. It took the Han government two reforms in 154 BC and 127 BC to disarm the new feudalism and restore the central authority. Such a destructive feudal pattern repeated itself during the Tang Period (618–907) when separatist military governors (*fanzhen*) waged wars in 755–63 and 783–87 and finally divided China into 10 kingdoms in 907–79. New strategies were then created by the empire-builder to tackle the Tang feudalism with a combination of 'strengthening the centre and weakening the regions' (*qianggan ruozhi*) and 'favouring civilian rule over military authority' (*zhongwen qingwu*).

The other option was to change ideology and governance. A historic switch to Confucianism took place in the lifetime of Dong Zhongshu (179–104 BC), an eminent scholar and educator of the time. Dong was summoned by Emperor Wudi (*r.* 140 BC–87 BC) three times to advise the monarch on the best way forward in ruling the empire. Dong pointed out that the lesson from the Qin was the bad policies of Legalism, which produced greedy officials, imposed excessive taxation to bankrupt farming, and led to widespread banditry.[13] Dong made particular points against Legalism that (1) laws tended to kill people but virtue saved them (*xingzhusha er dezhusheng*); (2) Heaven (*tian*) preferred virtue, not laws; and (3) the rule of law alone could not govern society properly (*xingzhe buke renyi zhishi*).[14]

Attitudes changed at the top. In 128 AD, the emperor issued an edict to promote Confucian values including good knowledge, virtuous ethnics,

---

[11] Gang Deng, *The Premodern Chinese Economy* (London, Routledge Press, 1999), pp. 363–76.

[12] Sima, *Book of History*, Vol. 68, Entry 'Shangjun Liezhuan', in *TFOH*, Vol. 1, p. 255.

[13] Ban, *History of the Han Dynasty*, Vol. 56, Entry 'Biography of Dong Zhongshu', in *TFOH*, Vol. 1, p. 599.

[14] *Ibid.*, Vol. 56, Entry 'Biography of Dong Zhongshu', in *TFOH*, Vol. 1, p. 599.

gentlemanly behaviour, filial piety, and benevolence as the criteria for assessing government officials. He even cited Confucius's motto 'among any three companies one will be my teacher'.[15] Earlier, Emperor Gaozu (*r.* 206 BC – 195 BC) already made the gesture by declaring Confucius' Memorial Temple to be a noble site.[16] In 1 AD, Confucius was given post-humously a Duke status (*xuanni gong*) and Confucius descendants were given hereditary marquis titles by Emperor Pingdi (*r.* 1–5 AD),[17] a practice followed by most regimes later.

This marked the beginning of Confucianisation of the statecraft and further bureaucratisation of the empire. In 3 AD, state–run schools were granted, at both prefecture and county levels, to teach *Book on Filial Piety* (*xiaojing*).[18] In 5 AD, an edict was issued to attract scholars who taught Confucian classics to serve the empire.[19] By 24 AD, of the 103 famous authors on the Imperial list, 58 were Confucians.[20] The days of Legalist dominance in China's politics were over.

The first consciously Confucianised ruler was Emperor Yuandi (*r.* 48–33 BC) who was described as 'soft-hearted, benevolent and attracted by Confucianism'.[21] In 42 BC, disasters struck and refugees and bandits emerged. The emperor blamed himself by saying, 'Poor governance of society is all but my lack of wisdom, ... I feel much ashamed. Being the parent of all citizens, my poor performance cannot be justified.'[22] To redeem himself, the emperor granted amnesty to criminals so that society, including the monarch, could start afresh all over again (*dashe tianxia*).[23] This set the precedence of 'self-blaming edicts' by the monarch (*zuijizhao*) in China.

By the turn of the first century AD, Confucianism had come a long way from its humble beginning to replay hard-line Legalism of the Qin to tame the newly established centralised state and stabilise the

---

[15] *Ibid.*, Vol. 6, Entry 'Biography of Emperor Wudi', in *TFOH*, Vol. 1, p. 383.

[16] Sima, *Book of History*, Vol. 47, Entry 'Kongzi Shijia', in *TFOH*, Vol. 1, p. 228.

[17] Ban, *History of the Han Dynasty*, Vol. 12, Entry 'Biography of Emperor Pingdi', in *TFOH*, Vol. 1, p. 397.

[18] *Ibid.*, Vol. 12, Entry 'Biography of Emperor Pingdi', in *TFOH*, Vol. 1, p. 398.

[19] *Ibid.*, p. 398.

[20] *Ibid.*, p. 529.

[21] *Ibid.*, p. 391.

[22, 23] *Ibid.*, p. 392.

newborn empire. The basic assumptions now were that (1) a benevolent rule of a soft autocratic state would make society content, and that (2) society-wide self-discipline and self-rule would minimise bureaucracy and hence tax extraction. Meanwhile, steps were taken to set the limits for state rent-seeking from the peasantry, known as 'light corvée and thin taxes' (*qingyao bofu*). The doctrine of balanced government budget (*liangru weichu*) was also adopted to avoid unchecked government spending under the previous Qin.

Moreover, the Han state began to treat the peasantry differently. From the dialogue between Emperor Wudi and Dong Zhongshu, Han monarchs already practised the annual ceremony of ploughing farmland (*gengji*) to identify the state with the peasantry.[24] In 122 BC, 'filial piety' (*xiaoti*) and 'devotion to farming' (*litian*) became the official criteria for good citizens' rewards, which became the norm for all the later regimes.[25] By 70 BC, farming had been regarded as the 'foundation for virtuous ethics' (*xingde zhiben*); redundant government employees were persuaded to take up farming;[26] the peasantry was officially regarded as a favoured stratum in China's social hierarchy;[27] and peasant property rights, including inheritance, were defined and protected.[28] Finally, in 81 BC by law the merchant class was excluded from the lucrative salt and iron trade, with the new policy of 'state monopoly of salt and iron' (*yantie guanying*), a policy that was inherited by most regimes after the Han.

All these measures marked the beginning of 'rationing government spending' and 'favouring farmers and confining merchants' (*zhongnong yishang*), or simply physiocracy, upon which a state-peasant alliance was

---

[24] *Ibid.*, p. 599.

[25] *Ibid.*, p. 385.

[26] *Ibid.*, p. 389.

[27] The hierarchy was made of (1) the literati on the top, (2) the peasantry, (3) artisans, and (4) merchants at the bottom. The only exception was the Yuan Dynasty under Mongol colonisation when the peasantry disappeared from a ten-scale social ranking of (1) officials (*guan*), (2) clerks (*li*), (3) Buddhists, (4) Taoists, (5) medical doctors, (6) artisans, (7) prostitutes, (8) thieves, (9) Confucians, and (10) beggars. Most peasants were forced into slavery. See Xing Tie, *Zhongguo Jiating Shi, Disi Juan* (*A History of Families in China*) (Guangzhou: Guangdong People's Press, 2007), Vol. 4, pp. 11, 19.

[28] Wang Lihua, *Zhongguo Jiating Shi, Diyi Juan* (*A History of Families in China*) (Guangzhou: Guangdong People's Press, 2007), Vol. 1, pp. 230–44.

officially forged and became the cornerstone of the 'moral economy' of the empire.

In short, in the post-Qin history, after centuries of trial and error, the political economy of the empire was finally set with an integrated system of three interlocking components: Confucianism, physiocracy, and state-peasant alliance.

(2) Long-term Impact of Confucianisation

The Confucianisation of the state and its related state-peasant alliance had profound impact on both society and the growth trajectory of China's economy. First of all, without a hereditary ruling class, officials had to be selected according to good deeds and/or schooling through open channels and competition. The new system of bureaucrat recruitment became the engine of social mobility. Human capital accumulation via education was appreciated in society. This was the positive side of the Confucian state.

Secondly, the Confucian state emphasized the function of role models and rule by consensus. Moral persuasion weighed heavily. Such an approach planted the seed of China's weakness in national security and hence China's vulnerability to foreign invasions and conquests, as evident in the cases of (1) the 'Five Nomad Groups' (*wuhu*, 304–439 AD) who scrambled for North China, (2) the 'Southern and Northern Dynasties' (*nanbei chao*, 420–589 AD) when large parts of North China were carved away by nomads, (3) the Southern Song Period (1127–1279) when North China was taken by nomads, (4) the Yuan Period (1279–1368) when the Mongols colonised the empire in its entirety, and (5) the Qing Period (1644–1911) when a Manchu monarchy replaced the Han Chinese one by force. This was the negative side of the Confucian state.

Meanwhile, governance by consensus led to autonomy at the grassroots level. It granted ordinary people freedom but left domestic law and order to private and communal hands. Typically, villages organised their own schools to teach their young and their police forces to defend their properties and crops on a regular basis.[29] It created a highly fragmented

---

[29] For a solid case study, see Sidney D. Gamble, *North China Villages, Social, Political and Economic Activities before 1933* (Berkeley: University of California Press, 1963).

internal security structure because no single village was able to prevent invaders of an overwhelming number from killing and looting its own villagers. This proved to be the case during the Taiping, Nian, Miao, and Muslim rebellions in the 1850s to 1870s, when organised riots seemed unstoppable across the empire.

Chapter Four

Key Institutions

Conceptually, laws have always been formal institutions; cultural values and ethics, informal institutions. Customary rules to govern families and clans are semi-formal institutions. Property rights are often considered a paramount economic institution that dictates the growth trajectory of an economy.[1] In essence, institutionalism argues that 'rules' determines how the 'game' should be played, not the other way round.[2]

1. Confucian Values to Discipline Power-Holders

Confucian values are embedded in nine classics: (1) *Analects of Confucius*, (2) *Great Learning*, (3) *Doctrine of the Mean*, (4) *Mencius*, (5) *Book of Songs*, (6) *Book of History*, (7) *Book of Changes*, (8) *Book of Rites*, and (9) *Spring and Autumn Annals*. They encompass about 437,000 characters and cover many aspects of nature and society. But the political and moral message is, quite simply, 'a harmonic order' as the sole purpose of social progress.

The criteria for judging whether or not a harmonic order are deadly plain, as the Confucian teaching can be boiled down to 'four patterns of

---

[1] D. C. North, and R. P. Thomas, *The Rise of the Western World: A New Economic History* (Cambridge: Cambridge University Press, 1973).
[2] See D. C. North's two publications: *Structure and Change in Economic History* (New York: W.W. Norton, 1981); and *Institutions, Institutional Change and Economic Performance* (Cambridge: Cambridge University Press, 1990).

behaviour' described by Confucius himself as: 'A monarch behaving like a monarch, a minister behaving like a minister, a father behaving like a father, and a son behaving like a son' (*junjun, chenchen, fufu, zizi*). Such an order is to be achieved voluntarily and not imposed by harsh law. This was how Confucian governance by consensus replaced Legalist rule by law. Here, voluntariness is determined by the Confucian doctrine of 'not to treat the others the way that you do not want to be treated yourself' (*jisuo buyu wu shiyu ren*).

Moreover, Confucius understood the concept of power asymmetry within society, and thus the challenge of achieving the lofty realm of 'a harmonic order'. For him, harmony began with a process of inculcating 'benevolence' (*ren*) among the power-holders: The monarch, ministers, and fathers.[3] Confucius mentioned *ren* more than a hundred times in his *Analects* alone. It is hence no exaggeration to call benevolence the very ethos of Confucianism.

Confucius explicitly defined *ren* as 'cherishing or loving one another' (*renzhe airen*).[4] In this regard, *ren* is about sympathy and empathy toward fellow human beings from a benefactor in a higher position, be it a monarch or a father. The implicit message has to be 'a monarch behaving like a sage king, a father behaving like a loving father'. Moreover, the relationships have to be reciprocal, hence 'a minister behaving like a professional bureaucrat, and a son behaving like a filial son' demonstrates the beneficiaries repaying the benefactors' benevolence. This reciprocity formed the foundation of China's moral economy and political economy.

What was so brilliant about *ren* — together with its observations on behavioural patterns, and its goal of 'harmonious order' within society — was that it used human-biological behaviour as the benchmark to regulate and gauge social behaviour. Confucius articulated this in his *Book on Filial Piety* (*xiaojing*) as 'Ancient sages governed society so well without the use of harsh measures. This was because they all followed the human filial nature. ... The loving relationship between the father and his children

---

[3] For the debate on the term *ren*, see D. L. Hall and R. T. Ames, *Thinking through Confucius* (Albany: State University of New York, 1987), pp. 110–46.

[4] *Kong Qiu* (Confucius), *Lunyu* (*Analects of Confucius*) (c. 479 BC), in Wu Genyou (ed.) *Sishu Wujing* (*Four Books and Five Classics*) (Beijing: China's Friendship Press, 1993), pp. 9–35, ch. 'Yan Yuan'.

comes from our human instinct. ... One owes nothing greater than his life given by his parents.'[5] As family members are genetically programmed to care for one another, what social harmony looks like, beyond the family circle, hence becomes self-evident. One therefore did not need literacy to understand the essence of Confucian teaching.

What Confucianism did so cleverly was to externalise such a family bond to other people beyond the family unit. In doing so, ordinary citizens were given a reliable and tangible set of criteria to judge government actions. In other words, they did not need to read constitutions or government regulations to know whether or not the emperor and his officials performed their duties. This inevitably strengthened China's secular civilian rule.

Of course, the Confucian ideology changed over time. During the Western Han Period, its key values were re-defined by Dong Zhongshu as 'three relationships' and 'five virtues' (*sangang wuchang*). The three relations were between the monarch and ministers, fathers and sons, and husbands and wives. The five virtues were 'benevolence', 'righteousness', 'etiquette', 'wisdom', and 'trustworthiness' (*ren yi li zhi xin*).[6] Dong's relationships and virtues offered nothing new but made criteria more straightforward for running a meritocracy.

A significant contribution made by Dong was his metaphysical concept of 'Heaven' as an almighty-omnipresent supernatural force, watching every move made by the emperor; expressing its resentment towards the emperor's wrong doings by inflicting natural disasters. In his *Many Dewdrops of Spring and Autumn (Chunqiu Fanlu)*, Dong asserted that 'the monarch yields to Heaven';[7] and that 'if evil and crimes committed by monarchs bring calamities to the people, Heaven will deprive the monarchs of their power to rule.'[8] The introduction of Heaven shows a great doubt among Confucians whether the monarch was able to discipline himself by *ren* alone. The introduction of Heaven made the power of the monarch more vulnerable, because the right to interpret Heaven's will and

---

[5] Anon., *Xiao Jing (Book on Filial Piety)*, ch. 'Shengzhi Zhang 9'.
[6] Zhu Xi, *Yu Lei (Philosophical Analects)* (1200 AD), Vol. 4.
[7] *Ibid.*, ch. 'Yubei'. For the debate on the term *tian*, see Hall and Ames, *Thinking through Confucius*, pp. 204–18, 237–49.
[8] Zhu, *Philosophical Analects*, ch. 'Yao Shun Bu Shanyi, Tang Wu Bu Zhuansha'.

mandate was monopolised by the Confucian literati, which laid the foundation of China's bureaucratic monarchy.

After Dong, there was neo-Confucianism emerging during the Song Period (960–1279). The leaders of this new sect were two brothers Cheng Hao (1032–85) and Cheng Yi (1033–1107), and another scholar by the name of Zhu Xi (1130–1200). Neo-Confucianism is also called the 'School of Principle' (*lixue*) or 'School of Morality' (*daoxue*) because it saw a conflict between human desires (*renyu*) and Heaven's Principle (*tianli*) or Heaven's Morality (*dao*).[9] The slogan of neo-Confucianism was 'keeping Heaven's Principle and eliminating human desires' (*cun tianli mie renyu*). This has often been interpreted as an ascetic movement in China's history. The later contributor to neo-Confucianism was Wang Shouren (also known as Wang Yangming, 1472–1529) of the Ming Period (1368–1644). Wang contemplated the right way to obtain 'Heaven's Principle' (*li*) and argued that it was impossible to detect 'Heaven's Principle' by observing and experiencing nature (*gewu zhizhi*). Rather, one has to find it from within in one's own mind (*xinxue*). Wang's approach simplified new-Confucianism, but made it more inward-looking. However, the fact that Wang saw no conflict between knowing and doing (*zhixing heyi*), i.e., knowing good behaviour can only be seen from conducting such behaviour and conducting good behaviour reveals 'Heaven's Principle',[10] made the Wang School pro-active in life at the same time.

However, the implications of these ideas have often been overlooked: e.g. (1) 'keeping Heaven's Principle and eliminating human desires' means to discipline power-holders in society, especially the monarch; (2) 'Heaven's Principle' obtained from years of hard work through schooling means also a limited number of practitioners in society;[11] (3) ordinary citizens were expected to keep their mundane desires intact.

---

[9] For the debate on the term *dao*, see Hall and Ames, *Thinking through Confucius*, pp. 226–36.

[10] Wang Yangming, *Chuanxi Lu* (*Analects for Propagating and Learning Knowledge*) (Reprint. Zhengzhou: Henan Classics Press, 2008).

[11] Bear in mind also, the oral language in China was highly fragmented by local dialects which made it very difficult to learn Confucian classics by word of mouth. Moreover, there was no church network for Confucian preaching. Classroom teaching, book reading, and correspondence between literati members remained the main forms of learning Confucianism.

To stress such differentiation, Cheng Yi wrote directly to the emperor, saying that 'the most important tasks in the empire are in the hands of Prime Minister (*zaixiang*) and Court Tutor for the Throne (*jingyan*). The Prime Minister runs the empire to rid it of chaos; the Court Tutor looks after the emperor's morals to help the monarch do the right thing.'[12] Similarly, Zhu Xi described the cardinal importance of Confucian teaching as 'getting the emperor's thinking right' (*zheng junxin*).[13] It is clear that Confucianism shifted its targeted audience steadily toward the top of China's social hierarchy so that the establishments — the monarch and bureaucrats — were subject to moral assessment.

Undoubtedly, Confucian doctrines and principles were 'informal institutions'; good ideas that had little teeth. Other institutions were needed to make Confucian doctrines and principles work.

2. Bureaucratic Monarchy and Bureaucratic Meritocracy

Conceptually, feudalism was ill suited for an empire that had expanding boundaries. The ultimate constraint faced by a feudal system was a demographic one: It depended on how many young male aristocrats were born in each generation to take up positions to rule. Institutionally, the jealously-guarded principles of primogeniture and internal marriages regulated the breeding of aristocrats and hence set the upper limit for the size of a polity under feudalism. In post-Qin China, unless aristocrats were able to multiply their numbers indefinitely to meet the huge demand for administrators when an empire marched in all directions, officials had to come from other classes. If so, feudalism had to be abandoned. What China's empire system was capable of doing was to supply any number of bureaucrats at a short notice to be deployed anywhere in the empire to keep the system going.

Post-Qin China had a monarchy — but that was where the similarity with the European feudal system of the Middle Ages ended. Most scholars have agreed that the power of monarchy in China's empire system was

---

[12] Cheng Hao and Cheng Yi, *Ercheng Ji* (*Collected Works by Cheng Hao and Cheng Yi*) (Beijing: Zhonghua Books, 1981), Vol. 2, p. 540.
[13] Li Jingde (ed.), *Zhuzi Yulei* (*Analects of Master Zhu Xi*) (Beijing: Zhonghua Books, 1986), p. 267.

very limited. Equating the Empire of China with 'absolutist and totalitarian rule' has almost certainly come from mistaking China's Imperial Court for European aristocratic monarchies like French *Ancien Régime* or Russian Tsarism under which the ruling class consisted of hereditary and landed aristocracy. In post-Qin China, such a class was absent. Landholding property rights in post-Qin China were purposely and thoroughly democratised among a large number of ordinary farmers. Landholding alone did not directly lead to office, and no office other than the throne was inheritable. If, in principle, no official was born to govern, post-Qin China was anything but feudal.

Instead, China's bureaucratic monarchy was based on meritocracy. Family wealth and lineage status alone had limited weight in one's chance to join the ruling club, if the candidate himself was not intelligent. Moreover, even the best-educated sons of the most capable ministers had to begin at junior ranks. During the post-Tang period, they were treated like other applicants and subjected to Imperial Examinations as well. Also, promotions were never guaranteed regardless of one's family background and how highly positioned one's father was within the imperial government. This was because the supply of candidates almost always exceeded the vacancies for official positions. So, if one did not perform in examinations or in his government job, there were plenty of qualified candidates waiting to replace him. This created competition and hence meritocracy.

China's selection for bureaucrats began in 178 BC during the reign of Emperor Wendi of the Han Period, aiming to spot 'the able, the virtuous, and the righteous who are good at remonstrating bluntly' (*xianliang fangzheng neng zhiyan jijian zhe*).[14] The system was commonly known as 'observation and recommendation' (*cha ju*). The recommendees were subject to formal examinations run by the authorities. It was the main form of bureaucrat recruitment until the end of the Sui Period (581–618 AD). This Han system had a tendency towards formation of patrons who controlled the process of recommendation, known as 'powerful lineages' or 'lineage clique' (*menfa*). Cronyism led to suboptimal performers. It did

---

[14]Ban, *History of the Han Dynasty*, Vol. 6, Entry 'Biography of Emperor Wendi', in *TFOH*, Vol. 1, p. 379.

not supply the bureaucracy the best qualified citizens and hence weakened the empire in the long run. Even so, it was still not feudalism that we know of.

A parallel and more open system of 'Imperial Examinations', (*keju*) emerged under Emperor Gaozong of the Tang Period (*r.* 650–683 AD). Examinations were regularly scheduled after 688 AD as the salvation of the corrupt observation and recommendation arrangement. The new examinations created a more equal footing to enter the bureaucracy and hence minimised the impact of powerful lineages. During the Northern Song Period, Imperial Examinations were standardised; all Confucian classics were compulsory readings. Three of them, *Book of Songs*, *Book of Rites*, and *Book of History*, were dubbed the 'major classics' (*dajing*) to signal their importance for all examinees.[15]

Gradually, the examination system opened to 'less desirable strata'. The Sui-Tang recruitment excluded sons of artisans and merchants.[16] Restrictions were lifted during the Northern Song Era. Also, the examinations became the only channel to get into officialdom. It proved to be a great success: During the Song Period, the annual number of candidates who received their Imperial Degrees was five times the number during the previous Tang Period, and 3.4 times the number in the subsequent Qing Period.[17]

Meritocratic selection was a costly business considering the number of years of education that was required to build up human capital, and the assessment which followed, all in accordance to rigid criteria. Not only was nothing guaranteed but each generation also had to start all over again to replace retired officials. However, the burden of such costs was born mainly by the private sector as most schools were privately run. It had practically no impact on the government budget apart from the costs of

---

[15]Tuotuo, *Song Shi* (*History of the Song Dynasty*), Vol. 155, Entry 'Xuanju Zhi', (Originally published in 1345 AD. Reprint), in *Er-shi-wu Shi* (*Twenty-Five Official Histories, or TFOH*) (Shanghai: Shanghai Classics Press, 1986), Vol. 7, p. 5641.

[16]Liu Xu, *Jiu Tangshu* (*Old History of the Tang Dynasty*), Vol. 43, Entry 'Zhiguan Zhi' (Originally published in 946 AD. Reprint), in *TFOH* (Shanghai: Shanghai Classics Press, 1986), Vol. 5, p. 3697.

[17]Yang Ling, *Songdai Chuban Wenhua* (*Printing Culture of the Song Period*) (Beijing: Cultural Relics Press, 2012), p. 47.

organising the regular Imperial Examinations. Undoubtedly, feudalism was cheaper to run regardless of human capital formation so long as one was born into the right family. He who had blue blood, ruled. There was no need to select constantly the best-qualified people among the general population, and there was no need for open competition, either.

In the every-day running of the empire in China, the monarch had to rely on his ministers, commissioners, and governors — without whom, the emperor was powerless. One key institution was the 'emperor-chaired conference' (*yuqian huiyi*) for policy debates with sometimes hundreds of officials attending. In Han times, 127 such conferences were held at an average of one for every 3.4 years.[18] The state monopoly of salt, wine, iron and weapons was a product of such a conference in 81 BC. For lesser matters, the throne depended on his team within the Imperial Court. In the Ming Period, Imperial Academicians (*neige daxueshi*) from five Imperial Colleges were actively involved in decision-making of the highest levels.[19]

The personnel of the imperial bureaucracy were only a part of China's governance system. To feed the centre with information of activities far afield, the empire depended on a network that had its tentacles reaching every county inside the empire. In the beginning of the Qin Period, the Prime Minister (*chengxiang*) was in charge of this network. It became the responsibility of the Imperial Secretariat (*shangshu tai*) in the following Han Period, and Bureau of Imperial Representatives (*yezhe Tai*) during the Sui Period, Imperial Academy (*hanlin yuan, xueshi yuan*) under the Tang and the Song Periods, Imperial Cabinet (*neige*) and, Imperial Secret Police (*dongxi chang, jinyi wei*),[20] and, Imperial Cabinet (*neige*) and Grand Council (*junji chu*),[21] during the Ming and Qing Periods respectively. The most important reform regarding information flux was the Qing 'confidential memorial to the throne' (*mizhe, mizou* or *zoushu*) which linked officials, including those of lower ranks, directly to the emperor to reduce information manipulation by the official pecking order.[22]

---

[18] Wu Yumin, *Wuxingde Wangluo* (*The Invisible Network — China's Traditional Culture from the Angle of Communication*) (Beijing: International Culture Press, 1988), p. 119.
[19] *Ibid.*, p. 100.
[20] Literally 'Eastern Depot', 'Western Depot', and 'Guards in Embroidered Uniforms'.
[21] Literally 'Department of Military Secrets'.
[22] Wu, *Invisible Network*, pp. 102–11.

However, the greatest challenge to the empire system was how to manage and minimise power abuse and corruption within the bureaucracy. The Chinese elite thought through it hard and gradually put some checks and balances in place. First of all, there was a balance between the monarch and the bureaucracy. China's bureaucracy did not depend on a monarch to function. At best, the monarch was a custodian to safeguard the bureaucracy from malfunction,[23] and a great many monarchs of China accepted such a role. In 648 AD, Emperor Taizhong of the Tang Period (r. 627–49) even compiled *How to Become a Model Emperor (Di Fan)* for his successors. He described the role of the monarch as a role model for society: 'Monarch is like the fountainhead. A clean fountainhead makes the entire river clean, and a cloudy fountainhead makes the river muddy.'[24] The catch here was that it was the Confucian literati's mission to educate all young princes from a very young age, and assist and supervise the emperor to behave like the 'Son of Heaven'.[25] The interpretation of 'Heaven' (*tian*) and 'Heaven's Way' (*dao*) was firmly monopolised by the literati. Therefore, Mencius stated that 'the purpose for a Confucian to work for the king is solely to guide him to reach benevolence' (*junzi zi shijun ye wuyin qijun yi dangdao zhiyu ren eryi*).[26] In this regard, the monarch himself needed a role model known as the 'sage king', or 'internally a sage who externalise him as a king' (*neisheng waiwang*).[27] Few monarch in China was able to achieve such a status by himself. It was hence imperative that the throne was surrounded by Confucian tutors, advisers, and ministers. The Imperial Court — consisting of the emperor and government ministers — held meetings routinely to discuss and decide matters that arose. It essentially involved teamwork.[28] Often, what the throne had to do was to act as a judicator between different options. It was a myth that the

---

[23] Deng, *Premodern Chinese Economy*, pp. 159–60.

[24] Li Shimin, *Di Fan (How to Become a Model Emperor)* (648 AD), ch. 1.

[25] For the Qing Dynasty, see Albert Feuerwerker, *State and Society in Eighteenth-Century China: The Ch'ing Empire in Its Glory* (Ann Arbor: Center for Chinese Studies of the University of Michigan, 1976), pp. 35–8.

[26] Mencius, *Mengzi (Master Meng's Book)* (Warring States Period: 475–221 BC), ch. 'Guozi Xia'.

[27] R. B. Dobson, *The Peasants' Revolts of 1381* (London: MacMillan, 1983), pp. 155–7.

[28] J. K. Fairbank, *The United States and China* (Cambridge [MA]: Harvard University Press, 1965), p. 114.

emperor decided everything alone; if this had been true, the bureaucracy would have become redundant.

Secondly, to minimise power abuse, the central administration was deliberately split up into departments. During the Sui Dynasty (581–618 AD), a 'three department system' (*san sheng zhi*) was invented: the Prime Ministry (*shangshu sheng*), Imperial Secretariat (*zhongshu sheng*), and Imperial Liaison Office (*menxia sheng*), taking charge of administration, legislation, and evaluation of policies, respectively. These departments were equally ranked and empowered. The Prime Ministry ran a network of six government ministries (*bu*) and 24 bureaus (*si*), but it had no role in legislation. The Imperial Secretariat was in charge of laws and law making, which was subject to evaluation by the Imperial Liaison Office. Each department had three to five senior officials to share responsibilities. This system was adopted by the dynasties that followed.

Thirdly, due to asymmetric information and the 'principle-agent problem', local officials had considerable autonomy in the running of provincial affairs, which was often depicted in the phrase, 'Heaven is high, and the emperor is far away' (*tiangao huangdiyuan*). The age-old problem of 'who watches the watchmen' (Latin: *Quis custodiet ipsos custodes*) remained. The main problem with officials was not so much their intellect but their integrity. It was a fact that capable officials with easy access to resources were likely to steal with great efficiency from the public. Autonomy of officials only made corruption easy. Without regular checks, it was inevitable for a local official to deviate from the Confucian guideline and government policies for some time before being detected. To prevent this from taking place, a network of surveillance (*micha*) was created, including vertically arranged 'Imperial Inspectors' (*xunxing*) and 'confidential memorials to the throne' (*mizou*). Officials and their performances were assessed by grades (*mokan*). In the Tang Period (618–907 AD), the assessment included nine grades from 'excellent' (*shangshang*) to 'poor' (*xiaxia*) in order to determine promotion, demotion, or dismissal. This system was inherited by the later dynasties, too.

In addition, there was a horizontally operated procedure of 'impeachment of fellow officials' (*tanhe*). Impeachment of fellow officials for their wrong doings was made part of official routine duties.[29] The penalty was progressive, ranking-wise. The 1820 law states that:

> *If a Governor-General [zongdu] is greedy while his [subordinate] Governor of Province [xunfu] does not report (him), the latter is to be demoted by three grades and re-appointed elsewhere regardless of whether the two parties are stationed in the same town or not. If a local official does not duly discover and report his subordinate's greediness before his superior [dufu] does, he is to be demoted by two grades and re-appointed elsewhere if (he is) holding an office as a prefecture magistrate [zhifu, zhizhou]; and to be demoted by one grade and re-appointed elsewhere if holding an office as a county magistrate [zhixian].[30]*

Such checks and balances did produce some results. There were over 200 major cases of corruption during the Qing Period. Seventy percent of them involved ranking officials of the Third Grade (*sanpin*) or higher.[31] The most sensational cases included Wang Danwang (Provincial Treasurer of Gansu) in 1781, Pu Lin (Governor of Fujian) in 1795, and He Shen (Senior Grand Secretary) in 1799. Wang, guilty of the embezzlement of a disaster relief fund, was sentenced to death. Pu, guilty of receiving bribes of 280,000 *taels* of silver (10.5 metric tons), also received the death penalty.[32] He Shen, guilty of embezzling 26,000 *taels* of gold and 3,000,000 *taels* of silver (112.5 metric tons), was forced to commit suicide.[33] Other corrupt ranking officials punished by death included Zhou Xuejian (1748), E Leshun (1755), Hen Wen (1757), Jiang Zhou (1757), Yang Hao (1757), Gao Heng (1768), Fang Shijun (1769),

---

[29] Silas Wu, *Communication and Imperial Control in China: The Evolution of the Palace Memorial System, 1693–1735* (Cambridge: Harvard University Press, 1970); T. A. Metzger, *The Internal Organization of Ch'ing Bureaucracy: Legal, Normative, and Communication Aspects* (Cambridge [MA]: Harvard University Press, 1973).

[30] Anon., *Jiaqing 25 Nian Qinding Libu Zeli (The 1820 Regulations of Ministry of Personnel, Made by Imperial Order)* (Originally published in 1820. Reprint. Taipei: Chengwen Press, 1966), p. 68.

[31] Zhao, *History of the Qing Dynasty*, in *TFOH*, Vol. 12, pp. 9798–10366.

[32] Dai Yi (ed.), *Er-shi-liu Shi Da Zidian (Encyclopaedia of the Twenty-Six Official Histories)* (Changchun: Jilin People's Press, 1993), pp. 1300–1.

[33] Zhao, *History of the Qing Dynasty*, in *TFOH*, Vol. 12, pp. 10000–1.

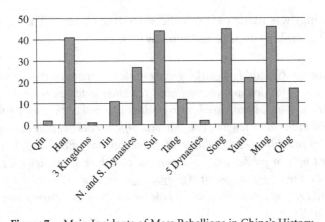

Figure 7.   Main Incidents of Mass Rebellions in China's History.

Source: Li Guangbi, Qian Junye and Lai Xinxia, *Zhongguo Nongmin Qiyi Lunji* (*Chinese Peasant Rebellions*) (Beijing: Sanlian Books, 1958); Fan Wenlan, *Zhongguo Tongshi Jian Bian* (*A Brief Panorama of Chinese History*) (Beijing: People's Press, 1964–5); Liu Zehua, Yang Zhijiu, Wang Yuzhe, Yang Yixiang, Feng Erkang, Nan Bingwen, Tang Gang, Zheng Kesheng and Sun Liqun, *Zhongguo Gudaishi* (*History of Pre-modern China*) (Beijing: People's Press, 1979); Zhang Shaoliang and Zheng Xianjin, *Zhongguo Nongmin Geming Douzhengshi* (*A History of Revolutionary Struggle of the Chinese Peasantry*) (Beijing: Qiushi Press, 1983).

Liang Qing (1769), Qian Du (1772), Chen Huizu (1782), Lu Jianzeng (1768), Guo Tai (1782), Hao Shuo (1784), Gao Pu (1788), Fu Song (1792), Wu Lana (1795), and Guang Xing (1808).[34]

Occasionally, the system completely broke down. The solution was a regime change (to a new monarch and new bureaucracy) via popular rebellions (see Figure 7). These rebellions were seen as 'acting on behalf of Heaven' (*tie tian xing dao*) in order to restore Heaven's order for the empire.

3. Physiocracy, Landholding Property Rights, Tax Burden, and Agricultural Assistance

The Qin Empire was created by spears and ploughs in the hands of farmer-soldiers in accordance with Shang Yang's 'farming and warring' strategy (*gengzhan*). The need for physically tough men to fight wars and occupy newly captured lands on a permanent basis made settled agriculture an

[34]Dai, *Encyclopaedia of the Twenty-Six Official Histories*, pp. 1299–1301, 1302, 1310.

ideal sector, and a land-holding peasantry an ideal social class for the Qin empire-building. Physiocracy, or 'agricultural fundamentalism', was hence, historically, a logical and effective policy that delivered desirable results.

In post-Qin history, when peace prevailed, physiocracy remained the cornerstone of government economic policy for a slightly different reason: It provided the population with employment, as Emperor Wendi of the Han Dynasty stated in 178 BC that 'farming is the cardinal foundation upon which people's livelihood depends. ... I thus lead all government ministers tilling in order to promote farming'.[35] What remained tacit in the emperor's statement was that predictable yield from faming also brought the state stable revenues. Here, the influence and importance of the state-peasant alliance was obvious.

An immediate consequence of physiocracy was the creation and entrenchment of landholding rights for the farmers, which was the antithesis of the previous feudal land ownership. Such rights included lease-holding and freehold rights, known as 'land for tillers'.[36] The Qin farmers took the lead. When Shang Yang's reforms were carried out in 390–338 BC, self-declared ownership over unclaimed land (*zhi shi tian*) kick-started the new ownership scheme. Later, during the Northern Song Period (960–1127), farmers were again permitted to self-declare ownership over unclaimed land; and most state-owned land was decisively privatised to that same end.[37]

In the post-Qin era, apart from outright free holding of land, a repertoire policy involved leaseholding of government-owned land. The best known empire-wide land allocation schemes were the 'Land Allowed to Citizens' (*zhantian*), 'Land Allocated to Citizens' (*shoutian*), and 'Land Equalization System' (*juntian zhi*) in exchange for tax in grain and corvée services.[38] The first national scheme was implemented in 280 AD. The distribution was modelled after the early chessboard-field system but

---

[35] Ban, *History of the Han Dynasty*, Vol. 6, Entry 'Biography of Emperor Wendi', in *TFOH*, Vol. 1, p. 379.
[36] 'Land for tillers' has often been mistaken for a modern approach among those who know little about China's past.
[37] Tuotuo, *History of the Song Dynasty*, Vol. 173, Entry 'Shihuozhi 126', in *TFOH*, Vol. 7, p. 5711.
[38] The Tang annual tax burden was about nine strings of bronze coins and 60 days corvée service by a male per household per year; see Zhang Guogang, *Zhongguo Jiating Shi, Dier Juan* (*A History of Families in China*) (Guangzhou: Guangdong People's Press, 2007), Vol. 2, p. 266.

without feudal lords to promote equality. The best-recorded arrangement was the Land Equalization System between the fifth and eighth centuries. In 485 AD, the system allocated each married couple 80 *mu* of land of which 60 *mu* for grain and 20 *mu* for 50 mulberry trees, five jujube trees and three elm trees.[39] Under Tang rule, farmland was allocated according to age and gender (Table 6).

Table 6.   Gender and Farmland.

Type	Farmland *mu*
Male, 18–60 years old	100
Male, over 60	40
Widows	30

Source: Zhang, *History of Families in China*, Vol. 2, p. 143.

Later, the average landholding declined to 40 *mu*, suggesting the inevitable re-distribution of land to accommodate population growth.[40] Table 7 shows the residual household landholding under the Tang Land Equalization System in the Dunhuang Region in the north-western frontier of the empire, along the Silk Road.

Another common form of private landholding was 'farming colonies' (*tuntian*) along China's frontiers as a means of consolidating the army's food supply as well as the empire's territorial control.[41] Song army soldiers for example were allocated 200 *mu* each in those colonies.[42]

These land-for-tiller schemes represented a state-run command economy. Farmers' leaseholding property rights were well defined and protected. In return, the state received corvée services and revenues from the peasantry. Under these schemes, the farming tenants paid both rent and taxes to the same government. There was no feudal lord involved in this state–peasant relationship.

---

[39]Wei Shou, *Wei Shu* (*History of the Wei Kingdom*) (Originally published in 554 AD. Reprint. Beijing: Zhonghua Books, 1974), ch. 'Shihuo Zhi'.

[40]*Ibid.*, Vol. 2, pp. 260–1.

[41]M. P. Lee, *The Economic History of China, with Special Reference to Agriculture* (New York: AMS Press, 1969), pp. 33–133.

[42]Xu Song, *Song Huiyao Jigao* (*Edited Administrative Statutes of the Song Dynasty*) (Originally published in 1809. Reprint. Taipei: Xinwenfeng Press, 1976), Vol. 7, Entry 'Bing 4/11', p. 6811. *Note*: 200 *mu* = 12 ha.

Table 7. Dunhuang Household Land Lease-holding in the Late Tang, *c.* 907 AD.

Size of holding (*mu*)	Percentage of total farmland	Percentage of households
<20	3.2	17.3
20–130	51.4	74.1
>130	45.4	8.6
Total	100.0	100.0

Source: Zhang Donggang, *Zhongguo Jiating Shi, Dier Juan* (*A History of Families in China*) (Guangzhou: Guangdong People's Press, 2007), Vol. 2, p. 260.

Under such schemes, individual farmers were granted, by law, permanent lease-holding rights until they retired. Even so, evidence shows that land was openly traded with formal written contracts.[43] In later times, this idea of permanent leaseholding rights was taken up by the private sector. A turning point occurred during the Northern Song Period when state land was systematically privatised and state ownership dropped to merely 1.4 percent of China's total farmland, much lower than the previous Tang.[44] From then on, private landownership was the dominant ownership type until 1949.

Physiocracy also set the upper limits for tax burden on the peasantry. In the post-Qin era, heavy taxation on the peasantry was a political taboo. The Western Han state imposed a low rate of three percent of the total output of the main crop of the year on the peasantry.[45] During the Qing Period, the annual revenue from the Land-Poll Tax (*diding*) was frozen unilaterally by the state on the level of 30 million *taels* of silver (1,125 metric tons) for over a century from 1715 to 1840. This was known as 'freezing the tax revenue' (*yongbu jiafu*), or 'Kangxi tax cut'.[46] During this period, the Chinese population increased around 5.7 times (between 1721 and 1833),[47] but the enlarged

---

[43] Zhang, *History of Families in China*, Vol. 2, p. 274.

[44] Liang Fangzhong, *Zhongguo Lidai Hukou Tiandi Tianfu Tongji* (*Dynastic Data for China's Households, Cultivated Land and Land Taxation*) (Shanghai: Shanghai People's Press), p. 290; Qi Xia, *Songdai Jingjishi* (*An Economic History of the Song*) (Beijing: Zhonghua Books, 2009), Vol. 1, p. 299.

[45] Ban, *History of the Han Dynasty*, Vol. 24, Entry 'Shihuo 4', in *TFOH*, Vol. 1, p. 477.

[46] Zhao, *History of the Qing Dynasty*, Vol. 121, Entry 'Economy', in *TFOH*, Vol. 11, p. 9261.

[47] Deng, 'Unveiling China's True Population Statistics'.

population paid roughly the same 30 million *taels* a year. In per capita terms, direct-tax burdens fell by a massive 79 percent. Per unit of land, the tax burden declined between 30 and 50 percent, given that arable land area also increased.[48] In the end, the Qing taxation rate was so light that people 'barely noticed the tax system, almost as if they suffered no tax burden at all'.[49]

To put the Qing tax burden into a wage perspective, according to Sidney Gamble, the average daily wage between 1807 and 1850 for unskilled labourers in Beijing was 0.09–0.15 *taels* of silver during the peak season. The Qing annual tax burden was thus about one to two days' unskilled wages.[50] In the nineteenth century, a Manchu cavalryman had an allowance of 36 *taels* a year plus of stipend rice.[51] The amount of 0.16 *taels* was 1.5 days' pay excluding his stipend rice as his wage goods. Tax holidays for newly reclaimed land or new crop type were common. For example, during the Northern Song Period, land under rice was once completely tax-free.[52] 'Negative taxation' applied in the form of disaster-famine relief, which we will come back to later.

Physiocracy also included government financial and technical assistance. For example, during the Northern Song Period, government loans were used to persuade farmers to stay in farming.[53] The 'Green-shoots Loan Scheme' (*qingmiao fa*), which consisted of low-interest government loans, was designed to help those whose winter-wheat crop failed.[54] Technical assistance included assimilation of best practices in farming tools, crop choices, field management, and food storage. The best example

---

[48]Ts'ui-Jung Liu and J. C. H. Fei, 'An Analysis of the Land Tax Burden in China, 1650–1865', *The Journal of Economic History*, 43/3 (1977), pp. 373, 375–6.

[49]Susan Mann, *Local Merchants and the Chinese Bureaucracy, 1750–1950* (Stanford: Stanford University Press, 1987), p. 16.

[50]For the wage data, see S. D. Gamble, 'Daily Wages of Unskilled Chinese Laborers, 1807–1902', *The Far Eastern Quarterly*, 3/1 (1943), p. 62. For the money exchange rate, see Yu, *History of Prices*, p. 860.

[51]He and Wei, *Qing Administration*, p. 868.

[52]Tuotuo, *History of the Song Dynasty*, Vol. 173, Entry 'Shihuozhi 126', in *TFOH*, Vol. 7, p. 5711.

[53]So much so, according to one source, only 30 percent of land under cultivation actually bore tax before 1069. See Xu, *Edited Administrative Statutes of the Song Dynasty*, chs. 'Shihuo 63/182', 'Shihuo 69/38', Vol. 7, pp. 6063, 6334; and Zhou Bodi, *Zhongguo Caizheng Shi* (*A Financial History of China*) (Shanghai: Shanghai People's Press, 1981), p. 249.

[54]Tuotuo, *History of the Song Dynasty*, Vol. 176, Entry 'Shihuozhi 129', in *TFOH*, Vol. 7, p. 5726.

Table 8. Agricultural Treatises, Total Numbers, and Frequency of Production.

Dynasty	Duration in years (I)	No. of book titles (II)	II/I
Han	426	14	30.4
Tang	289	28	10.3
Song	319	105	3.0
Ming	276	127	2.2
Qing	267	199	1.3

Source: Wang Yuhu, *Zhongguo Nongxue Shulu* (*Bibliography of Chinese Classical Agronomy*) (Beijing: Agriculture Press, 1964).

is the compilation and circulation of agricultural treatises (*nongshu*) that increased steadily over time due to strong support from the authorities (see Table 8).

4. Marriages, Family Structures, and Inheritance

Universal marriages were practised in post-Qin China. Singletons counted for about only two percent of the total population (as of the 1930s).[55] The marriage market was very local, with 50 percent of married couples coming from the same prefectures among the gentry class, and 65 percent among the peasantry.[56]

The official policy was to encourage couples to marry young. During the Eastern Han Period (25–220 AD), the average age for marriage was 30 for men and 20 for women.[57] During the Three Kingdoms Period (220–280), the average marriage age for both male and female dropped to 17. By 316 AD, the age declined to 13 for females and 15 for males.[58] After that, changes in marriageable age were but marginal.[59] Only in the

[55]Yang Zihui (ed.), *Zhongguo Lidai Renkou Tongji Ziliao Yanjiu* (*China's Historical Population Statistics in the Long Run*) (Beijing: Reforms Press, 1996), p. 1439.

[56]Yu, *History of Families in China*, Vol. 4, pp. 67–8.

[57]Wang, *History of Families in China*, Vol. 1, p. 246.

[58]*Ibid.*, Vol. 1, p. 416; Li Yanshou, *Beishi* (*History of Northern Kingdoms*) (Originally published in 659 AD. Reprint), in *Er-shi-wu Shi* (*Twenty-Five Official Histories, or TFOH*) (Shanghai: Shanghai Classics Press, 1986), Vol. 4, p. 2913.

[59]Jiang Tao, *Renkou Yu Lishi* (*Population and History*) (Beijing: People's Press, 1998), p. 272; Yu, *History of Families in China*, Vol. 4, p. 76.

Table 9. Proportion of Nuclear Families in China, 2 AD–1928.

Year	Nuclear families in China's total (%)
2 AD	97 (China-wide)
900	52 (Dunhuang)
1600	48 (upper classes)
1880	65 (Anhui)
	45 (Sichuan)
1928	63 (China-wide)

Source: Liang, *Dynastic Data*, pp. 4–11; also Wang, *History of Families in China*, Vol. 1, p. 221; Zhang, *History of Families in China*, Vol. 2, p. 12; Yu, *History of Families in China*, Vol. 4, pp. 31, 47; Zheng, *History of Families in China*, Vol. 5, p. 31.

1920s, did the earliest marriage ages on average increase to 19.7 years for males and 17.7 for females.[60]

Monogamy was, without a doubt, China's dominant marriage pattern. The much publicised phenomenon of polygamy only applied to about five percent of all families during the Qing era.[61] Much publicised extensive families (made of more than two families) were not considered the mainstream. Rather, the nuclear family (a married couple with children) was the long-term norm since the early Han Period (see Table 9). Such a family structure was undoubtedly the legacy of the Qin institution that aimed to increase the number of taxpayers.[62]

Moreover, population control, including infanticide and abortion, was quite common.[63] As a result, the average size of families from various samples remained stable (see Table 10).

Feudal primogeniture was not practised in post-Qin China. Rather, *de jure* equal inheritance among sons (and brothers) was the norm.

---

[60] Zheng Quanhong, *Zhongguo Jiating Shi, Diwu Juan* (*A History of Families in China*) (Guangzhou: Guangdong People's Press, 2007), Vol. 5, pp. 102–6.

[61] Yu, *History of Families in China*, Vol. 4, pp. 99–100.

[62] Wang, *History of Families in China*, Vol. 1, pp. 230–44.

[63] James Lee and Wang Feng, 'Malthusian Models and Chinese Realities: The Chinese Demographic System 1700–2000', *Population and Development Review*, 25/1 (1999), pp. 33–65; Li Bozhong, *Duoshijiao Kan Jiangnan Jingjishi, 1250–1850* (*Multiple Aspects of Economic History of the Lower Yangzi, 1250–1850*) (Beijing: Sanlian Books, 2003), pp. 236–40.

Table 10. Average Size of Family in China, 2 AD–1947.

Year	Persons/Household
2 AD	4.9
262	5.3
370	4.1
464	5.2
516	5.2
609	5.2
740	5.7
821	6.6
1100	5.5
1291	4.5
1491	5.9
1620	5.3
1753	4.7
1781	4.5
1911	5.2
1928	5.3
1936	5.4
1947	5.3

Source: Liang, *Dynastic Data*, pp. 4–11; Zhang, *History of Families in China*, Vol. 2, pp. 9–11; Xing, *History of Families in China*, Vol. 3, p. 25; Yu, *History of Families in China*, Vol. 4, pp. 16–24; Zheng, *History of Families in China*, Vol. 5, p. 61; Yang, *China's Historical Population Statistics*, pp. 1439, 1449.

According to the *Complete Record of the Tang Dynasty* (*Tang Huiyao*), if a father passed away, his property was to be equally divided and inherited by all of his sons; if any of his sons was dead by the time of inheritance, his grandsons took that share; if he did not have a son, his widow inherited his property.[64] The Ming–Qing (1368–1911) Inheritance Law stipulated that 'all the family land property is subject to equal division among all the sons

---

[64]Wang Pu, *Tang Huiyao* (*Complete Record of the Tang Dynasty*) (961 AD), Vol. 84, Entry 'Zalu', cited in Zhang, *History of Families in China*, Vol. 2, p. 212.

regardless of their mothers' legal status in the household, be it the wife, concubines or maids; a son of adultery inherits half of such a share'.[65] Without a doubt, equal inheritance matched well with the empire, whose territory was not permanently fixed (see Figure 1), and the empire was rather thinly populated until *c.* 1700 AD (see Figure 2). The empire needed to replicate family farms anywhere the empire ruled.

5. Anti-Merchant Attitudes, State Trade Monopoly and Peasant Commercialisation

Confucian physiocrats in post-Qin history held negative views about occupations other than government service and farming. Such an attitude was simplified as 'favouring farmers and confining merchants' (*zhongnong yishang*). From the viewpoint of empire building, this was deeply rooted in the aforementioned state-peasant alliance.

The technical reason for farming and farmers to be singled out and treated differently from other sectors and groups was that settled farming communities were less mobile and their outputs more visible outdoors, which made governance and taxation easy. Moreover, the image of farmers of being less cunning than artisans and merchants also granted farmers a desirable moral character in a morally charged Confucian society. In addition, the Confucian elite were rurally based: The majority of serving bureaucrats had land properties and a large majority of them also retired to their home villages. Students from the rural sector (*nong*) were always encouraged to take Imperial Examinations. 'China's dream' then was described as 'a young man who lives in a rural hut in the morning mounts the Palace of the Son of Heaven in the dusk; army generals and government ministers are not inherited, they are but men of high expectations' (*zhaowei tianshe lang, modeng tianzi tang; jiangxiang ben wu zhong, nan-er zi dang qiang*).[66] Such a channel for social mobility was often unavailable for sons of artisans and merchants (with the exception of the Song and Qing Periods). Inevitably, a vested interest group of 'physiocrats'

---

[65] Yu, *History of Families in China*, Vol. 3, p. 117.

[66] This is part of a long poem composed by the Northern Song prodigy, Wang Zhu, to preach young sons of farmers to take up education for officialdom. See Zhang Wei (ed.), *Shengtong Shi* (*The Song Prodigy's Poem on Schooling*) (Beijing: Zhonghua Books, 2013).

became well entrenched in the politics of the empire who made sure the same policy continued.

A policy package to confine merchants began with Emperor Gaozu (*r.* 206–195 BC) of the Western Han Period who decided that merchants were not permitted to wear silk or ride on carts, and they had to pay heavy taxes; Emperor Huidi (*r.* 194–188 BC) forbade merchant descendants to join the bureaucracy.[67] In addition, merchants were not entitled to get farmland allotments from the state (*mingtian*).[68] Emperor Wudi (*r.* 140–87 BC) went further by viewing merchants as parasites 'living on others' and 'getting rich by arbitraging rare goods from mountains and seas', which rationalised the state monopoly over 'key markets' for goods like salt and iron. These items were chosen not because of their scarcity, but because of their income and price inelasticity (such as salt and wine) and their importance in national security (metals and weapons).

The Han government imposed in 114 BC an empire-wide audit of merchants' wealth in order to tax more (*suanmin*); those who evaded and concealed their wealth faced the penalty of exile and property expropriation (*gaomin*).[69] The auditing process was so severe that most medium and larger merchant houses went broke.[70] The number of properties confiscated by the state amounted for several hundred million strings of cash together with tens of thousand family servants and unknown quantities of farmland.[71] Such institutional discrimination against merchants perpetuated in the long run with the exception of the Song and, to a lesser extent, the Qing Periods.

Policies of confining merchants were however, not identical with policies which were catered to commerce and commercial sectors. The market and market exchange were largely tolerated, simply because both the state and private citizens needed the market. With its monopoly over key markets, the state was the single largest market agent inside the empire.

[67] Sima, *Book of History*, Vol. 30, Entry 'Pingzhun Shu', in *TFOH*, Vol. 1, p. 178.
[68] Ban, *History of the Han Dynasty*, Vol. 24, Entry 'Shihuo Zhi Xia', in *TFOH*, Vol. 1, p. 480.
[69] *Ibid.*
[70] Sima, *Book of History*, Vol. 30, Entry 'Pingzhun Shu', in *TFOH*, Vol. 1, p. 180.
[71] Ban, *History of the Han Dynasty*, Vol. 24, Entry 'Shihuo Zhi Xia', in *TFOH*, Vol. 1, p. 480.

During the Northern Song Period, government market operations developed further to the stage of mercantilism.

Petty market operation by small landholders was rarely viewed as a threat to China's social stability; rather, they were seen as China's social lubricant. This was because China's private households in the rural sector had the incentives to produce surpluses and they enjoyed a high degree of freedom to exchange goods and services. During the Qing Period, China's local trading networks had 45,000 fairs, each serving 15–20 villages.[72] The state did not impose taxes on these fairs. During the Ming–Qing Period, 20–40 percent of peasant outputs were traded there by peasants and for peasants.[73] Merchants' involvement was minimal.

In this context, merchants' operations in terms of scale and scope were capped. The most common form of merchant operation was to procure ready-made cloth from rural households. But rural producers had no obligation to sell their textiles to these merchants; ordinary peasants were part-time traders themselves. So, the scale of merchants' operations was small.[74] A putting-out system (*fangsha shoubu*) emerged late and sporadic.[75] In the early twentieth century, the largest firm Guang Heng Tong controlled about 10,000 weavers, a trivial proportion in the most productive Lower Yangzi Delta where about 70 percent of the 5.4 million households produced their own cotton cloth.[76]

6. Relaxation of State Monopoly

It is worth noting that government market monopoly was relaxed from time to time. During the Northern Song Period, a new system of dealership permits (*yin*) for salt, wine and tea was implemented. After paying

---

[72]G. W. Skinner, 'Chinese Peasants and Closed Community: An Open and Shut Case', *Comparative Studies in Society and History*, 13/3 (1971), pp. 272–3; G. W. Skinner, 'Marketing and Social Structure in Rural China', *The Journal of Asian Studies*, 24/1 (1964), pp. 3–44; 24/2 (1965), pp. 195–228; 24/3 (1965), pp. 363–400.

[73]Perkins, *Agricultural Development in China*, p. 115; Feuerwerker, *State and Society*, p. 86.

[74]Xu Xinwu (ed.), *Jiangnan Tubu Shi* (*A History of Home-made Cotton Cloth in the Lower Yangzi Delta*) (Shanghai: Shanghai Social Science Academy Press, 1989), pp. 549–55, 642–4, 671–5.

[75]*Ibid.*, pp. 644–6, 699–701.

[76]*Ibid.*, pp. 200–1700. For household numbers (as of 1912), see Liang, *Dynastic Data*, p. 268.

their license fees, merchants became government tax-farmers. Salt fields remained state-run through which the state still controlled the forward linkages. Large quantities of salt, 400 million *catties* (238,600 metric tons) a year,[77] were released, but to licensed dealers only. Government income from the salt dealership fees grew from 2.8 billion bronze coins in 1049 to 23 billion in 1078.[78] Similarly, wine yeast was produced by state workshops and then sold to private breweries by government agents.[79] It was mandatory for all breweries' output, about 100 million Chinese decilitres (*sheng*) per annum, to private be sold through a government channel.[80] By law, tea-growers also sold their outputs exclusively to government agents. The system handled 23–29 million *catties* (13,730–17,300 metric tons) of tea a year.[81] Such a policy continued until the Qing Period. In the 1840s, 10 million *taels* of silver (375 tons) were collected annually from salt levies (*yanke*) together with internal customs duties (*guanshui*).[82]

On the export front, similarly, trade dealers were selected by the government and enjoyed the right as the sole agents to operate China's imports and exports. In return, the dealers were responsible for customs control, payment of commercial taxes, and liaison between foreign traders and ordinary Chinese merchants, as well as between foreign traders and the Chinese authorities.[83] Until the signing of the Nanking Treaty in 1842, these merchants were practically in charge of the entire Sino-foreign seafaring trade. Such power and responsibility of merchants were unprecedented in China's

---

[77] Hu Xiaopeng, *Zhongguo Shougongye Jingji Tongshi, Song Yuan Juan* (*A General History of Handicraft Industry in China, the Song and Yuan Periods*) (Fuzhou: Fujian People's Press, 2004), pp. 353, 402.

[78] Li Xiao, *Songchao Zhengfu Goumai Zhidu Yanjiu* (*Government Procurement Systems during the Song Period*) (Shanghai: Shanghai People's Press, 2007), p. 222.

[79] Wei Tian-an, *Songdai Guanying Jingji Shi* (*A History of State-owned Sector during the Song Period*) (Beijing: People's Press, 2011), pp. 356, 361.

[80] Hu, *General History of Handicraft Industry*, p. 353.

[81] Hua Shan, *Songshi Lunji* (Jinan: Qilu Books, 1982), pp. 76, 109.

[82] Zhou, *History of State Finance in China*, pp. 419–21, 426.

[83] For a case, see Chen Guodong, 'Pan Youdu (Pan Qiguan Ershi): Yiwei Chenggongde Yanghang Shangren' (Pan Youdu, Pan Qiguan, the Second: A Successful Chartered Foreign Trade Dealer), in Zhang Bincun and Liu Shiji (eds.), *Zhongguo Haiyang Fazhanshi Lunwenji* (*Selected Essays on the Maritime History of China*) (Taipei: Academia Sinica, 1993), Vol. 5, pp. 245–300.

history: For the first time, the Imperial government gave a group of private merchants such a position in an area that was traditionally viewed as the exclusive domain of the government since the Han Period.

Now, the Qing government faced a constant dilemma: (1) According to the Confucian doctrine the merchant class was useful but untrustworthy, yet (2) according to the rule of the 'market game', the merchant class was the most qualified player at all accounts, and thus they should be trusted. The fact that those merchants were all chartered showed enormous trust by the state, a very un-Confucian approach. In this context, it becomes easy to understand (1) Why the Qing authorities viewed the chartered sea merchants as money-making machines of the government and (2) why business failures of those merchants often gave provocation to the throne and losers were often extraordinarily heavily punished for their business failures. The Qing government had great expectations of these privileged dealers with an express provision that no bankruptcy should ever occur. Therefore, it is misleading to view harsh penalties upon chartered maritime merchants as hard evidence of government antitrade policy. The merchants were chartered voluntarily and penalties were regarded as a reasonable price for the monopolistic power given to them.

During the Ming–Qing Period, merchants also enjoyed noticeable freedom in silver imports. Foreign silver was purchased by China's exports. Silver imports and silver trade were deliberately left unregulated, despite its easy controllability, because of a long dispute between the state and importers over taxes imposed on imported silver. The Ming–Qing government viewed silver imports as commodities subject to customs duties, while the importers viewed silver as a currency and thus should be tax-free.[84] It was thus in the best interest of the Imperial authorities to recognise foreign silver as bullion only to tax it. And tax they did. As a direct result of this policy, there was silver heterogeneity in shapes, sizes and purity everywhere in China.[85] The heterogeneity however, was left to the merchant

---

[84] P. A. van Dyke, *The Canton Trade, Life and Enterprise on the China Coast, 1700–1845* (Hong Kong: Hong Kong University Press, 2005), p. 119.

[85] Zhao Dexin, *Zhongguo Jingjishi Cidian* (*Dictionary of Chinese Economic History*) (Wuhan: Hubei Dictionary Press, 1990), pp. 613–4; Yen-p'ing Hao, *The Commercial Revolution in Nineteenth-Century China* (Berkeley: University of California Press, 1986), pp. 35–46.

class to sort out.[86] Silver *sycee* ingots (that were refined from foreign coins through remarkable chemical and physically changes), the only standard-ised silver pieces which were affected by the Qing government in their creation, were used for tax payment but not for market circulation.[87]

Consequently, there was no single weight measure for silver *tael* (*liang*). There were as many as 56 official weight standards (*shiping liang*) in opera-tion, varying from 35.14 to 37.50 grams.[88] Only four of the standards over-lapped across the empire.[89] Even the measures used by the central government, the 'Treasury Weight Standard' (*kuping liang*) and the 'Customs Weight Standard' (*guanping liang*) were different: One was 37.30–37.31 grams; and the other, 37.68 grams. There were several hundred private

---

[86] Kent Deng, 'Miracle or Mirage? Foreign Silver, China's Economy and Globalisation of the Sixteenth to Nineteenth Centuries', *Pacific Economic Review*, 13/3 (2008), pp. 320–57. Generally, there are three main arguments: (1) China had a *de facto* silver standard from the mid-Ming Period; see D. O. Flynn and Arturo Giraldez (eds.), *Metals and Monies in an Emerging Global Economy, An Expanding World: The European Impact on World History, 1450–1800* (Aldershor: Variorum, 1997); D. O. Flynn and Arturo Giráldez, 'Cycles of Silver: Global Economic Unity through the Mid-Eighteenth Century', *Journal of World History*, 2 (2002), pp. 391–427. (2) China had a bi-metallic monetary system from the mid-Ming Period; see Lin Manhong, 'Jiadao Qianjian Xianxiang Chansheng Yuanyin, Qianduo Qianlie Lunzhi Shangque' (On 'Over-supply of Inferior Currency' as the Causes of Devaluation of Money in China during 1808–1850), in Zhang Bincun and Liu Shiji (eds.), *Zhongguo Haiyang Fazhanshi Lunwenji* (*Selected Essays on the Maritime History of China*) (Taipei: *Academia Sinica*, 1993), Vol. 5, pp. 357–426; Richard von Glahn, *Fountain of Fortune, Money and Monetary Policy in China, 1000–1700* (Berkeley: University of California Press, 1996). (3) China had a copper currency all the way until the end of the Qing Period; see Kuroda Akinobu, 'Copper Coins Chosen and Silver Differentiated: Another Aspect of the 'Silver Century' in East Asia', *Acta Asiatica* (Tokyo), 88 (2005), pp. 65–86; Chen Chunsheng and Liu Zhiwei, 'Gongfu Shichang Yu Wuzhi Shenghuo — Shilun Shiba Shiji Meizhou Baiyin Shuru Yu Zhongguo Shehui Bianqianzhi Guanxi' (Tributary Market and Material Life — The Relationship between Silver Imports from the Americas from the Eighteenth Century and Changes in Chinese Society) *Qinghua Daxue Xuebao* (*Bulletin of Tsinghua University*), 25/5 (2010), pp. 65–81.

[87] In Richard von Glahn's view, *sycee* was 'uncoined silver', a crude, regressive form of money through melting down coins; see von Glahn, *Fountain of Fortune*, p. 253.

[88] Zhang Huixin, 'Yinliangde Pingse Ji Mingcheng' (Qualities and Names of Silver), *Gugong Wenwu Yuekan* (*Palace Museum Cultural Relics Monthly*) (Taipei), 52 (1987), p. 130.

[89] These were: (1) 35.84 grams shared by Hunan's Xiangtan and Yunnan, (2) 36.00 grams shared by Tianjin and Shenyan, (3) 36.05 grams shared between Beijing, Changsha and Chongqing, and (4) 36.56 grams, also known as 'the Grand Canal Standard', shared between Shanghai, Yangzhou, Anqing, Jiujiang and Kulun; see Zhang, 'Qualities and Names of Silver', p. 130.

weight measures varying from place to place and from trade to trade.[90] In Zhili Province, there were six silver weight standards (35.16 grams, 36.00 grams, 36.05 grams, 36.18 grams, 36.80 grams, and 37.43 grams). Hankou, in the middle reached of the Yangzi, had over 40 different silver weight measures in as late as the early twentieth century.[91] The 'Shanxi native banks' (*piaohao*) used their own 'internal weight standards' (*zanping yin*, *benping yin*).[92] In contrast to this complete mess, the government policies on China's own bronze coins (*qian*) were well defined; and its supply, regulated and monitored most of the time.

As a result of this heterogeneity, when and where foreign silver changed hand, traders had to barter every time to assess each silver piece. This was another market over which the government did not impose control and the peasantry did not enter. It created a niche for merchants (now money dealers) across the empire to tackle the new market transaction costs. These money dealers assayed silver quality (*guse*),[93] converted different weights (*kouping*),[94] and arbitrage between various silver coins, and between silver bullions and silver coins (*yangli*).[95] One service they provided was assessment of silver coins with a chop of approval chiselled permanently on the face of those coins. As no single dealer had the universal authority, coins were often chopped repeatedly until they were defaced on both sides. The business thrived until the Qing Dragon Dollar (*longyang*, *dayang*) was finally inaugurated in 1889, after over three centuries since Spanish silver coins first landed in China. By 1913, a total of 220 million

---

[90] Yeh-chien Wang, 'Evolution of the Chinese Monetary System, 1644–1850', in Hou Chi-ming (ed.), *Modern Chinese Economic History* (Taipei: The Institute of Economics, *Academia Sinica*, 1979), p. 433.

[91] Kuroda, 'Copper Coins Chosen and Silver Differentiated', p. 84.

[92] Shanxi School of Finance and Economics and Shanxi Office of People's Bank of China (eds.), *Shanxi Piaohao Shiliao* (*Materials of Shanxi Native Banks*) (Taiyuan: Shanxi People's Press, 1990), pp. 135–6.

[93] This often involving cutting up coins; see Joe Cribb, *Money in the Bank: An Illustrated Introduction to the Money Collection of The Hongkong and Shanghai Banking Corporation* (London: Spink & Son Ltd, 1987), pp. 121, 122. Manuals on silver assaying were available since the early nineteenth century. The known items include Huang Yousong and Liang Enze, *Xinjuan Yinjing Fami* (*Unveiling the Secret of Silver, New Edition*) (c. 1821); Yang Qing, *Yin Lun* (*On Silver*) (1865); Su Fuyuan, *Xinzeng Yin Lun* (*On Silver, Enlarged*) (1874).

[94] Chen Mingguang, *Qianzhuang Shi* (*A History of Native Banks*) (Shanghai: Shanghai Arts Press, 1997), pp. 150–1.

[95] *Ibid.*, pp. 149–50.

Qing silver coins (5,247 tons), the 'Silver Yuan', were issued.[96] This finally drove out all foreign coins and ended money dealers' business.

So, most of the time during the Qing Period, silver was a rather inconvenient medium for market transactions. Exchanges were predominantly facilitated by China's own bronze coins. Indeed, by the 1850s, up to 90 percent of commercial dealings in the north were in fact silver-free.[97] The same pattern occurred in the more commercialised south: Anhui, Hunan, Sichuan, Guangxi, Jiangsu, and Fujian.[98]

Pawning was also not controlled by the government despite the heavy involvement of officials especially during the Qing Period. Pawnshops functioned as both short-term lenders for customers and pension providers for investors. During the Qing, the 'normal' interest rate charged by the pawning sector was between 1 percent and 3 percent per month.[99] The Qing regulation exempted all taxes on pawnshops.[100] The sector also functioned as the channel to siphon silver from market circulation. Typically, loans were originally issued in bronze coins or low-quality foreign silver pieces, but repayments had to be made in *sycee*.[101] So, beside the Imperial Treasury, the pawning sector was where silver was and consequently became the looters' prime target during civil unrest and foreign invasions.[102]

In term of business scale, during the Ming, the capital Nanjing alone had 500 pawnshops, one shop per 2,000 residents of the city. During the Qing, Beijing had 600 pawnshops, also one shop for every 2,000 residents.[103]

---

[96] *Yinhang Zhoubao* (*Baking Weekly*) (Shanghai), Vol. 9, No. 8, 10th March 1925, p. 25.

[97] Wang, 'Evolution of the Chinese Monetary System', pp. 436–7, 440, 446; Huang Jianhui, 'Qingchu Shangyong Huipiao Yu Shangpin Jingjide Fazhan' (Commercialisation and the Rise of Bank Drafts during the Early Qing), *Wenxian* (*Literature*), 1 (1987), pp. 3–15.

[98] Lin, 'Over-Supply of Inferior Currency', pp. 397–9.

[99] Zhou Hui, *Jinling Suoshi Shenglu* (*More on Everyday Life in Nanjing*) (Originally Published in 1610. Reprint. Beijing: Literature and Classics Press, 1955), Vol. 3; Ling Mengchu, *Chuke Pai-an Jingqi* (*Table-Slapping Stories*) (Originally published in 1632. Reprint. Beijing: People's Press, 1991), p. 250.

[100] Liu Jiansheng, Liu Pengsheng, Liang Sibao, Yan Hongzhong, Wang Ruifen and Fan Jiangchun, *Jinshang Yanjiu* (*Shanxi Merchants*) (Taiyuan: Shanxi People's Press, 2005), pp. 217–21.

[101] Peng Zeyi, *Zhongguo Gongshang Hanghui Shiliao Ji* (*Historical Materials of China's Industrial and Commercial Guilds*) (Beijing: Zhonghua Books, 1995), p. 847; Qu, *Pawning, A Journey through Time*, p. 207.

[102] Qu, *Pawning, A Journey through Time*, pp. 191–5.

[103] *Ibid*, pp. 17, 21, 58.

Pawning also operated on the township level.[104] The number of pawnshops increased by a factor of three from 1685 to 1812 (see Table 11).

With a total of 23,139 pawnshops the Qing population was served 36 times better by the pawning sector than by China's native banks: There was one pawnshop for every 16,000 people on average.[105] Investments in pawnshops were often related to a pension scheme.[106] Individual and institutional investors across a wide spectrum flocked in, including Emperors Yongzheng (r. 1723–35) and Qianlong (r. 1736–95) themselves.[107] Most pawnshops were collectively owned by shareholders to reach the critical mass. A well-established shop could be worth 30,000–40,000 *taels* (1.1–1.5 tons).[108] The smallest might start with only 1,000–2,000 *taels*.[109] But the average size seems to have been in the region of 10,000–20,000 *taels*.[110] By 1812, the total silver invested in the 23,139 pawnshops was likely to be 300 million *taels*,[111] an equivalent about half of China's total silver stock prior to 1800. By 1912, the pawning sector had remained at the top of the league table for investors (see Table 12).

Evidence indicates that the commercial sector seldom used pawnshops to raise money for investment purposes.[112] Ordinary peasants took the majority

---

[104] *Ibid.*, p. 67. *Note*: Grassroots pawnshops at the village level are not included; see Zhao Lianfa, *Zhongguo Diandangye Shuping* (*Survey of the Pawning Sector in China*) (Taipei: Shishi Press, 1978), p. 148.

[105] For more details on the Qing population of the time (as of 1812), see Deng, 'Unveiling China's True Population', Appendix 2.

[106] Liu Qiugen, *Mingqing Gaolidai Ziben* (*Usury Capital during the Ming–Qing Period*) (Beijing: Social Science Literature Press, 2000).

[107] Qu Yanbin, *Diandang Shi* (*Pawning, A Journey through Time*) (Taipei: Huacheng Books, 2004), pp. 184–90. Also see Wei Qingyuan, *Mingqingshi Bianxi* (*Scrutiny of the Ming-Qing History*) (Beijing: China's Social Sciences Press, 1989); Liu *et al.*, *Shanxi Merchants*, pp. 217–8; Qu, *Pawning*, pp. 71–2, 180–2.

[108] In the early twentieth century, the minimum amount required to establish a pawnshop in Shanghai was 30,000 silver *yuan*; see Yang Yong, 'Jingdai Jiangnan Diandangyede Shehui Zhuanxing' (Transition of the Pawning Sector in Early Modern Jiangnan), *Shixue Yuekan* (*Study of History Monthly*), 5 (2005), p. 103. See also Qu, *Pawning*, pp. 70–1, 179, 185.

[109] Liu, *Usury Capital*, p. 78; Liu *et al.*, *Shanxi Merchants*, p. 205; Qu, *Pawning*, pp. 70–4.

[110] See Ai Na, the Lay Buddhist, *Doupeng Xianhua* (*Gossip from a Bean Shed*) (N.d. Reprint. Shanghai: Shanghai Classics Press, 1983), ch. 3; Luan Chengxian, 'Mingmuo Dianye Huishang Yili: Chongzhen Ernian Xiuning Cheng Xuyu Li Fenshu Yanjiu' (*A Case Study of Family Property Division Document by Cheng Xuyu of Xiuning County in 1629*), *Huizhou Shehui Kexue* (*Social Sciences in Anhui*), 3 (1996), pp. 30–40.

[111] This is slightly lower than Liu's estimate of 347 million *taels*, see Liu, *Usury Capital*, p. 81.

[112] Qu, *Pawning*, p. 209.

Table 11. Growth in the Number of Pawnshops, 1685–1812.

Year	North	South	Total	Index
1685	5,210	2,485	7,695	100
1724	7,265	2,639	9,904	129
1753	12,141	5,934	18,075	234
1812	12,085	11,054	23,139	301

Source: Liu Jiansheng, Liu Pengsheng, Liang Sibao, Yan Hongzhong, Wang Ruifen and Fan Jiangchun, *Jinshang Yanjiu* (*Shanxi Merchants*) (Taiyuan: Shanxi People's Press, 2005), p. 199.
Note: Grassroots pawnshops at the village level are not included; see Zhao Lianfa, *Zhongguo Diandangye Shuping* (*Survey of the Pawning Sector in China*) (Taipei: Shishi Press, 1978), p. 148.

Table 12. Investments Recipients.

Pawn shops	Native banks	Industrial enterprises	Total
89.8 (million dollars)	75.1	54.8	219.8
2,141.7 (tons)	1,791.1	1,307.0	5,239.8
41%	34%	25%	100%

Source: Wang Jingyu, *Zhongguo Jindai Gongyeshi Ziliao* (*Historical Materials of Early Modern Industries in China*) (Beijing: Sciences Press, 1957), Vol. 2, p. 1017.

of loans: In Zhejiang, peasants took over 50 percent of the total value of loans, and in Jiangsu, up to 80 percent. These loans were mainly 'debts for survival' (*shengcun jiekuan*), and often seasonal.[113] Only 14 percent of the total value of the loans was devoted to capital spending (on land, tools, seed, and fertilizers).[114] The cost of borrowing was 1–3 percent per month.[115] A considerable proportion of pawnshop capital lay idle during low seasons.[116]

[113] Yang Yong, 'Transition of the Pawning Sector', p. 107.
[114] Zhao Lianfa, *Zhongguo Diandangshi Shuping* (*Survey of the Pawning Sector in China*) (Taipei: Stone House Press, 1978), pp. 151–2. Liu, *Usury Capital*, p. 254.
[115] Zhou, *More on Everyday Life in Nanjing*, Vol. 3; Ling, *Table-Slapping Stories*, p. 250. Also, Qu, *Pawning*, pp. 58, 183, 204, 207.
[116] The total earning per unit of pawnshop capital was halved from the late Qing to early Republic Periods, which suggests the amount of idle capital increased; see Pan, 'A Study of the Pawning Sector', p. 307.

Chapter Five

Public Goods Provision

Many historians remain puzzled as to how China's empire system was able to fulfil its obligations of providing public goods such as supply of farmland, technical aid, social welfare, external security (or national defence), and internal security (or law and order), with its relatively small state bureaucracy.

1. Physiocracy, Territorial Expansion, and Farmland Supply

It is obvious from Figure 1 that territorial expansion was part of China's behavioural pattern. China's expansion stopped when it finally reached the physical limits for farming on East Asian Mainland. Behind this expansion was physiocracy, or agricultural fundamentalism. It came with a range of institutions to convert land to farms and labourers to farmers, all of which dictated China's growth pattern and growth trajectory. Physiocracy also linked government performance to the health of the rural sector. This, in turn, laid the foundation of the state-peasant alliance whereby the state gained its legitimacy to rule.[1] In the end, physiocracy became a political issue of paramount importance.

---

[1] This causal relationship between physiocracy and China's territorial expansion cannot be explained by the orthodox Marxian 'historical materialism' which asserts that government and government policies (called 'superstructure') are dictated by the existing economy (called 'infrastructure'). Theoretically, China did not have to farm so extensively.

Historically, it took a long time for physiocracy to become a leading thought. During the Shang Period (*c.* 1520–1030 BC), commerce and merchants were the 'chosen' ones. In the following Zhou Period (*c.* 1030–771 BC), China at best had a mixed economy. Farmers were not prominent in the social hierarchy. However, in searching for a way to stabilise society, Confucius (? – 479 BC) began to pay attention to farming and farmers. He was reported to say that:

> *The greatest business of the people is agriculture. From agriculture, the millet which is used for the sacrifice to God is produced; the density of population grows; the expense of the business is supplied; social harmony and peace arise; the multiplication of wealth begins; and the characters of honesty, great-mindedness, integrity and solidity become a general habit of the people.*[2]

By the time of the Warring States (475–221 BC), agricultural prosperity was recognised as the prerequisite to making a political unit powerful. This ushered in the era of 'agriculture as the foundation of society' (*nongben*). The unification of China by the Qin Kingdom, which was known for its farming performance and private land ownership for ordinary farmers, proved that point. So, historically, physiocracy was backed by military supremacy. After the unification when the shelf life of the Qin military supremacy was over, physiocracy was no longer linked to war but to peace and people's livelihoods. This was described *Master Guan's Book* (*Guanzi*) as follows: 'When the granaries are full, people will know propriety and moderation; when their clothing and food is adequate, people will know [the distinction between] honour and shame.'[3]

Physiocracy had several aspects. First, agriculture was officially recognised as being the fundamental sector of the economy.[4] Second, farmers were ranked in society above other commoners such as artisans (*gong*) and merchants (*shang*).[5] Third, it was considered the duty of the

---

[2] Cited in Huan-chang Chen, *The Economic Principles of Confucius and His School* (New York: Columbia University Press, 1911), p. 381.

[3] W. A. Rickett (trans.), *Guanzi: Political, Economic, and Philosophical Essays from Early China* (Princeton: Princeton University Press, 1985), p. 52.

[4] Denis Twitchett, 'Merchant, Trade and Government in Late T'ang', *Asia Major*, 14/1 (1968), pp. 63–95.

[5] D. C. Lau (trans.), *Mencius* (Hong Kong: The Chinese University Press, 1984), p. 21.

Table 13. Expansion of China's Arable Land.

Period	*Circa*	Arable land (10⁴ km²)	Index
Zhou	1030 BC	40.5	100
Western Han	24 AD	279.5	690
Tang	907	380.7	940
Qing	1800	554.9	1,370
PRC	1980	534.6	1,320

Source: Based on Chen Dunyi and Hu Jishan, *Zhongguo Jingji Dili* (*Economic Geography of China*), Beijing: China's Perspective Press, 1983), ch. 2; Hou Wailu (ed.), *Zhongguo Dabaike Quanshu Zhongguo Lishi* (*Encyclopaedia of Chinese History*) (Beijing and Shanghai: China's Encyclopaedia Publisher, 1992), pp. 5, 811, 1538; Tan Qixiang, *Jianming Zhongguo Lishi Dituji* (*Concise Maps of Chinese History*) (Beijing: China's Map Press, 1991), pp. 15–18, 39–40, 57–8, 67–8.

government to encourage the growth of the agricultural sector to maintain social stability.[6]

When physiocracy was translated into actions, alongside China's ambitions for territorial expansion, the supply of arable land increased absolutely (see Table 13).

The process has been defined as China's 'internal colonisation' which has been positively tested by textual, archaeological, linguistic, and anthropological studies.[7] To put this in the demographic perspective, land supply in China was in general abundance in relation to China's population (see Figure 2 where China's total population was under 70 million most of the time). Only by the late Qing Period in 1800 did the supply of arable land

---

[6] Early measures employed included the protection of private land ownership, as in the deeds of Shang Yang (*c.* 390–338 BC); land distribution, as proposed by Li Anshi (443–493 AD); control of grain prices by Li Kui (*circa* 455–395 BC); irrigation projects under Sang Hongyang (152–80 BC). See Lee, *The Economic History of China*, pts. 1–2.

[7] Zhao Tongmao, 'Zhonghua Minzu Qiyuandide Xin Tansuo' ('A New Inquiry into the Original Regions of the Chinese'), *Dazong Yixue* (*Popular Medical Science*), 3 (1986), pp. 5–6; Mao Hanwen, 'Zhonghua Minzude Liang Da Fayandi' ('Two Major Geographic Origins of the Chinese'), *Xinhua Wenzhai* (*New China Readers' Digest*), 1 (1987), pp. 199–200; Liu Bima, 'Xiandai Zhongguoren Tizhi Tezheng Yanjiude Xishouhuo' (New Achievements in the Study of Modern Chinese Physical Characteristics), *Keji Ribao* (*Science and Technology Daily*), October 6 (1987), p. 4; Yuan and Zhang, *Chinese Surnames, Group Genetics and Demographic Distribution*, pp. 6–57.

become tight. Of course, there existed the 'relative shortage of land' in many locations inside the empire before 1800. Resource re-allocation via internal migration however, was designed precisely to deal with such a shortage so that the equilibrium was still maintained (see Figures 4 and 5, and Table 1).

After 1800, expanding and gaining new territory on East Asian Mainland came to a halt. There was also a lack of input of modern land-saving technology in farming. Even so, food surpluses enabled China's population to increase during much of the twentieth century, often in defiance of Malthusianism.

2. Public Works

The Great Wall and the Grand Cannel were by far the main public work projects which the Imperial administration completed. The much cited projects for irrigation were a myth. Most (70 percent) of China's main water-related public works aimed at transport, communication and flood control (see Table 14).

In China, irrigation was the *sine qua non* for rice farming across all regions in China. If one uses modern China's annual precipitation as a

Table 14.   Cross-regional Water-related Public Works in China's History.

Years	Canals*	Dykes†	Irrigation§	Other
221–1 BC	2	2	3	1
1–200 AD	0	1	0	1
201–400	2	1	2	0
401–600	0	1	0	0
601–800	3	1	0	0
801–1000	1	0	0	0
1001–1200	0	2	1	0
1201–1400	1	1	0	0
1401–1600	0	0	0	0
1601–1800	0	1	0	0
Total	9	10	6	2
% in all	33.3	37.0	22.2	7.5

Source: Yao Hanyuan, *Zhongguo Shuili Fazhanshi* (*Development in Water Control in China*) (Shanghai: Shanghai People's Press, 2005), Appendix.
Note: * Transport and communication, † Flood control, § Food production.

Table 15. Distribution of Water in Rice Farming (mm per Day).

Region	Seepage loss	Plant evaporation	Water deficit
Yellow River	360–1,560	480–840	840–2,280
Yangzi Delta	30–1,120	280–800	350–1,800
Pearl Delta	30–160	270–540	300–700

Source: Zhao *et al.*, *Sorted Rice Types in China*, p. 100.

proxy,[8] no single region was irrigation-free for rice cultivation. The universal need for man-made irrigation in China to compensate water deficit can be illustrated above (see Table 15).

But, irrigation for food production was not given priority in Imperial projects. The best example was the Northern Song Period (960–1127 AD) during which the state most visibly promoted irrigation: It amassed 200,000 workers to build an irrigation system in Hangzhou in 973 AD.[9] But the scale of these projects was tiny. In 1011–69, six irrigation projects created just 42,800 *qing* irrigated land, merely one percent of the Song total of 4.4 million *qing* (as of 1065).[10] The state-owned land did not fare any better: Merely 0.5 percent of all irrigated land belonged to the Song state.[11] By the end of the Northern Song Period, the scale of irrigation remained 7–8 percent of all farmland with the Song territory (see Table 16).[12]

By as late as 1919, the irrigation rate of China's total farmland was 24 percent.[13] Consequently, despite the much talked about double

---

[8] As a rule of thumb, the annual precipitation in modern China is as follows: the Yellow River region: 500–1,000 mm; the Yangzi River Region: 1,000–1,500 mm; the Pearl River region: >1,500 mm; and the Loess Plateau: 100–500 mm.

[9] Tuotuo, *History of the Song Dynasty*, Vol. 97, Entry 'Hequzhi 49', in *TFOH* (Shanghai: Shanghai Classics Press, 1986), Vol. 7, pp. 5503, 5504.

[10] *Ibid.*, Vol. 173, Entry 'Shihuozhi 126', in *TFOH*, Vol. 7, p. 5712. In fact, one cannot assume *shili* (water projects) were all for irrigation. Many large Song *shuili* projects were devoted to channel building and flood control, and not to rice-farming.

[11] See Shiba, *Songdai Jiangnan Jingjishi Yanjiu*, p. 203.

[12] I.e., a total of 30,794,365–36,117,800 Song *mu* was irrigated rice-farming land, out of 443,792,405 Song *mu* of farmland. Based on Liang, *Dynastic Data*, pp. 290–1; Cheng Minsheng, *Songdai Diyu Jingji* (*Regional Economies during the Song Period*) (Zhengzhou: Henan University Press, 1992), p. 87. See also Perkins, *Agricultural Development in China*, p. 342. The higher figure of 36,117,800 comes from Tuotuo, *History of the Song Dynasty*, Vol. 173, Entry 'Shihuozhi 126', in *TFOH*, Vol. 7, p. 5712.

[13] Perkins, *Agricultural Development in China*, pp. 16, 64.

Table 16.   Scale of Irrigation by 1077.

Region	Irrigated *mu* (I)	Total *mu* (II)	I/II (%)
China-wide (1)	30,794,365	443,792,405	6.9
China-wide (2)	36,117,800*	443,792,405	8.1
North China (1)	14,441,299	143,175,394	10.1
North China (2)	14,444,540*	143,175,394	10.1
South China (1)	16,353,066	300,617,011	5.4
South China (2)	21,592,320*	300,617,011	7.2
Unspecified	80,900*		

Source: Liang, *Dynastic Data*, pp. 290–1; Cheng, *Regional Economies*, p. 87. *A different set of figures; see Tuotuo, *Song Shi* (*History of the Song Dynasty*), Vol. 173, in *Er-shi-wu Shi* (*Twenty-Five Official Histories or TFOH*), Vol. 7, p. 5712; Sibo Yixin (Shiba Yoshinobu), *Songdai Jiangnan Jingjishi Yanjiu* (*An Economic History of the Lower Yangzi Region during the Song Period*), translated by Fang Jian and He Zhongli (Nanjing: Jiangsu People's Press, 2001), pp. 217–8.

cropping of rice,[14] in the 1930s, only four percent of China's farmland catered to such farming practice.[15] China was simply not qualified as a

---

[14] Li Bozhong, *Tangdai Jiangnan Nongyede Fazhan* (*Development of Jiangnan Agriculture during the Tang Period*) (Beijing: Peking University Press, 1990), pp. 119–20; and his 'Songmo Zhi Mingchu Jiangnan Nongmin Jingyingde Bianhua' (Changes in Peasant Production Pattern in the Lower Yangzi Region from Late Song to Early Ming Times), *Zhongguo Nongshi* (*Agricultural History of China*), 2 (1998), pp. 30–9; Liang Gengyao, *Nansongde Nongcun Jingji* (*The Rural Economy in the Southern Song Period*) (Beijing: New Star Press, 2006); Cheng, *Songdai Diyu Jingji*, pp. 98–101; Chao, *Man and Land in Chinese History*, p. 199. See also Chen Chun and Zheng Jianming, 'Daozuo Qiyuande Kaogu Tansuo' (Archaeological Discoveries of the Origin of Rice Cultivation), *Fudan Xuebao* (*Research Bulletin of Fudan University*), 4 (2005), pp. 126–31; Ting Ying, 'Zhongguo Zaipei Daozhongde Qiyuan Jiqi Yanbian' (The Origin and Differentiation of Cultivated Rice in China), *Nongye Xuebao* (*Acta Agriculturae Sinica*), 8/3 (1957), pp. 243–60; Yan Wenming, 'Zhongguo Daozuo Nongyede Qiyuan' (The Origin of Rice Cultivation in China), *Nongye Kaogu* (*Agricultural Archaeology*), 1 (1982), pp. 19–31; Lin Chengkun, 'Changjiang Qiantanjiang Zhongxiayou Diqu Xinshiqi Shidai Dili Yu Daozuode Qiyuan He Fenbu' (The Origin and Geographic Distribution of Rice Cultivation during the Neolithic Period in the Middle and Lower Reaches of the Yangzi and Qiantang Rivers), *Nongye Kaogu* (*Agricultural Archaeology*), 1 (1987), pp. 283–91; Cao Keping, 'Jiangxi Wannian Xianrendong Yicun Zaiyanjiu Ji Zhongguo Daozuo Nongye Qiyuan Xin Renshi' (Re-examination of Remains of the 10,000 Year Old Cave of Immortals in Jiangxi and the New Insight into the Origin of Rice Farming in China), *Dongnan Wenhua* (*South-eastern Culture*), 3 (1998), pp. 25–31; Fan Yuzhou, 'Jiangnan Diqude Shiqian Nongye' (Pre-historical Farming in the Lower Yangzi Region), *Zhongguo Nongshi* (*Agricultural History of China*), 2 (1995), pp. 1–8.
[15] Perkins, *Agricultural Development in China*, pp. 16, 44.

'hydraulic empire' for rice output maximisation. Dry crops dominated the vast area of China until the 1920s.[16] In this context, the much-circulated hypotheses of 'Oriental Hydraulic (Irrigational) Empire' and 'Oriental Despotism' have to be groundless.

3. Technical Aid

The impact of physiocracy was apparent in the form of technical aid with tools, seed and information of good practice and so forth. The Western Han (206 BC–24 AD) government ran a sophisticated network to aid agricultural production with Supervisor of Grain Production (*sousu duwei*) in charge of grain production for the whole country, 13 Grand Agricultural Missionaries (*da nongzheng*) working in the 13 provinces, and District Supervisors of Agriculture (*sanfu jiaotianguan*) and Agricultural Administrators (*tianguan*) looking after local districts.[17] On the input side, there were Administrators of Iron Production (*tieguan*), who promoted iron tools, especially iron ploughs, and Administrator of Water (*shuiguan*) who oversaw flood control and irrigation.[18] It was during this period that fallow land finally made way for annual farming in the same plot.

Seed of high output was promoted often by the political centre. Emperor Zhenzong of the Song (*r.* 998–1022) was documented to have the Champa Rice distributed in the Yangzi River region to prevent a foreseen famine,[19]

[16] J. L. Buck, *Land Utilization in China: Atlas* (London: Oxford University Press, 1937).
[17] Zhongguo Wenhua Yanjiusuo (The Institute for the Advanced Chinese Studies) (ed.), *Zhongwen Dacidian* (*An Encyclopaedic Dictionary of the Chinese Language*) (Taipei: Institute of Chinese Culture, 1962–8), p. 1893; Li Jiannong, *Xianqin Lianghan Jingjishi Gao* (*An Economic History of the Period from Pre-Qin to the Western and Eastern Han Dynasties*) (Beijing: Zhonghua Books, 1962), pp. 154–8; Qiao Shuzhi, 'Pufan Tianguanqi Kao' (A Study of the Bronze Container of the Agricultural Administrator in the Pufan Region), *Lishi Yanjiu* (*Research in History*), 4 (1987), pp. 67–70.
[18] Zheng Zhaojing, *Zhongguo Shuili Shi* (*History of Water Control in China*) (Taipei: Taiwan Commercial Press, 1970), ch. 8; Deng Zhixing and Tien Shang, 'Shilun Dujiangyan Jingjiubushuaide Yuanyin' (The Reasons for the Endurance of Dujiangyan Irrigation System), *Zhongguoshi Yanjiu* (*Research in Chinese History*), 3 (1986), pp. 101–10.
[19] One *hu* = 50 litres (*sheng*); see Zhao, *Dictionary of Chinese Economic History*, p. 412.

> *There was a light drought in the Jiangnan, Huainan and Liangzhe provinces, which would reduce the anticipated paddy rice harvest. In the Fifth Month of Fourth Year of the Dazhong Xiangfu Reign [1011], Emperor Zhenzong sent his envoy to Fujian for 30,000 hu of the Champa rice seed to be distributed amongst the three provinces. ... Instructions for growing the new rice were posted for the public by the Transportation Commissioners.*

Two years later, the emperor partook in the harvest in this new rice species; it was reported: 'In the Ninth Month of 1013, Emperor Zhenzong displayed the newly harvested Champa Rice to all his ranking officials at Jade Palace.'[20] The promotion of the new rice seems to have been a success.

Another example was Emperor Kangxi (*r.* 1661 to 1722) who was involved in a nation-wide project to promote a new high-yield rice variety which was discovered by the Emperor himself. The new rice was consequently dubbed the 'Imperial Rice' (*yu daomi*).[21] His predecessor Emperor Shengzu (1661–1722), a keen agricultural promoter, also had a botanical encyclopaedia *Guang Qunfangpu (Complete Thesaurus of Botany, Enlarged)* compiled in 1708, which provided details about 25 varieties of wheat and barley, 100 varieties of rice, and 167 varieties of millet.[22]

This led to the unique phenomenon in China's history of agricultural treatises (*nongshu*) that were produced and circulated among government officials and their literati associates to promote good farming practices. Evidence also shows that *nongshu* were always included in government collections of books, such as the Qing *Gujin Tushu Jichen (A Collection of Ancient and Current Books)*, *Siku Quanshu (The Qing Imperial Complete Collection of Books)*, and *Huangchao Jingshi Wenbian (A Collection of*

---

[20] Tuotuo, *History of the Song Dynasty*, Vol. 8, in *TFOH*, Vol. 7, p. 5205.

[21] Kong Xiangxian, 'Jiangnan Geshengde Shuangjidao Shizai Kangxi Houqi Kaishi Tuiguangde' (Promotion of Double-Cropping Rice in the Late Years of the Kangxi Reign), *Nongye Kaogu (Agricultural Archaeology)*, 1 (1983), pp. 33–8. Eight ranking officials were made responsible for the campaign: Wu Chunli, Xu Yuanmeng, Tong Guorang, Zhao Shixian, Wang Xishun, He Shou, Li Xu and Chao Fu.

[22] Wang Hao, *Guang Qunfangpu (Complete Thesaurus of Botany, Enlarged)* (Originally published in 1708. Reprint. Shanghai: Commercial Press, 1936), Vols. 7–10.

Table 17. Agricultural Authors: Number and Identification.

Dynasty	A	B	C	D	E	F	G	Total
Pre-Qin	1	2	—	—	4	—	1	8
Han	1	6	—	—	—	—	8	15
Jin	—	1	—	—	—	—	1	2
N + S	1	5	—	—	—	—	1	7
Sui	—	1	—	—	1	—	22	24
Tang	4	5	1	1	4	—	17	32
Song	3	21	14	2	11	3	53	107
Yuan	2	5	—	—	3	—	19	29
Ming	2	6	13	14	20	10	48	113
Qing	14	23	25	37	14	1	93	207
Total	28	75	53	54	57	14	263	544
% of total	5.2	13.8	9.7	9.9	10.5	2.6	48.3	100.0

Source: Based on Wang, *Bibliography of Chinese Classical Agronomy*.

Note: A = Government-sponsored cases, B = Authors who had official positions, C = Authors who were imperial degree-holding officials, D = Authors who can only be identified as imperial degree holders, E = Authors who can only be identified as scholars, F = Author who were royal family members, G = Authors who cannot be identified. N + S = Northern and Southern Dynasties.

Applied Books for the Qing Dynasty), as an inseparable part of useful and reliable knowledge of the Chinese civilisation.

The authors' identities are revealed in Table 17, which shows an intimate link between the state and literati on one side and the peasantry on the other.

It was not uncommon for the head of the state to get involved. In 1020 AD Emperor Zhenzong of the Northern Song ordered two books, *Qimin Yaoshu* and *Sishi Zuanyao* (*Important Rules for the Four Seasons*), to be published and distributed to all officials in charge of agricultural administration.[23] Between 1304 and 1307 AD, Emperor Chengzong (*r.* 1295–1307) of the Yuan Dynasty ordered *Wangzhen Nongshu* (*Wang*

---

[23] Wan Guoding, 'Han E *Sishi Zuanyao*' (Han E and *Important Rules for the Four Seasons*), *Zhongguo Nongbao* (*Chinese Agricultural Journal*), 11 (1962), p. 33; Hu Daojing, *Nongshu Nongshi Lunji* (*Selected Works on Agricultural Books and Agronomic History*) (Beijing: Agriculture Press, 1985), p. 46.

Table 18.   Government Sponsorship of Agricultural Treatises.

Period	A	B	C	D	Total
Tang	2	—	—	—	2
Song	10	—	1	1	12
Yuan	3	2	—	—	5
Ming	7	5	1	3	16
Qing	10	12	10	6	38
Total	32	19	12	10	73

Source: Based on Wang, *Bibliography of Chinese Classical Agronomy*, Appendix III.

Note: A = Central government; B = Provincial government; C = Prefectural government; D = County government.

Zhen's Agriculture Treatise) to be published and distributed.[24] Later, in 1318, the Yuan Emperor Renzong (*r.* 1311–19) ordered *Zaisang Tushuo* (*Illustrations of Mulberry Growing*) to be printed and issued throughout the country.[25] In 1708, Emperor Kangxi instructed a scholar by the name of Wang Hao to write *Guang Qunfangpu* (*Enlarged Flora*).[26] In 1808 Emperor Jiaqing (*r.* 1796–1820) commanded Dong Hao to compile *Shouyi Guangxun* (*Instructions for Textile Production*).[27]

In the 73 known cases of government publications, all three levels of government were involved, but the central government took the lead (see Table 18).

The purpose of these books was reflected by a statement made by Emperor Qianlong (*r.* 1736–95 AD) who wrote the preface for a comprehensive treatise *Compendium of Works and Days* (*Shoushi Tongkao*), which runs in part as follows:[28]

> *The foundation of society is agriculture. … [I] gave my edict to the court scholars to search widely to collect information regarding the significance of*

[24] Hu, *Selected Works on Agricultural Books and Agronomic History*, p. 5.
[25] Song Lian, *Yuan Shi* (*History of the Yuan Dynasty*) (Originally published in 1370. Reprint. Beijing: Zhonghua Books, 1976), ch. 'Biography of Emperor Renzong'.
[26] Wang Yuhu, *Zhongguo Nongxue Shulu* (*Bibliography of Chinese Classical Agronomy*) (Beijing: Agriculture Press, 1964), p. 214.
[27] *Ibid.*, p. 244.
[28] E-Ertai, *Shoushi Tongkao* (*Compendium of Works and Days*) (Originally published in 1742. Reprint. Beijing: Zhonghua Books, 1956), p. 1.

Table 19. Spread of Rice Varieties across South China during the Qing Period.

Type of rice	A	B
1. *Xiangdao* (Fragrant Rice)	61	28.1
2. *Hupinuo* (Tiger Skin)	51	23.5
3. *Liushiri* (Sixty Days)	45	20.7
4. *Jinbaoyin* (Golden Husk)	31	14.3
5. *Tiengannuo* (Iron Stem)	26	12.0
6. *Jiugongji* (Saviour)	25	11.5
7. *Xiamakan* (Eye-catcher)	24	11.0
8. *Zhancheng* (Champa Rice)	23	10.6
9. *Wushiri* (Fifty Days)	13	6.0
10. *Xiaoniangnuo* (Delicate Girl)	5	2.3
Total	304	140.0*

Source: Based on E-Ertai, *Shoushi Tongkao* (*Compendium of Works and Days*) (Originally published in 1742. Reprint. Beijing: Zhonghua Books, 1956), pp. 437–76.

Note: A = Number of Districts Reporting, B = Percentage in Total Rice-growing Districts. * The total is great than 100% here, meaning that there were overlaps of rice adoption in the same region.

phenology, the different soil types in the north and south, the timing of tillage, methods of storage and the management of sericulture and animal husbandry. ... This compilation contains all works written on agriculture and [states that] the peasantry will receive respect, and that people will work hard.

In terms of information, these treatises typically contain useful and reliable knowledge of (1) soil types and soil preparations (such as ploughing and irrigation), (2) choices of crops (including crop rotation and inter–planting), (3) timing for various tasks, (4) field management (such as inter–tilling, fertilisation, and weeding), (5) household economy (food storage and marketing). Table 19 exemplifies information of rice varieties commonly available across vast regions in South China.

Equally important was the scale on which these agricultural treatises were circulated in society. In 686 AD the Tang Empress Wu Zetian (r. 690–704) issued a treatise entitled *Zaoren Benye* (*Fundamental Occupation for Ordinary People*) to her high-ranking officials.[29] Later, in

---

[29] Wang, *Complete Record of the Tang Dynasty*, ch. 36.

828 AD, Emperor Wenzong (*r.* 827–40) ordered the same book to be copied in all prefectures and counties and issued to villages across the empire.[30] In 1008 and 1014 AD, Emperor Zhenzong (*r.* 998–1022) of the Song Dynasty ordered two veterinary books to be issued nationwide.[31] Over time, many such books were able to reach villages where some members of the local communities were always literate. From the data for the Qing, it is known that there was a large reserve army of Imperial degree-holders in relation to the Imperial bureaucracy with a ratio of 57 to 1; and, only a small percentage of the school goers were able to obtain an Imperial degree.[32] As a result, the popular literacy rate in China was high by premodern standards.[33] At least one person in each village was able to read such treatises.

Moreover, there was a channel of official posters (*wengao*) for public viewing. For instance, in 1829, *Pan Fengyuzhuang Benshu* (*Essential Farming Method for Pan's Village*) was posted extensively in Suzhou Prefecture to spread a good farming practice.[34] There were at least other five official farming bulletins in Zhili, Jiangsu, Jiangxi, Hubei, and Sichuan provinces.[35] In addition, stelae, cut in intaglio, were used as a cheap means of duplicating text. In 1765, Fang Guancheng, the Governor of Zhili, had a set of twelve stelae engraved for such a purpose. The text was entitled *Mianhua Tu* (*Pictures of Cotton Production*), containing in detail 16 processes of cotton production, including sowing, irrigation, inter-tillage,

---

[30] Liu Xu, *Jiu Tang Shu* (*Old History of the Tang Dynasty*) (Originally published in 945. Reprint. Beijing: Zhonghua Books, 1975), ch. 'Biography of Emperor Wenzong'.

[31] Tuotuo, *History of the Song Dynasty*, ch. 'Economy'; Xu, *Edited Record of the Song Dynasty*, Vol. 184, Entry 'Horse Administration VI'.

[32] Based on the facts that 90 percent of the Qing population (359 million in 1833) was rural, living in 1,672 counties. The long-term ratio between degree-holders and official openings was 30:1 and 100:1; see Deng, *Development versus Stagnation*, p. 102; Chang, *The Chinese Gentry*, pp. 83–92; Fairbank, *Chinese Thought and Institutions*, pp. 251–68; Ho, *Ladder of Success in Imperial China*, p. 262; Deng, *History of the Chinese Imperial Examination System*, pp. 163–4; and Wang, *Civil Examinations of the Qing Dynasty*, pp. 65–6; Zhao, *History of the Qing Dynasty*, Vol. 131, Entry 'Military', in *TFOH*, Vol. 11, pp. 9305, 9307.

[33] It has been estimated that literacy rates were over 30 percent among the male and over 10 percent among the female population; see E. S. Rawski, *Education and Popular Literacy in Ch'ing China* (Ann Arbor: The University of Michigan Press, 1979).

[34] Chen Zugui, *Dao* (*Rice*) (Beijing: Zhonghua Books, 1958), pp. 357–67, 371–4.

[35] Wang, *Bibliography of Chinese Classical Agronomy*, pp. 137, 260, 275, 283, 290.

pruning, harvesting, drying, storage, stoning, fluffing, carding, spin-
ning, wearing, sizing, and dyeing. Emperor Kangxi composed a poem
to each process, as part of the production.[36]

Government involvement can be seen from assessment of agricultural
supervision and administration by individual officials.[37] According to the
Tang regulations, county magistrates who managed to have agricultural
output increased by 20 percent were promoted by one rank with a 30 percent salary increase. For those counties which suffered a 10 percent decline
in agricultural output, the magistrates were demoted by one rank with a
loss of 30 percent income.[38] Indeed, under Song law, agricultural supervision and administration were the principal criteria for making assessment
of different levels of administration.[39] This explains why even military
officers became seriously concerned about agriculture. For example, in
1775, Gao Ji (1707–78), a high-ranking Qing officer, submitted to the
throne a proposal that in the Yangzi Valley cash crops which pushed rice
production aside should be controlled, although his mission had little to
do with agriculture.[40] In another case, Lin Zexu (1785–1850), a well-
known Qing officer, wrote three lengthy memorials to the throne to con-
vince the emperor that rice production in Hebei Province should be
encouraged.[41] In the 1740s and 1750s Chen Dashou (Governor of Anhui
Province) and Hao Yulin (Governor of Fujian and Zhejiang and later

---

[36] Wang Jinke and Chen Meijian, 'Zongjie Woguo Gudai Mianhua Zhongzhi Jishu Jingyande Yishu Zhenpin, Mianhuatu Kao' (The Essence of Technology for Cotton Production in Premodern China), *Nongye Kaoku* (*Agricultural Archaeology*), 2 (1982), pp. 157–66.

[37] Lee, *Economic History of China*, pp. 110–11; J. R. Watt, *The District Magistrate in Late Imperial China* (New York: Columbia University Press, 1972), pp. 108–9; Zhong Xiangcai, 'Zhongguo Gudai Nongye Guanli Sixiang Shulun' (On the Thought of the Agricultural Administration in Ancient China), *Zhongguo Nongshi* (*Chinese Agricultural History*), 4 (1985), pp. 1–10; for the situation in a non-Chinese dynasty see Gao Shulin, 'Jinchao Hukou Wenti Chutan' (Inquiry into the Census of the Jin Dynasty), *Zhongguoshi Yanjiu* (*Research in Chinese History*), 2 (1986), pp. 31–9.

[38] Zheng Ziming, *Zhongguo Lidaide Xianzheng* (*County Administration in Premodern China*) (Shanghai: Cangjie Publishing Co, 1938), p. 154.

[39] Deng Guangming and Qi Xia, 'Songdai Guanzhi' (Bureaucracy of the Song Dynasty), *Baike Zhishi* (*Encyclopaedia Knowledge*), 5 (1987), pp. 29–31.

[40] Chen, *Rice*, pp. 238–9.

[41] *Ibid.*, pp. 444–59.

Governor of Jiangsu and Jiangxi) were responsible for the spread of maize, a new crop from overseas.[42]

4. Social Welfare

Social welfare of the empire was derived from the Confucian ideology of *ren* (benevolence) and *minben* (people as the foundation of the ruler). The main evidence of such a state can be found in the state-run granary system from the early Han, called 'ever-even granaries' across the empire.[43] Such a system was justified as: 'Grain storage is vital for the order of society ... Pearls, jade, gold, and silver cannot fill one's stomach during hunger or make one warm when it is cold.'[44] In this context, accumulation of real wealth had to be in the form of grain.

Large food stock was distributed by the states during disasters. The granary system thus played a key role in China's traditional social welfare. During the reign of Emperor Wudi of the Han, the state granary system accumulated so much stock that food spoilage became a serious problem.[45] During the Qing Period even when the occurrence of disasters declined, the government relief scheme maintained its intensity (see Figure 8).

5. National Security and its Weakness

After the formation of the empire in 221 BC, internal security and external defence in China were organised completely differently from its feudal past. First of all, the empire maintained a standing army along China's northern borders to face nomads. China's permanent defence line against nomad invaders, the Great Wall, was built and rebuilt several times until the Ming Period with two parallel walls of an average six meter high and four metres wide and a total length

---

[42] Luo Ergang, 'Yushushu Chuanru Zhongguo' (How Maize Was Introduced to China), *Lishi Yanjiu* (*Study of History*), 3 (1956), p. 70.
[43] Ban, *History of the Han Dynasty*, Vol. 24, Entry 'Shihuo 4', in *TFOH*, Vol. 1, p. 478.
[44, 49] *Ibid.*, Vol. 1, p. 477.
[45] *Ibid.*, Vol. 1, p. 477.

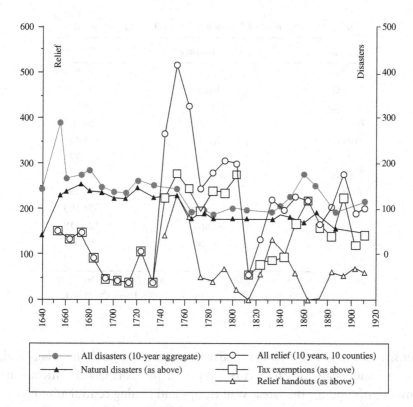

Figure 8. Disasters vs. Qing Relief, 1644–1911.

Source: Disasters based on Chen Gaoyong, *Zhongguo Lidai Tianzai Renhuo Biao* (*Chronological Tables of Chinese Natural and Man-made Disasters*) (Shanghai: Jinan University Press, 1937). Data for Qing disaster aid are from Zhao, *History of the Qing Dynasty*, Vols. 4–25, 'Biographies of the Qing Emperors', in *TFOH*, Vol. 11, pp. 8827–8937; and Vols. 54–81, Entry 'Administrative Geography', Vol. 11, pp. 9071–9131.

of 8,850 kilometres.[46] The Ming Great Wall defence system had a five-layer system, which consisted of (1) strategic points (*zhen*), (2) main branches (*lu*), (3) passes (*guan*), (4) castles (*cheng*) and (5) beacon towers (*tai*).[47] It took about one million troops to guard the wall (see Table 20).

To support the northern defence, there was a sophisticated logistics network which was marked by the 1800-kilometre long Grand Cannel

---

[46] See 'Changcheng', zh.m.wikioedia.org.
[47] See Zhao Xiukun, Tian Zhaolin, Kang Ning, Tao Wenhuan, Shi Shibi, Chen Yangping, Zhu Ansheng, Xu Fei, Zhang Chunyi and Zhang Shufang, *Zhongguo Junshishi* (*A Military History of China*) (Beijing: PLA Press, 1991), Vol. 6, pp. 111–36, 244–79.

Table 20.   Provision of Troops for the Great Wall Defence Line.

Location	Province	Troops
Beizhen	Liaoning	99,875
Qianxi	Hebei	107,813
Changping	Hebei	19,039
Baoding	Hebei	34,697
Xuanhua	Hebei	151,452
Datong	Shanxi	135,778
Taiyuan	Shanxi	57,611
Yulin	Shaanxi	80,196
Yinchuan	Ningxia	71,693
Guyuan	Ningxia	126,919
Zhangye	Gansu	91,571
Total	6	976,644

Source: Zhang Tingyu, *Ming Shi* (*History of the Ming Dynasty*) (Originally published in 1735. Reprint. Beijing: Zhonghua Books, 1974), ch. 'Military'.

constructed in 605–10 AD to link five river systems (the Yellow, Hai, Huai, Yangzi, and Qiantang) to secure supply to the northern frontiers. The amount of food for the Great Wall troops and Beijing central administration alone, known as the 'annual stipend rice via the canal' (*caomi*), amounted to four million *shi* (289,960 tons) from the fourteenth to nineteenth centuries.[48] This amount was enough to feed 1.5 million adults a year at the subsistence level.[49] Considering the enormous input of land, labour, and capital, the construction and maintenance of the Great Wall defence line embodied China's economic capabilities.

China's Great Wall defence (fortification in nature) was passive. Very rarely China's military went beyond the wall to confront nomads. The Great Wall defence was ineffective, too. The wall was breached at least 45 times from 206 BC to 1644 AD,[50] and was completely lost to nomads for 50 years during the end of the Tang Period and for another 167 years

---

[48] Liang, *Dynastic Data*, pp. 366–73.
[49] Zhou, *Financial History of China*, pp. 419–21, 426. See also Yeh-chien Wang, *Late Taxation in Imperial China, 1750–1911* (Cambridge [MA]: Harvard University Press, 1973), p. 70.
[50] Deng, *Chinese Premodern Economy*, p. 268.

Table 21.   Foreign Territories along Sea Routes Reported in Official Histories.

Foreign Territory	A	B	C	D	E	F	G	H	J	Total
Samboja ('Sanfuoqi', Sumatra)						√	√		√	3
Vnam ('Funan', Cambodia)		√	√	√		√	√			5
Siam Reap ('Zhenla', Thailand)					√	√	√		√	4
Malay peninsular				√	√	√	√		√	5
Java ('Shepo')	√			√		√	√	√	√	6
Southeast Asian islands				√		√	√	√	√	5
India's coast	√			√		√	√	√	√	6
Total	2	1	1	5	2	7	7	3	6	34

Source: Based on Feng Chengjun, *Zhongguo Nanyang Jiaotong Shi* (*A History of Communication between China and Southeast Asia*) (Hong Kong: Pacific Books, 1963), pt. II.

Note: Abbreviations for historical periods: A = Eastern Han, B = Three Kingdoms, C = Jin, D = Southern and Northern, E = Sui, F = Tang, G = Song, H = Yuan, J = Ming.

during the following Northern Song. The weakness of China's northern defence was obvious.

China's eastern and southern coasts were far more open and tranquil thanks to the absence of external threat from the sea prior to the fourteenth century. China seas served the empire as open highways for commerce, communication, and diplomacy. The empire did reach out along sea routes to many parts of Southeast and South Asia from the first century AD onwards (see Table 21).

The noticeable threat from the sea to China's national security was more of maritime smuggling than naval attacks. Early accounts for maritime smuggling appeared in the beginning of the Ming Period. Under Emperor Taizu (*r.* 1368–98), Chinese smugglers were reported to operate twenty large ships in Champa Kingdom ('Zhanpo', in now Vietnam).[51] The Ming armada under Zheng He (1405–33) once confronted Sumatra-based Chinese smugglers of 5,000 men on 17 large warships.[52] At that stage, smugglers kept a safe distance from China. About a century later, they moved to China's coasts. A permanent smuggling base emerged in the

---

[51] Dong Lun, *Ming Taizu Shilu* (*Veritable Records of Emperor Taizu of the Ming Dynasty*) (Originally published in 1399. Reprint. Taipei: *Academia Sinica*, 1966), Vol. 48.
[52] Yang Shiqi, *Ming Chengzu Shilu* (*Veritable Records of Emperor Chengzu of the Ming Dynasty*) (Originally published in *c.* 1425. Reprint. Taipei: *Academia Sinica*, 1966), Vol. 52; Zhang, *History of the Ming Dynasty*, ch. 'Sanfuoqi Zhuan'.

Shuangyu Islands (122° 2' E, 31° 4' N) at China's doorstep.[53] A smuggling group under the command of Zhang Lian and Lin Zhaoxi had several hundred thousand followers.[54] It took 200,000 Ming troops to crack down on their network.[55] But the Ming victory was short-lived. In 1552–7, a group of smugglers under Wang Zhi launched multiple frontal attacks on China's coastal cities.[56]

The tactics of these smugglers were very similar to the ones used by nomads along China's northern frontiers and outmanoeuvred a standing army of the empire. Known as the 'Piracy Calamity during the Jiajing Reign' (*jiajing wonan*), attacks trawled China's coast for about half a century. Evidence indicates that from the sixteenth century onwards, the alleged Japanese pirates (*wokou* in China or *wako* in Japanese) were mainly Japan-based Chinese smugglers.[57] Ming officials identified over 70 percent of *wokou* as Chinese fakes (*jiawo*).[58] Evidence also shows that most *wokou* vessels were built in China's coastal province Fujian.[59]

In response to the *wokou* challenge, the Ming government imposed a maritime ban (*haijin*). From 1452 to 1533, the Ming state banned maritime activities six times. Such a policy was copied by the Qing state in 1661–83 and 1717–27. However, such a passive measure hardly produced any desirable result. During the 1661–83 ban, as many as 450 ships sailed

---

[53] Xu Jie and Zhang Juzheng, *Ming Shizong Shilu* (*Veritable Records of Emperor Shizong of the Ming*) (Originally published in *c.* 1567. Reprint. Taipei: *Academia Sinica*, 1961), Vol. 350.

[54] C. R. Boxer, *South China in the Sixteenth Century* (London: Robert Maclehose, 1953), p. 193.

[55] Wang Qi, *Xu Wenxian Tongkao* (*Continued Comprehensive Study of Historical Records*) (1586), Vol. 236, Entry 'Sanfuoqi'.

[56] Ji Liuqi, *Mingji Beilue* (*A Short History of North China*) (1671), Vol. 11, Entry 'Zhengzhilong Xiaozhuan'; Zhang, *History of the Ming Dynasty*, ch. 'Riben Zhuan'.

[57] Zhang Xie, *Dongxiyang Kao* (*A Comprehensive Maritime History*) (Originally published in 1616. Reprint. Beijing: Zhonghua Books, 1981), ch. 'Shuixiang Kao'.

[58] Zhang, *History of the Ming Dynasty*, ch. 'Riben Zhuan'; Zhang Bincun, 'Shiliu Shiji Zhoushan Qundaode Zousi Maoyi' (Illegal Trade Activities from Zhoushan Archipelago during the Sixteenth Century), in Editing Committee for *Maritime History of China* (ed.), *Zhongguo Haiyang Fazhanshi Lunwenji* (*Selected Essays on the Maritime History of China*) (Taipei: *Academia* Sinica, 1984), Vol. 1, p. 71.

[59] Lin Renchuan, *Mingmo Qingchu Siren Haishang Maoyi* (*Private Maritime Trade during the Late Ming and Early Qing Period*) (Shanghai: East China Normal University Press, 1987), pp. 48–9.

Table 22.   Reported Departure Events for Smuggling Ships, 1661–83.

Year	Jiangsu	Zhejiang	Fujian	Guangdong	Taiwan	Other	Total
1661–5	6	3	56	26	15	31	137
1666–70	3	5	11	2	44	48	113
1671–5	7	1	4	14	54	4	84
1676–80	6	9	14	9	44	—	82
1681–3	2	—	1	4	27	—	34
Total	24	18	86	55	184	83	450
Share (%)	5.3	4.0	19.1	12.2	40.9	18.5	100

Source: Zhu Delan, 'Qingchu Qianjieling Shi Zhongguo Chuan Haishang Maoyizhi Yanjiu' (On Trade Activities of Chinese Ships under the Qing Law of Anti-maritime Immigration from the Coastal Region), in Editing Committee for *Maritime History of China* (ed.), *Zhongguo Haiyang Fazhanshi Lunwenji* (*Selected Essays on the Maritime History of China*) (Taipei: *Academia Sinica*, 1986), pp. 110–35.

to Japan (see Table 22). During the 1717–27 ban, over 1,000 ocean-going ships sailed overseas (as in 1720).[60]

In the early Qing, the Ming loyalist movement under Zheng Chenggong (1624–62, nickname 'Guoxing Ye', known to the West as 'Koxinga') had 8,000 ships and controlled much of China Seas.[61] During 1647 to 1654, Zheng's navy attacked China's long coast from Shandong Peninsula to Guangdong, entered the Yangzi River and laid siege to Nanjing. In 1662, Zheng's men captured Penghu Islands and Taiwan from the Dutch.[62] It was not until 1683 did the Qing navy gained the upper hand in the war with the help of 20 Dutch warships.[63]

A century later, China's coast was once again infested with smuggling — this time, opium-related. Large quantities of imports made the narcotic cheaper; and the business was booming (Table 23).

The Qing draconian ban on the trade in 1839 without naval back up failed. British gunboats disarmed the entire Qing coastal defence during

[60] Qi Zhaonan, *Qingchao Wenxian Tongkao* (*Comprehensive Study of Qing Records*) (1787), Vol. 33.
[61] Sun Guangqi, *Zhongguo Gudai Hanghaishi* (*A Nautical History of Premodern China*) (Beijing: Maritime Press, 1989), p. 596.
[62] *Ibid.*, pp. 296–8.
[63] Zhang Dechang, 'Qingdai Yapian Zhanzheng Qianzhi Zhongxi Yanhai Tongshang' (Sino-Western Maritime Trade in Qing Times prior to the Opium Wars), *Qinghua Xuebao* (*Bulletin of Qinghua University*), 10/1 (1935), p. 104.

Table 23.   Opium Prices, Selected Years, 1820–35.

Year	Chests *	Weight (*catties*)	Value (*pesos*)	Pesos [*taels*]/*catty*
1820–5	6,774	729,320	33,502,440	45.9 [29.4][64]
1825–30	12,108	1,312,440	56,930,593	43.4 [27.8]
1830–5	20,546[65]	2,217,260	63,866,684	28.8 [18.5]
Annul %	7.7	7.7	4.4	–3.2

Source: H. B. Morse, *The Chronicles of the East India Company Trading to China, 1635–1834* (Oxford: Oxford University Press, 1926–9), Vols. 3–5; Timothy Brook and B. T. Wakabayashi (eds.), *Opium Regimes: China, Britain, and Japan, 1839–1952* (Berkeley: University of California Press, 2000), p. 204 (for the 1838 figure); E. H. Pritchard, *Anglo-Chinese Relations during the Seventeenth and Eighteenth Centuries* (Urbana: The University of Illinois Press, 1929), p. 160; *cf.* Yen-p'ing Hao, *The Commercial Revolution in Nineteenth-Century China* (Berkeley: University of California Press, 1986), p. 117; Gong Yingyan, *Yapiande Chuanbo Yu Duhua Yapian Maoyi* (*Spread of Opium Consumption and Opium Imports by China*) (Beijing: Orient Press, 1999), pp. 284–90, 292.
Note: Figures in parentheses are in metric tons. All the figures are higher if all smuggling is included.[66] Chest-weight conversion is based on Gong, *Spread of Opium*, pp. 281, 284–90, 292. *A chest contained 40 opium balls (the same size as a cannon ball, 15 cm in diameter, 3 *catties* each) of 100–120 *catties* (133.3–140 lb) in total.[67] A *tael* weighed 37.5 grams.

the 1840 Opium War. China's defence weakness was soon exploited by other powers in the following decades:

1856–60   Second Opium War (also known as the 'Arrow War') over a dispute about a Hong Kong ship and treatment of a French missionary;

1883–5   Sino-French War (also known as *Guerre Franco-chinoise*) over the control of present-day Vietnam;

[64] One Qing catty was 16 *liang*. So, the average opium price per catty was higher than silver in weight. High-quality opium cost up to four times its weight in silver, see Qi Sihe, *Yapian Zhanzheng* (*The Opium War*) (Shanghai: Shanghai People's Press, 2000), Vol. 1, p. 537.
[65] Chinese sources often put a figure of 25,000 to 35,500 chests a year for the late 1830s including smuggling, e.g., History Society of China, *Yapian Zhanzheng* (*The Opium War*) (Shanghai: Shenzhou Guoguang Press, 1954), Vol. 2, p. 543; Kuang Haolin, *Jianming Zhongguo Jindai Jingjishi* (*A Brief Economic History of Early Modern China*) (Beijing: Central National University Press, 1989), p. 38. Morse's data here are taken as the minimum.
[66] This is based on a comparison between Morse and Wu: (1) 22.2 million *taels* (832.5 tons) a year in the 1830s on the official record (see Morse, *Chronicles*, Vols. 4–5), and (2) 43.4 million *taels* (1,627.5 tons) including smuggling; see Wu, *China's Modernization*, p. 286.
[67] Martin Booth, *Opium: A History* (New York: St. Martin's Press, 1996), ch. 1.

1894　　　First Sino-Japanese War (also known as the '1894 War') over the control of present-day two Koreas;

1900　　　Invasion of the Eight-Nation Alliance to take revenge on the Boxer Rioters who had targeted Chinese Catholic converts. [68]

In the end, 26 treaties with 12 foreign powers were signed (see Table 24). These treaties aimed to end China's economic independence. [69]

Chin's wealth was also forcefully transferred to foreign powers. From 1842 to 1900, China's war reparations to foreign powers totalled 713 million *tales* of silver (26,600 metric tons). [70] By 1938 China had paid out 913 million *taels* of silver (34,055 tons), [71] equivalent to 30 years of the Qing annual Land-Poll Tax revenue. [72] China's coastal defence failure cost the empire dearly.

6. Internal Public Goods and Internal Crises

Internally, the empire kept substantial troops in the capital city against potential unrest and rebellions. Outside the capital, smaller army units

---

[68] As far as we can work out, only 230–250 foreigners were killed during the riot compared with the deaths of 20,000 Chinese Christians. So, the boxers were not really after foreigners. In all, 49,300 invading troops were deployed by Britain, France, Germany, Italy, Austria, Russia, USA, and Japan. It was absurd that non-Christian Japan joined most enthusiastically in the crusade by contributing 42 percent of all soldiers and 35 percent of all warships. Russia, whose citizens suffered no casualty at all in the riot, put in another 27 percent of soldiers and 20 percent of warships. So, it was practically a war of Japan and Russia against China. The real purpose of the alliance was extremely dodgy. See R. C. Forsyth, *The China Martyrs of 1900* (London: Publishers unknown, 1904); Marshall Broomhall, *Martyred Missionaries of China Inland Mission* (London: Morgan & Scott and CIM, 1901); see also C. C. Tan, *The Boxer Catastrophe* (New York: Columbia University Press, 1955); Fairbank and Liu, *Cambridge History of China*, Vol. 11, pt. 2, pp. 115–30; Tang Degang, *Wanqing Qishinian, Yihetuan Yu Baguo Lianjun* (*The Last Seventy Years of the Qing, the Boxer Riot and the Eight-Nation Alliance*) (Taipei: Yuanliu Press, 1998), Vol. 4; Diana Preston, *The Boxer Rebellion; The Dramatic Story of China's War on Foreigners That Shook the World in the Summer of 1900* (New York: Walker & Company, 2000).

[69] Tang Xianglong, *Zhongguo Jindai Haiguan Shuishou He Fenpei Tongji* (*Statistics of Customs Revenue and its Distribution in Modern China*) (Beijing: Zhonghua Books, 1992), pp. 34–41.

[70] Zhang, *Dictionary of Chinese Economic History*, pp. 874–80; Tang, *Statistics of Customs Revenue*, p. 33.

[71] Xia Zhengnong (ed.), *Cihai* (*Encyclopaedia*) (Shanghai: Encyclopaedia Publisher, 1989), p. 961.

[72] Liang, *Dynastic Data*, pp. 387, 397–98, 401, 415–16.

Table 24. 'Unequal Treaties' with China, 1842–1901.

Date	No of treaties	Beneficiary	Main benefit
1842–50	5	UK, USA, Fr	Pt, Rp, Tr, PR, UMF, CJ, CCD RD
1851-60	5	UK, USA, Fr, Rs	Pt, Rp, Tr, UMF, CJ, RD, CCD RL, FA
1861–70	2	UK, USA	FT, RR
1871–80	2	UK, USA	Pt, UMF, CJ, FA, RL
1881–90	3	Fr, Prl	CCD, Pt, UMF, CJ, Tr, PR
1891–1901	9	UK, USA, Fr, Atr, Sp Blm, Fr, Gm, Hld, Itl Rs, Jp	Tr, Rp, Pt, CCD, RF, UMF RD, RR
Total	26	12	

Source: Based on Zhang Doqing, *Zhongguo Jingjishi Cidian* (Encyclopaedia of Chinese Economic History) (Wuhan: Hubei Books, 1990), pp. 874–80.
Note: Atr = Austria, Blm = Belgium, Fr = France, Gm = Germany, Hld = Holland, Itl = Italy, Jp = Japan, Prl = Portugal, Rs = Russia, Sp = Spain. CCD = Cut in Customs Duty; CJ = Consular jurisdiction; FA = Free access to the interior; FT = Free trade of goods; PR = Permanent residency for foreigners; Pt = Free access to trading ports; RD = Right to deploy foreign armed forces; RF = Right to build factories; RL = Right to recruit Chinese labour for overseas markets; Rp = War reparation; RR = Right to build railways; Tr = Territorial gain including cession and concession of land; UMF = Unilateral most-favoured-nation treatment for trade.

were scattered across the vast empire so thinly that their presence became more or less symbolically. That included provincial government head quarters. According to the Qing record, there were commonly 1,000–2,000 troops under a Brigadier-General (*fu dutong*, the Second Grade) in charge of defence of a province.[73] In 1853, only 5,000 Qing soldiers guarded the strategic city of Nanjing's 13 gates and 34 kilometres long wall (67 *li*).[74] A large town had a few hundred soldiers under a Post Commandant (*fang-wei wei*, the Third Grade).[75] There were in all 35,300 troops in 44 stations

[73] Zhao, *History of the Qing Dynasty*, Vol. 131, Entry 'Military', in *TFOH*, Vol. 11, pp. 9307–8. See Zhao Xiukun, Tian Shaolin, He Shaoheng, Cai Zhipu, He Shaoheng, Wei Zhenfu and Zhang Jiyin, *Zhongguo Junshi Shi* (*A Military History of China*) (Beijing: PLA Press, 1987), Vol. 3, p. 441.
[74] Nie Bochun and Han Pinzheng, *Taiping Tianguo Tianjing Tushuo Ji* (*Illustrated Maps of the Capital City of the Heavenly Kingdom of Great Peace*) (Nanjing: Jiangsu Classics Press, 1985), pp. 8–10, 11.
[75] Zhao *et al.*, *Military History of China*, Vol. 3, p. 442.

in the Manchu homeland Manchuria (as of 1824), with were 800 soldiers in each station.[76] In this context, Imperial China was not a militarised society, and the Imperial state *did not* monopolise violence.

At the grassroots level, where the Imperial bureaucracy had little control, internal security was organised autonomously by citizens themselves. According to Sidney D. Gamble's survey, in North China villages were self-governed (regarding internal law-making, censuses, cadastral surveys, religious festivals, taxes, and public spending) with own provision of public goods (internal judiciary, local policing, and local education). The key institutions were village assembly, village neighbourhood watch, village militia, and village schools. The village assembly (*cunmin dahui*) was responsible for law making and selecting the head of the village. The 'neighbourhood watch' (*baojia*) ensured tax payments and crime control in a collective manner. The village militia (*tuanlian*) ran night watching and crop-guarding against thieves and bandits. Village schools provided four-fifths of villagers with one-year rudimentary education, and one-fifth with three years of schooling.[77] All these institutions served the village's economy.[78] All such services were financed by villages themselves.[79]

The best example of grassroots autonomy was shown by how disputes were handled. China had a long tradition to view disputes and lawsuits harmful to social tranquillity and public morale. Confucius thus famously said that 'I am concerned about lawsuits in society. It is necessary to eliminate them'.[80] As a result, bureaucrats were assessed by how few lawsuits they handled in any given period as an indicator of their moral leadership in local communities. Local officials were thus reluctant to take on law cases. The tiny size of the Qing state was unable to handle heavy workload anyway.

---

[76] Zhao, *History of the Qing Dynasty*, Vol. 130, Entry 'Military', in *TFOH*, Vol. 11, p. 9303.

[77] S. D. Gamble, *North China Villages, Social Political, and Economic Activities before 1933* (Berkeley: University of California Press, 1963), pp. 62, 139, 140, 167, 171–4, 179, 181–4, 187–91, 196–208, 216–20, 232–9, 266–84, 324–30, 322, 335–6, 339–41.

[78] E.g., J. L. Buck, *Land Utilization in China: Statistics* (London: Oxford University Press, 1937); Hsiao–t'ung Fei, *Peasant Life in China; A Field Study of Country Life in the Yangtze Valley* (London: Paul, Trench, Trubner, 1939); Skinner, 'Marketing and Social Structure in Rural China'.

[79] Zhao, *History of the Qing Dynasty*, Vol. 133, Entry 'Village Guards', in *TFOH*, Vol. 11, p. 9315.

[80] Wu Genyou (ed.), *Sishu Wujing (The Annotated Four Books and Five Classics of Confucianism)*, ch. 'Yanyuan', (Beijing: China's Friendship Press, 1993), p. 23.

A Qing county court typically opened for business for just two open days (*gaofang ri*) per month for a total of six months a year.[81] It was often mutually agreed between the villagers and the country magistrate that disputes were submitted to officials only after all non-official means and channels were exhausted.[82] In majority cases, therefore, customary rules (*suli*, literally 'customary precedents') dominated dispute settlements.[83] So much so that even if an official ruling was handed down, villagers were still allowed to seek for a different settlement according to village's customary rules.[84] For example, divisions of family property amongst sons (*fenjia*) were entirely governed by local customary rules.[85] Mediators — either a relative on the mother's side or the clan/village head — could be brought in. Final decisions were binding and written contracts were not necessary. Similarly, inheritance (*jicheng*) was mainly governed by customary rules.[86] These rules were

---

[81] Dang Jiangzhou, *Zhongguo Songshi Wenhua* (*The Shysters' Culture in Traditional China*) (Beijing: Peking University Press, 2005), pp. 64–6; Derk Bodde and Clarence Morris, *Law in Imperial China* (Philadelphia: University of Pennsylvania Press, 1967).

[82] Madeleine Zelin, 'The Rights of Tenants in Mid-Qing Sichuan: A Study of Land-Related Lawsuits in the Baxian Archives', *Journal of Asian Studies*, 45/3 (1986), pp. 521–2.

[83] Bourgon Jerome, 'Uncivil Dialogue: Law and Custom Did not Merge into Civil Law under the Qing', *Late Imperial China*, 23/1 (2002), pp. 50–90; J. A. Cohen, R. R. Edwards, and F. C. Chen, *Essays on China's Legal Tradition* (Princeton: Princeton University Press, 1980); Liang Zhiping, *Qingdai Xiguanfa: Shehui Yu Guojia* (*Customary Law during the Qing Period: Society and the State*) (Beijing: Chinese University of Law and Politics Press, 1996); see also P. C. C. Huang, *Civil Justice in China: Representation and Practice in the Qing* (Stanford: Stanford University Press, 1996); P. C. C. Huang, 'Civil Adjudication in China, Past and Present', *Modern China*, 32/2 (2006), pp. 135–80.

[84] Kathryn Bernhardt and P. C. C. Huang (eds.), *Civil Law in Qing and Republican China* (Stanford: Stanford University Press, 1994), p. 116; Cohen *et al.*, *Essays on China's Legal Tradition*, pp. 78–84.

[85] Numerous works cite examples of this: e.g., Fei, *Peasant Life in China*, pp. 65–9; Yueh-hwa Lin, *The Golden Wing: A Sociological Study of Chinese Familism* (London: Kegan Paul, 1947), pp. 122–8; Shūzō Shiga, 'Family Property and the Law of Inheritance in Traditional China', in D. C. Buxbaum (ed.), *Chinese Family Law and Social Change in Historical and Comparative Perspective* (Seattle: University of Washington Press, 1979), pp. 109–50; M. L. Cohen, *House United, House Divided: The Chinese Family in Taiwan* (New York: Columbia University Press, 1976), pp. 205–10.

[86] Kathryn Bernhardt and P. C. C. Huang (eds.), *Civil Law in Qing and Republican China* (Stanford: Stanford University Press, 1994), pp. 137–8, 170–1; Qu Tongzu, *Zhongguo Falü He Zhongguo Shehui* (*Chinese Law and Chinese Society*) (Beijing: Zhonghua Books, 1981); Xie Hui and Chen Jinduo, *Minjian Fa* (*Customary Law*) (Jinan: Shandong People's Press, 2002); Zhang Renshan, *Li, Fa, Shehui* (*Rights, Laws and Society*) (Tianjin: Tianjin Classics Press, 2002), pp. 28–39.

so powerful that even totalitarian Maoism could do little to change them.[87] It was these customary rules that granted grassroots communities *de jure* autonomy politically and economically.[88]

It is important to note the long-term dichotomy of Chinese 'laws' rooted in two separate traditions. Mainstream customary rules came from the Western Zhou rites (*li*) dating back *c*. 1030–771 BC. It had a strong sense of fairness (being fair within one's social standing) but not necessarily equality (being treated indiscriminately like everyone else). This approach is consistent with famous Confucian maxims of 'seeing no rites-less, hearing no rites-less, speaking no rites-less and acting no rites-less' (*feili wushi, feili wuting, feili wuyan, feili wudong*),[89] and 'not doing to others what you would not want done to yourself' (*ji suo buyu, wushi yu ren*) and 'cherishing or loving one another' (*airen*).[90] These rites aimed to bring out inner goodness, conscience, and virtues of individuals in order to create and maintain social harmony in a hierarchical society through moral persuasion. The sanction from customary rules consisted of monetary payments and ostracism from the community. Consequently, the rites-cum-rules operated on social formalities and individual reputation (known as *mianzi*, or 'face'). They were subtle and often more effective than political coercion and legal punishments. So, after the empire was established, the rites-based customary rules (*lizhi*,

---

[87] M. L. Cohen, 'Family Management and Family Division in Contemporary China', *The China Quarterly*, 130/2 (1992), pp. 357–77.

[88] For a classical study, see Milton Katz (ed.), *Government under Law and the Individual* (Washington D.C.: American Council of Learned Societies, 1957), pp. 28–39. Also, Fu-mei C. Chen and R. H. Myers, 'Customary Law and the Economic Growth of China during the Ch'ing Period', *Ch'ing-shih Wen-t'i*, 3/5 (1976), pp. 1–32, and 3/10 (1978), pp. 4–27. For a more recent debate, see Bernhardt and Huang, *Civil Law in Qing and Republican China*, pp. 27–32.

[89] Wu, *Four Books and Five Classics of Confucianism*, p. 22. They are often translated into 'seeing no evil …' which is not accurate because the concept of 'evil' suggests that bad things have already gone too far.

[90] Kong Qiu (Confucius), *The Analects*. Later, Zhu Xi (1130–1200 AD.), the founder of Neo-Confucianism, interpreted *ren* as what separates human beings from the animal Kingdom in a package of benevolence, righteousness, etiquette and intelligence (*ren yi li zhi*); see Zhu, *Philosophical Analects*, Vol. 4. See also R. L. Taylor, *The Cultivation of Sagehood as a Religious Goal in Neo-Confucianism* (Missoula [Mont.]: Scholars Press, 1978), pp. 101–20, 121–34.

meaning 'rule by rites') survived everywhere, although they became localised and often unwritten.[91] Rules and regulations of guilds reflected such an approach.[92]

The second tradition of codified laws began with the rise of the Legalist School (*fajia*). This school argued that everyone was equal before a universal law because individuals were potential cheaters. The Legalists saw coercion as necessary in maintaining social order. The Legalist approach proved to be efficient in dealing with impersonal situations and relationships. In particular, it served the purpose of building up a large political unit which transcended regional and communal differences. Indeed, the Qin Kingdom which unified China in 221 BC was to a great extent *the* product of the Legalist approach.[93] However, the Legalist approach was associated with higher costs and a greater danger of power abuse which were eventually brought down the Qin regime in 207 BC. In the following Western Han Period (206 BC–24 AD), the Legalist approach was relaxed and replaced by Confucian code of conduct and customary rules. The Ming-Qing state strongly endorsed both customary rules and village autonomy as the norm.[94]

The downside of customary rules and village autonomy was the absence of the state monopoly over violence, which planted the seed of social unrest if village autonomy was shaken. Moreover, village autonomy lacked the economies of scale. Any sizeable bandits were able to bring down village-based security. This was the mechanism behind the phenomenon of recurring 'peasant rebellions' across the two-millennium history of the empire.[95] In the nineteenth century, this downside was fully exploited by the Taiping, Nian, and Miao rebels who swept quickly and easily from one

---

[91] Fei Xiaotong, *Xiangtu Zhongguo* (*Rural Life in China*) (Beijing: Beijing Press, 2004), pp. 68–99; also Feng Er-kang, *Zhongguo Zongzu Shehui* (*Clans in China*) (Hangzhou: Zhejiang People's Press, 1994).

[92] Peng, *Selected Historical Materials of Handicraft and Trade Guilds*, Vols. 1–2.

[93] For a good summary, see J. W. Head and Yanping Wang, *Law Codes in Dynastic China* (Durham: Carolina Academic Press, 2005), pp. 14–18, 49–50.

[94] Zhao, *History of the Qing Dynasty*, Vol. 133, Entry 'Village Guards', in *TFOH*, Vol. 11, pp. 9314–5; see also Niu Guanjie, 'Cong Shouwang Xiangzhu Dao Lizhi Yingyi Tuanlian Weixian: You Tuanlian Zuzhide Fazhan Yanbian Kan Guojia Zhengquan Yu Jiceng Shehuide Hudong Guanxi' (From Vigilante to Local Order: The Interplay between the State and Grassroots Society), *Zhongguo Nongshi* (*Agricultural History of China*), 23/1 (2004), pp. 73–80.

[95] Deng, *Chinese Premodern Economy*, Appendix J.

end of the empire to another apart from Manchuria, Mongolia and Tibet.[96] At their peak, the Taipings had about 600,000 troops.[97] They marched in a straight line from Guilin (Guangxi) all the way to Nanjing (Jiangsu) with little resistance,[98] taking over seven provinces on their way.[99] It took only 1,000 Taiping rebels to overpower a major city Zhangzhou.[100] Other large urban centres, including Hankou, Yangzhou and Hangzhou,[101] allowed the Taiping rebels to walk straight in.[102] Similarly, the Nians rampaged across five provinces freely with their 200,000 troops.[103]

In contrast, the backbone of the Qing government forces, the Green Standing Army, had in total just 350,000 men (as of 1851). In many towns and cities, local defence was all but symbolic. The entire Qing forces in Zhejiang Province (as of 1857) were 5,100.[104] Qing generals often borrowed troops from each other in order to keep their defences barely afloat.[105] In 1853 when 100,000 Taiping rebels attacked Nanjing,[106] there were only 5,000 Qing soldiers guarding the huge city.[107] Nanjing fell, as expected. Along the Yangzi River, the largest concentration of the Qing troops was 46,000 men in Ningguo in Anhui.[108] The Ningguo defence was no match to the invading 100,000 Taipings.[109] In 1853 the Qing government mobilised

---

[96] Kent Deng, *China's Political Economy in Modern Times* (London: Routledge, 2011), ch. 4.

[97] Zhao, *History of the Qing Dynasty*, Vol. 475, Entry 'Biography of Hong Xiuquan', in *TFOH*, Vol. 12, pp. 10259–10273.

[98] J. D. Spence, *The Search for Modern China* (New York: W. W. Norton, 1990), p. 173.

[99] F. H. Michael (ed.), *The Taiping Rebellion, History and Documents* (Seattle: University of Washington Press, 1966–71), Vol. 1, pp. 205–15, Maps 4–14.

[100] Luo Ergang, *Zhongwang Li Xiucheng Zizhuan Yuangao Jianzheng (Annotated Confession of Li Xiucheng)* (Beijing: Zhonghua Books, 1957), p. 218.

[101] Yangzhou Prefecture governed 3.3 million residents, while Hangzhou governed 27.4 million (as of 1820); see Liang, *Dynastic Data*, pp. 273, 275.

[102] Luo, *Annotated Confession of Li Xiucheng*, pp. 203, 218. See also A. F. Lindley, *Ti-Ping Tien-Kwoh: the History of the Ti-ping Revolution* (London: Day and Son, 1866), p. 65.

[103] Zhao, *History of the Qing Dynasty*, Vol. 405, Entry 'Biography of Zeng Guofan', in *TFOH*, Vol. 12, p. 10144.

[104] Chinese Historical Society (ed.), *Taiping Tianguo (Heavenly Kingdom of Great Peace)* (Shanghai: Shenzhou Guoguang Press, 1952), Vol. 6, p. 593.

[105] Luo, *Annotated Confession of Li Xiucheng*, p. 205.

[106] Nie and Han, *Illustrated Maps of the Capital City*, pp. 35, 48–9.

[107] *Ibid.*, pp. 8–10, 11.

[108] For the local population, see Liang, *Dynastic Data*, p. 273.

[109] Luo, *Annotated Confession of Li Xiucheng*, pp. 222, 227–8; see also Ssu-yü Teng, *The Taiping Rebellion and the Western Powers* (Oxford: Clarendon, 1971), pp. 331–5.

24,800 soldiers to retake Nanjing.[110] They were no march with the 100,000 Taipings.[111] The Qing military tried again in 1858 by laying siege on Nanjing with 40,000 troops.[112] They were once again overpowered by 100,000 Taiping rebels in 1860.[113]

Miraculously, the Qing state survived the empire-wide unrest during the 1850s to 1870s. It was however a costly victory. Financially, the war against the Taiping rebels alone cost the Qing Treasury 167 million *taels* of silver (about 6,229 metric tons).[114] Another 31.7 million *taels* were spent on the campaign against the Nians, 101.1 million *taels* on the campaign against rebels in the southwest, and 118.9 million *taels* on the campaign against the Muslims.[115] They totaled 251.7 million *taels* (about 9,388 tons) and all came from Beijing. Another 420 million *taels* was footed by provincial establishments.[116] The aggregate war bill was 838.7 million *taels* (about 31,283 tons),[117] about 28 years of the Qing annual Land-Poll Tax revenue.

Moreover, China's internal unrest sharply reduced the Qing government tax incomes (Table 25).[118]

Table 25.   Annual Losses of the Land-Poll Tax to the Taiping Unrest, 1850–60.

	Revenue (million *taels*)*	Stipend rice (million *shi*)*
China's total in peace time	30.2	7.4 (7.4)[†]
Amount lost to Taipings	12.6	5.8 (5.8)[†]
Losses in China's total (%)	41.6	78.0

Source: Based on Liang, *Dynastic Data*, pp. 401–11.

Note: * Estimation is based on the data for 1820. [†] Minimum value, based on one *tael* of silver per *shi*.

[110] Nie and Han, *Illustrated Maps of the Capital City*, p. 41.

[111] *Ibid.*, pp. 46–50.

[112] Luo, *Annotated Confession of Li Xiucheng*, pp. 218–9.

[113] Nie and Han, *Illustrated Maps of the Capital City*, pp. 65, 72–5.

[114] Zhao, *History of the Qing Dynasty*, Vol. 125, Entry 'Economy', in TFOH, Vol. 11, p. 9283.

[115] Sun Xiugang, *Jianming Zhongguo Caizheng Shi* (*A Concise History of Government Finance*) (Beijing: China's Finance and Economics Press, 1988), p. 220; Peng Zeyi, *Shijiu Shiji Houbanqide Zhongguo Caizheng Yu Jingji* (*China's Finance and Economy during the Second Half of the Nineteenth Century*) (Beijing: Chinese Finance Press, 1990), p. 136.

[116] Peng, *China's Finance and Economy*, pp. 130, 137.

[117] Zhou, *History of State Finance*, pp. 151–3.

[118] Zhao, *History of the Qing Dynasty*, Vol. 125, Entry 'Economy', in *TFOH*, Vol. 11, p. 9283.

The 14-year long Taiping outbreak reduced the Qing Land Poll tax income for 200 million *taels* minimum. Similarly, after 1853, the normal salt trading routes from Anhui to Jiangxi and Hunan were all blocked.[119] The losses in salt taxes counted for another 100 million *taels*.

In all, the 1850–70 unrest cost Qing state about 1,138 million *taels* (42,447 tons). As any increase in domestic tax burden was politically dangerous, the only way out of this grim situation was to raise funds from foreign sources which in turn put the Qing government in a very bad light in China's domestic politics.

---

[119] Zeng Guofan, *Zeng Wenzhenggong Quanji, Wenji (Complete Collection of Master Zeng Guofan's Works, Essays)* (N.d. Reprint. Taipei: Wenhai Press, 1966–83), Vol. 6, pp. 20–1; also Peng Zeyi, *Zhongguo Jindai Shougongyeshi Ziliao (Historical Materials of Handicraft Industry in Early Modern China)* (Beijing: Sanlian Books, 1957), Vol. 1, p. 592.

Chapter Six

Highlights of the Economy
of the Empire

1. General Pattern: Extensive Growth

There has been much debate on what sort of economic growth the empire of China experienced from its beginning until 1800. There is a tendency to portray China's economy as one of gradual linear growth in which farming communities faced a Malthusian crisis due to fixed farm land and the law of diminishing returns.[1] What has often been overlooked was the fact that land supply in China remained highly elastic on the macro-level (see Figures 1, 2, 4 and 5). On the micro-level, private landholding property rights were well defined and protected to safeguard good use of land. More fundamentally, China's population did not grow very much for about 1.5 millennia (from 2 AD to *c.* 1000, and from *c.* 1279–1700), maintaining remarkably stable between 50 and 60 million.

---

[1] Lee, *Economic History of China*; Perkins, *Agricultural Development in China*; Elvin, *Pattern of the Chinese Past*; P. C. C. Huang, *The Peasant Economy and Social Change in North China* (Stanford: Stanford University Press, 1985); Chao, *Man and Land in Chinese History*; T. G. Rawski and L. M. Li (eds.), *Chinese History in Economic Perspective* (Berkeley: University of California Press, 1992); Maddison, *Chinese Economic Performance*.

To work out the size of the economy, one can take the minimalistic approach of subsistence living. To assume (1) that it takes 0.5 kilograms of husked/milled cereal each day to sustain an adult and half of that amount to maintain a child under the age of 15, and (2) that children consist of one-third of the total population, it requires about 425 metric tons to sustain a million people per day (350 tons for adults and 75 tons for children), or 155,125 tons or 2,139,700 *shi* of husked/milled cereal a year.[2] Rice and wheat lose about 30 percent of weight to the husking/milling process. So, the grass total becomes 221,600 tons or 3,056,600 *shi*. To use this as a benchmark, the annual total amount of food required by China's standing population during various periods, and the amount of farmland for food production can be calculated.

The fact is that the registered farmland by the Imperial government was always greater than the minimum amount to support the standing population, China's farming sector had over-capacity most of the time in the long run (see Table 26, measured by II > I in the long run). If so, a Malthusian crisis was not imminent most of the time in Imperial China.

Four factors explain this: First, China's private property right of land warranted farmers' incentives to feed themselves. Second, there is the 'diseconomies of scale in farming' (hence no advantages for large farms to achieve a higher yield), which suited perfectly China's household-based small farms. Third, food is perishable. A self-sufficient farming household would not want to produce too much food beyond its consumption. Fourth, if most households produced their own staple food, market volatility would not affect the majority in society. Besides, even if in the beginning good prices attract more food for sale, too much food then pushes the price down, which in turn discourages over-production.

A stable population in China did not necessarily mean a poor population. From the perspective of Engel Coefficient (i.e., proportion

---

[2] Loose rice in *shi* weighs 72.5 kilogram; see Liang, *Dynastic Data*, p. 545; Chao, *Man and Land in Chinese History*, p. 209.

Table 26.   Farmland *vis-à-vis* Food to Sustain China's Standing Population, 2–1887 AD.

AD	A	B	C (I)	D (II)	D′ (II′)	II:I	II′:I
2	59.6	174.3	174.3*	827.1	590.9Δ	4.7	3.4
145	49.5	151.3	151.3*	695.7	496.9Δ	4.6	3.3
609	46.0	140.6	140.6*	1940.4§	—	13.8	—
1100	115.2	352.1	234.8†	524.9¶	472.4‡	2.2	2.0
1381	60.0	183.4	122.3†	366.8	—	3.0	—
1701	56.1	171.5	114.3†	598.7	—	5.2	—
1766	208.1	636.1	424.1†	741.4	—	1.7	—
1887	377.6	1154.3	769.5†	912.0	—	1.2	—

Source: Deng, 'Unveiling China's True Population Statistics', Appendix 2; Liang, *Dynastic Data*, pp. 4–11. *Note*: A = Population in million persons. B = Unhusked/unmilled grain required in million *shi*. C = Land required in million *mu*. D = Actual registered farmland in million *mu*. Noted here, the government-registered farmland was subject to under-report by about 30 percent.[3] D′ = Period land measures adjusted. II:I = Ratio between registered landholding and minimum land required for food for subsistence living. II′:I = Ratio between landholding and land required with period land measures adjusted. * Dry farming on land of the medium soil fertility: one *shi* per *mu*. † A mixed dry and paddy farming economy: one *shi* per *mu* from dry farming and two *shi* per *mu* from paddy farming and hence 1.5 *shi* per *mu* on average on land of the medium soil fertility.[4] § Year 589 figure. ¶ Year 1021 figure. Δ One *mu* during this period was 1.4 standard *mu*.[5] ‡ One *mu* during this period was 0.9 standard *mu*.[6]

of households' income spent on food) China's population had reasonable standards of living over the long run (Table 27). This is compatible with the findings by the 'California School'.[7]

---

[3] Zhao Yun, 'Jishu Wucha, Zhemu Jiqi Juli Shuaijian Guilü Yanjiu' (Technical Errors: Land Unit Conversion and the Law of Diminishing Distance), *Zhongguo Shehui Jingjishi Yanjiu* (*Research in Chinese Social and Economic History*), 3 (2007), pp. 1–13.

[4] Wu Hui, *Zhongguo Jingjishi Rugan Wentide Jiliang Yanjiu* (*Quantitative Studies of Chinese Economic History*) (Fuzhou: Fujian People's Press, 2009), p. 115. For a similar conclusion, see also, Ge Jinfang and Gu Rong, 'Songdai Jiangnan Diqude Liangshi Muchan Jiqi Gusuan Fangfa Bianxi' (Estimation and Evidence of Yield Level in the Lower Yangzi Region during the Song Period), *Hubei Daxue Xuebao* (*Bulletin of the University of Hubei*), 3 (2000), pp. 78–83.

[5] Liang, *Dynastic Data*, p. 546.

[6] One Song *mu* = 0.9 modern *mu*, see Liang, *Dynastic Data*, p. 545.

[7] Their main works include R. B. Wong, *China Transformed, Historical Change and the Limits of European Experience* (Ithaca and London: Cornell University Press, 1997); A. G. Frank, *ReOrient: Global Economy in the Asian Age* (Berkeley: University of California Press, 1998); Pomeranz, *Great Divergence*.

Table 27.   Estimated Engel Coefficient in China over the
Long Run.

Year, *circa*	Engel coefficient*
2	0.50
640	0.72
1800[†]	0.65
1930 (urban)	0.54[§]
1933	0.56
1947[§]	0.61
Average	0.60

Source: Wang Lihua, *Zhongguo Jiating Shi, Diyi Juan* (*A History of Families in China, Vol. 1*) (Guangzhou: Guangdong People's Press, 2007), p. 281; Yu Xinzhong, *Zhongguo Jiating Shi, Disi Juan* (*A History of Families in China, Vol. 4*) (Guangzhou: Guangdong People's Press, 2007), pp. 146–7; Zheng Quanhong, *Zhongguo Jiating Shi, Diwu Juan* (*A History of Families in China, Vol. 5*) (Guangzhou: Guangdong People's Press, 2007), pp. 277–8, 281–2, 311–2, 335. Bureau of Social Affairs of Shanghai, *The Cost of Living Index Numbers of Laborers, Great Shanghai, January 1926–December 1931* (Shanghai: Bureau of Social Affairs of Shanghai, 1932), p. 18; Li Wenhai, Xia Mingfang and Huang Xingtao (eds.), *Minguo Shiqi Shehui Diaocha Congbian, Chengshi Laogong Shenghuojuan* (*Selected Social Surveys of the Republican Period, Volume on Urban Workers*) (Fuzhou: Fujian Education Press, 2005), Vol. 1, pp. 25, 26, 358; Vol. 2, pp. 2, 758, 827, 1225.

Note: * Percentage of total household income spent on food. [†] After the 1750 population take-off. [§] After the Second World War.

It is worth noting that in the 1960s to 70s, modern China's national Engel coefficient deteriorated to 0.7.[9]

---

[8] Comparable with Britain, Japan and India at the time; see Li Wenhai, Xia Mingfang and Huang Xingtao (eds.), *Minguo Shiqi Shehui Diaocha Congbian, Chengshi Laogong Shenghuojuan* (*Selected Social Surveys of the Republican Period, Volume on Urban Workers*) (Fuzhou: Fujian Education Press, 2005), Vol. 1, pp. 273, 359. For Meiji Japan's Engel Coefficient, see S. B. Hanley, *Everyday Things in Premodern Japan* (Berkeley: University of California Press, 1997), p. 171 and *passim*.

[9] He Bochuan, '2000 Nian Zhongguo Mubiao Xitongde 20 Ge Cuiruodian' (Twenty Weak Points in China's Targets for the Year 2000), *Xinhua Wenzhai* (*Xinhua Compilation*), 5 (1994), p. 8.

2. Exceptional Population Growth during the Northern Song Period

A fast population growth only occurred in 1000–1127 and post-1750, barely three centuries put altogether (see Figure 2). This was exceptional because the fast population growth counts for about one-seventh the empire's life span (221 BC – 1911 AD).[10] The Northern Song Period (960–1127) was a period of climate change and nomad invasion and conquest. The 'Little Ice Age' of that time caused the average temperature to drop 1–2° C in China.[11] During 1000–1120, the frequency of warm weather declined by 90 percent than before.[12] North China was hit particularly hard with the combination of increasing droughts,[13] delayed harvest season,[14] and 10–20 percent less yield (see Figure 9).[15] This climate change drove China's cereal production belt towards the Yangzi River in the south.[16]

---

[10] Zhang, *History of Families in China*, Vol. 2; Yu, *History of Families in China*, Vol. 4; Zheng, *History of Families*, Vol. 5.

[11] Zhu Kezhen, 'Woguo Jinwuqiannianlai Qihou Bianqiande Chubu Yanjiu' (Preliminary Analysis of Climatic Changes in China in the Past 5,000 Years), *Kaogu Xuebao* (*Bulletin of Archaeology*), 1 (1972), pp. 15–38; Hermann Flohn (ed.), *World Survey of Climatology, Vol. 2, General Climatology* (New York, 1969), p. 236; S. H. Schneider and Clifford Mass, 'Volcanic Dust, Sunspots, and Temperature Trends', *Science*, 190/4216 (1975), pp. 741–6. Also see Craig Loehle, 'A 2000-Year Global Temperature Reconstruction Based on Non-Treering Proxies', *Energy and Environment*, 7–8/18 (2007), pp. 1048–58.

[12] Song Zhenghai, Gao Jianguo, Sun Guanlong, and Zhang Binglun, *Zhongguo Gudai Ziran Zaiyi Dongtao Fenxi* (*Dynamic Analysis of Natural Disasters in Premodern China*) (Hefei: Anhui Educational Press, 2002), p. 343.

[13] *Ibid.*, p. 123.

[14] Tuotuo, *History of the Song Dynasty*, Vol. 174, Entry 'Shihuozhi 127', in *TFOH*, Vol. 7, p. 5716.

[15] Zheng Xuemeng, *Zhongguo Gudai Jingji Zhongxin Nanyi He Tangsong Jiangnan Jingji Yanjiu* (Southward Shift of China's Economic Centre of Gravity and the Economy of the Lower Yangzi Delta during the Tang and Song Periods) (Changsha: Yuelu Books, 1996), pp. 39–43; Song *et al.*, *Dynamic Analysis of Natural Disasters*, p. 187; Zhang Jiacheng, *Qihou Yu Renlei* (*Climate and Humankind*) (Zhengzhou: Henan Science and Technology Press, 1988), pp. 123–4.

[16] Zhao Hongjun and Yin Bocheng, 'Gongyuan 11 Shijihoude Qihou Bianleng Dui Songyihou Jingji Fazhande Dongtai Yingxiang' (Dynamic Impact of Cooling Down in Climate after the Eleventh Century on Economic Development in Post-Song China), *Shehui Kexue* (*Social Sciences*), 4 (2011), p. 71; Cheng, *Regional Economies during the Song Period*, pp. 13–14.

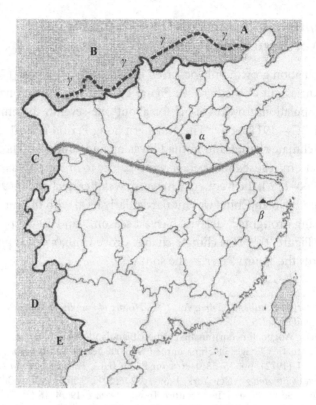

Figure 9.   Disaster Zone in North China.

Source: Based on Tan Qixiang, *Jianming Zhongguo Lishi Ditu Ji* (*Concise Historical Atlas of China*) (Beijing, 1991), pp. 51–4.

Note: Along borders, A = Liao Kingdom (Khitans); B = Xixia Kingdom (Tanguts); C = Tibet Kingdom; D = Dali Kingdom; E = Yue Kingdom. The grey line = the divide between the disaster zone of the 'Little Ice Age' in the north and the normal zone in the south; γ–γ = the line where the Great Wall had laid; α = Kaifeng, the capital of the Northern Song; β = Lin-an (Hangzhou), the capital of the Southern Song.

Farmers began to abandon farming in the north on a noticeable scale. In 996, the court official Chen Jing (948–1026) reported that 'Across 30 prefectures of 1,000 *li* surrounding the capital Kaifeng, only 20–30 percent arable land is actually cultivated.'[17] In 1007, as recorded, government land tax revenue declined by 718,000 *shi*.[18] Farming in the north declined.

---

[17] Tuotuo, *History of the Song Dynasty*, Vol. 173, Entry 'Shihuozhi 126', in *TFOH*, Vol. 7, p. 5711. Here, 1,000 Song *li* ≈ 500 km.

[18] *Ibid.*, Vol. 174, Entry 'Shihuozhi 127', in *TFOH*, Vol. 7, p. 5717. *Note*: One Song *shi* = 46.2 kg.

Table 28.1.   North–South Ratio in the Growth of Farmland.

	980 AD	1101 AD	Annual increase (%)
North	2,117,719	5,099,338	0.74
South	4,052,048	12,415,291	0.93

Source: Liang, *Dynastic Data*, p. 164; and Wu Songdi, *Zhongguo Renkoushi, Disan Juan, Liao, Song, Jin, Yuan Shiqi (Demographic History of China: Vol. III, the Liao, Song, Jin and Yuan Periods)* (Shanghai: Fudan University Press, 2000), pp. 122–35.

Note: Figures are numbers of households.

Table 28.2   North–South Ratio in the Growth in Households.

	South–North ratio
Number of households	1.2
Farmland (*mu*)	1.4

Source: Qi, *Economic History of the Song*, Vol. 1, pp. 68–9.

Fortunately, China's farmland overcapacity kicked in as shown in Table 28.1. The Song population became mobile and mass migration to the south accelerated.[19] Accordingly, the population in the south grew faster than that in the north. By 1085, more households living in the south; and so was more land cultivated (see Table 28.2).

It is worth noting that commonly alleged 'double-cropping of Champa Rice' during the Northern Song Period is a myth.[20] First, Champa Rice on China's record during the Song was a normal-ripening species: According to both *Thesaurus of Rice* (*Hepu*, 1094 AD) and *Chen Fu's Treatise on Agriculture* (*Chefu Nongshu*, 1149 AD), Champa Rice had a growth cycle of five to six months.[21] This was confirmed by the Imperial political centre: 'In the *Ninth Month* of 1013, Emperor Zhenzong displayed the newly harvested Champa Rice to all his ranking officials at

---

[19] Liang, *Dynastic Data*, pp. 126–9.

[20] Ping-ti Ho, 'Early-Ripening Rice in Chinese History', *Economic History Review*, 9/2 (1956), pp. 200–18.

[21] Zeng Anzhi, *He Pu* (*Thesaurus of Rice*), 1094 AD; in Cao Shuji, 'He Pu Jiaoshi' (Annotated Thesaurus of Rice), *Zhongguo Nongshi* (*Agricultural History of China*), 3 (1985), pp. 74–84; Chen Fu, *Chenfu Nongshu* (*Chen Fu's Treatise on Agriculture*) (Originally published in 1149 AD. Reprint. Beijing: Agricultural Press, 1956), p. 2. *Note*: A Chinese calendar month has 29 days.

Table 29.   Rice Crops in Suzhou (Lower Yangzi) during the Northern Song.

Month*	3rd	4th	5th	6th	7th	8th	9th
Rice α	↓			↑			
Rice β†	↓				↑		
Rice γ†		↓				↑	
Rice δ†		↓					↑

Source: Liang Gengyao, *Nansongde Nongcun Jingji* (*The Rural Economy in the Southern Song Period*) (Beijing: New Star Press, 2006), p. 117.

Note: * Chinese calendar. † With the same growth cycle as that of Champa Rice. ↓ Seed-sowing; ↑ Crop-harvesting.

Jade Palace.'[22] Champa Rice could ripen too late, as described by the Song poet Su Shi (1037–1101):[23]

> *So late Champa Rice ripens this year,*
>
> *Frost comes with an autumn rain,*
>
> *On green mad fall all the golden ears.*
>
> ...
>
> *It sells at fodder's price.*

All evidence shows thus that during the Northern Song Period, there was not enough time for a second rice crop to mature during the same calendar year (Table 29).[24]

The earliest known case of double-cropping of rice was dated in 1178 when the Northern Song Period was over.[25] Double-cropping of

---

[22] Tuotuo, *History of the Song*, Vol. 8, in *TFOH*, Vol. 7, p. 5205.

[23] Su Hua, *Songci Jianshang Zidian* (*Annotated Song Poems*) (Shanghai: Shanghai Books, 1987), p. 341.

[24] A similar point has been made in Zeng Xiongsheng, 'Songdaide Shuangji Dao' (Double-cropping of Rice in the Song Period), *Ziran Kexueshi Yanjiu* (*Study of History of Natural Sciences*), 21/3 (2002), pp. 255–68.

[25] For the first recorded double-cropping of rice, see Zhou Qufei, *Lingwai Daida* (*Knowledge about South China and Beyond*), in Ji Jun (ed.), *Wenyuange Siku Quanshu* (*The Qing Imperial Complete Collection of Books in the Wenyuan Library*) (Originally published in 1178. Reprint. Taipei: Taiwan Commercial Press, 1983), Vol. 8.

rice became modestly common during the Ming Period (1368–1644).[26] Its spread was extremely limited even in the twentieth century: In the 1930s only four percent of China's farmland was under double-cropped rice.[27] To reflect this, of a collection of 5,959 traditional farmers' proverbs published in the 1940s, double-cropping of rice was not even mentioned once.[28]

In the Yangzi region where farming was less affected by the Little Ice Age during the Northern Song, a different green revolution took place with the adoption of winter-wheat (*sumai*, or 'across-the-year wheat').[29] The new cropping system was as follows: a summer crop in Year One (including rice, 145–175 days) → a winter crop (±175 days) → another summer crop in Year Two (145–175 days).[30] Winter-wheat grew as a second crop only in the Yangzi region because China's further south was too hot for it.

It is known that towards the end of the tenth century, the regional distribution of land and population was as follows in 1078: (1) the 'Little Ice Age' disaster zone accounted for 32 percent of the Song farmland; (2) the south accounted for 68 percent of the Song farmland; (3) within the south, the Yangzi region accounted for 46 percent of the Song farmland.[31]

---

[26] Liang, *Rural Economy in the Southern Song Period*, p. 117; Cheng, *Regional Economies during the Song Period*, pp. 98–101; Chao, *Man and Land in Chinese History*, p. 199. See also Chen and Zheng, 'Archaeological Discoveries of the Origin of Rice Cultivation'; Ting, 'Origin and Differentiation of Cultivated Rice'; Yan, 'Origin of Rice Cultivation'; Li Genpan, 'Changjiang Xiayou Daomai Fuzhongzhide Xingcheng He Fazhang' (Formation and Development of the Rice-Wheat Multi-cropping System in the Low Yangzi Reaches), *Lishi Yanjiu*, 5 (2002), pp. 3–28; Cao, 'Re-examination of Remains of the 10,000 Year Old Cave'; Fan, 'Pre-historical Farming in the Lower Yangzi Region'.

[27] Perkins, *Agricultural Development in China*, pp. 16, 44.

[28] Zhu Jiefan, *Zhongguo Nongyan* (*Traditional Chinese Farmers' Proverbs*) (Originally published in 1941. Reprint. Taipei: Tianyi Press, 1974).

[29] Cheng, *Regional Economies during the Song Period*, pp. 98–100.

[30] Numerous references; e.g., Ge Jingfang, *Song Liao Xia Jin Jingji Yanxi* (*Analysis of the Song, Liao, Xia, Jin Economies*) (Wuhan: Wuhan Press, 1991), pp. 103–13; Li, 'Formation and Development of the Rice-Wheat Multi-cropping System', p. 7; Kong Qingfeng, 'Jianlun Zhongtang Yilai Chuantong Nongyede Yaosu Shengchanlü' (Factor Productivities of Traditional Agriculture since the Mid-Tang Period), *Wen Shi Zhe* (*Literature, History and Philosophy*), 6 (2006), pp. 100–107.

[31] Liang, *Dynastic Data*, pp. 164, 290–1; Cheng, *Regional Economies during the Song Period*, p. 87; Gao Wangling, 'Zhongguo Chuantong Jingjide Fazhan Xulie' (Developmental Sequence in China's Traditional Economy), *Shixue Lilun Yanjiu* (*Study of Historiography*), 3 (1994), p. 73; also Perkins, *Agricultural Development in China*, p. 342.

Table 30.   Food Output Increase during the Northern Song Period.

	Pre-second cropping	Annual yield index
North	1 *shi* per *mu* on 32 percent of land	32
South	2 *shi* per *mu* on 68 percent of land	136
Total (A)		168
	With second cropping	**Annual yield index**
North	1 *shi* per *mu* on 32 percent of land	32
Yangzi	2.8 *shi* per *mu* on 46 percent of land	129
Rest of the South	2 *shi* per *mu* on 22 percent of land	44
Total (B)		205
Gain in food: B/A		1.22

Source: Land distribution, based on Liang, *Dynastic Data*, pp. 164, 290–1; Cheng Minsheng, *Songdai Diyu Jingji* (*Regional Economies during the Song Period*) (Zhengzhou: Henan University Press, 1992), p. 87; Gao Wangling, 'Zhongguo Chuantong Jingjide Fazhan Xulie' (Developmental Sequence in China's Traditional Economy), *Shixue Lilun Yanjiu* (*Study of Historiography*), 3 (1994), p. 73. Output levels, based on Wu Hui, *Zhongguo Jingjishi Ruogan Wentide Jiliang Yanjiu* (*Quantitative Studies of Chinese Economic History*) (Fuzhou: Fujian People's Press, 2009), p. 115; Ge Jingfang and Gu Rong, 'Songdai Jiangnan Diqude Liangshi Muchan Jiqi Gusuan Fangfa Bianxi' (Estimation and Evidence of Yield Level in the Lower Yangzi Region during the Song Period), *Hubei Daxue Xuebao* (*Bulletin of the University of Hubei*), 3 (2000), pp. 78–9; Hua Shan, *Songshi Lunji* (*Collected Essays on Song History*) (Jinan: Qilu Press, 1982), pp. 4–5.

It is also known that, (1) the yield level from the medium fertile land was about one *shi* per *mu* in the north and about twice that in the Yangzi region; (2) winter-wheat from the medium fertile land produced about 0.8 *shi* per *mu*.[32] If so, the net gain from this green revolution was likely to be an extra 22 percent of food (Table 30).

Moreover, from 976 to 1083, the total farmland increased 56 percent from 295.3 to 461.7 million *mu*.[33] To assume the increased 166.4 million *mu* had the same split between regions and yields, the compounded gain

---

[32] Wu Hui, *Zhongguo Jingjishi Ruogan Wentide Jiliang Yanjiu* (*Quantitative Studies of Chinese Economic History*) (Fuzhou: Fujian People's Press, 2009), p. 115; Ge and Gu, 'Estimation and Evidence of Yield Level', pp. 78–9; Hua, *Collected Essays on Song History*, pp. 4–5; Qi Xia, 'Songdai Shehui Shengchanlide Fazhan Jiqizai Zhongguo Gudai Jingji Fazhan Guochengzhongde Diwei' (Productivity Increase in Song Times and Its Importance in China's Premodern Economic Growth), *Zhongguo Jingjishi Yanjiu* (*Research into Chinese Economic History*), 1 (1986), pp. 29–52.
[33] Liang, *Dynastic Data*, pp. 7–8.

in food supply was 90 percent for the period *circa* 1000 to *circa* 1090 with an annual rate of 1.07 percent. If most new farmland was situated in the south, the gain would be well over 90 percent due to the higher yield level there. Either way, the gain in food supply matched well the doubled population of the time (also at 1.07 percent per year).

However, cash prices of rice increased about 500 percent, more than doubled the rate of population increase (*wen/shi* of rice, see Table 31.1). Such a price increase was also reflected by rice prices relative to iron and silk.[34] The food relative prices increased also faster than that of the population (see Table 31.2).

The only explanation is that food production faced competition from more profitable input options for labour, land, capital, and technology. Inside agriculture most cash crops vied with staple crops during the same growing season (see Table 32), so the latter had to be scarified until the returns from staple food matched those from cash crops. This could only be done through the market mechanisms with which relative shortage of food must have occurred first which pushed the food price up to make staple food production worthwhile again.

To show how profitable cash crops became, in the Kaifeng region the income from 10 *mu* vegetable garden matched the income from 100 *mu* under food crops.[35] There was also a trade-off between silkworm-raising and rice-farming:[36]

> In Ji-an, many people make their livelihood exclusively from raising silkworms. A household of 10 people is able to raise 10 containers of worms. Each container yields 12 catties of cocoons. Each catty of cocoons produces 1.3 liang of raw silk. Each 5 liang of such silk produces a bolt of plain cloth, worth 1.4 shi of rice. In doing so, both ends of the household are guaranteed to be met.

---

[34]For the Northern Song inflation, see Peng Xinwei, *Zhongguo Huobi Shi* (*A History of Currencies in China*) (Shanghai: Shanghai People's Press, 1965), p. 505; Guo Dongxu, 'Songchaode Wujia Biandong Yu Jizang Lunzui', *Zhongguo Jingjishi Yanjiu*, 1 (2004), p. 72; Qi, *Economic History of the Song*, Vol. 2, pp. 1104–7. For multiple currencies and exchange rates, see Guo Zhengzhong, *Liansong Chengxiang Shangpin Huobi Jingji Kaolue* (*The Commercial and Cash Economy of the Northern and Southern Song Periods*) (Beijing: Economics and Management Press, 1997), pp. 287–321, 331.

[35]Cited in Qi, *Economic History of the Song*, Vol. 1, p. 162.

[36]Chen, *Chen Fu's Treatise on Agriculture*. One Song teal = 37.3 grams.

Table 31.1.   Increase in Rice Prices (*Wen/shi*).

Kaifeng (North)		Hedong (North)		Liangzhe (Yangzi)	
AD	Price	AD	Price	AD	Price
989	300 (100)	979	100	970	200 (100)
1074	1,500 (500)	1086	500	1098	1,000 (500)
Annual %	1.9		1.5		1.3
Annual % population					1.07

Source: Cheng Minsheng, *Songdai Wujia Yanjiu* (*Research into Song Commodity Prices*) (Beijing: People's Press, 2009), pp. 125, 132–4, 139–41.

Note: These figures only serve as rough indications. Kaifeng was the capital city where food was persistently more expensive. Hedong was one of the oldest northern farming provinces; Liangzhe was a new farming province at the time.

Table 31.2.   Increase in Rice Prices Relative to Iron and Silk.

AD	Amount iron/*shi* of rice	AD	Bolts silk cloth/*shi* of rice
997	16 (100)	997	0.24 (100)
1080	56 (350)	1108	0.95 (396)
Annual %	1.5		1.2
Annual % population			1.07

Source: R. M. Hartwell, 'Markets, Technology, and the Structure of Enterprise', *Journal of Economic History*, 26/1 (1966); and Yu Yaohua, *Zhongguo Jiage Shi* (*A History of Prices in China*) (Beijing: Price Press, 2000), pp. 602, 610.

Table 32.   Cash Crop Choices during the Song Period.

Crop type	Growth months	Growth cycle (days)
Hemp	1st–6th	145
Sugarcane*	2nd–10th	230
Early sesame	3rd–7th	116
Late sesame	5th–9th	116
Tea, fruits, mulberry trees	3rd–10th	201

Source: Chen Fu, *Chenfu Nongshu* (Originally published in 1149 AD. Reprint. Beijing, 1956), pp. 2–5; Wang Zhuo, *Tangshuang Pu* (*Treatise on Sugar-making*) (1154 AD); Guo Zhengzhong, *Liansong Chengxiang Shangpin Huobi Jingji Kaolue* (*The Commercial and Cash Economy of the Northern and Southern Song Periods*) (Beijing: Economics and Management Press, 1997), pp. 258, 264–8; Liang, *Rural Economy in the Southern Song Period*, p. 117; Cheng, *Regional Economies during the Song Period*, pp. 98–100.

Note: * Perennial, re-planting once every three years.

This means that some rural households gave up farming completely and became specialised with growing vegetables and silkworms. They contributed to a higher food prices as they began to depend on the market for their food supply.

Beyond agriculture, unprecedented commercial growth involved all strata in society. Many new devices were invented to facilitate the new growth including securities (trade licences for wine, tea, salt and so forth),[37] and the first paper currency in the world.[38] Furthermore, more resources were devoted to new technology, including deep drilling, furnaces, water mills, ceramics (genuine porcelain), textiles, magnetic compass, sea-going cargo ships, and firearms (cannons and rockets).[39] All these people who were involved in such non-farming activities often did not live on their own food.

Evidently, China's iron output increased about six-fold from *c.* 806 to 1078 AD with an annual growth rate of 0.7 percent.[40] In North China, where the Little Ice Age prevailed, iron production took off.[41] It is documented that in around 1040 in Shaanxi it took 700 households

[37]Tuotuo, *History of the Song Dynasty*, Vols. 180–6, Entries 'Shihuozhi 134, 135', in *TFOH*, Vol. 7, p. 5741–54; Hua, *Collected Essays on Song History*, pp. 76, 109; Hu, *General Economic History of Handicraft Industry*, pp. 353, 402.

[38]Shiba Yoshinobu, *Commerce and Society in Sung China* (Ann Arbor: University Michigan Press, 1970); Elvin, *Pattern of the Chinese Past*, pt. 2.

[39]Joseph Needham, *Science and Civilisation in China* (Cambridge: Cambridge University Press, 1954–2008); Gang Deng, *Chinese Maritime Activities and Socioeconomic Development* (New York, London and West Port, 1997); Joel Mokyr, *The Lever of Riches* (Oxford: Oxford University Press, 1990), ch. 8; von Glahn, *Fountain of Fortune*; Denis Twitchett and P. J. Smith (eds.), *The Cambridge History of China, Vol. 5, Part One* (Cambridge: Cambridge University Press, 2009); Qi Xia, *Songdai Jingjishi*, Vol. 2, chs 13, 18, 19, 28; Li Xiao, *Songchao Zhengfu Guomai Zhidu Yanjiu* (*Government Procurement System of the Song*) (Shanghai: Shanghai People's Press, 2007), p. 466.

[40]R. M. Hartwell, 'A Revolution in the Chinese Iron and Coal Industries during the Northern Sung, 960–1126 A.D.', *Journal of Asian Studies*, 21/1 (1962), pp. 153–62.

[41]Including weapons, religious statues, musical instruments (e.g., gongs and cymbals), farming and handicraft tools, shipbuilding (iron nails/rivets), bridge-building (iron chains), domestic kitchen (knives, pots and woks); see Patricia B. Ebrey, *The Cambridge Illustrated History of China* (Cambridge: Cambridge University Press, 1999), p. 144.

to produce 60 tons of iron (100,000 Song *catties*).[42] To maintain an annual output of 75,000 to 125,000 tons of the metal, as recorded in history, the industry needed a workforce from 0.9–1.6 million such households (or a total of 4.5–8.0 million people),[43] not including iron mining, coal mining,[44] charcoal marking (hence lumbering), and transportation. Iron production was also carried in South China. In 1102, there were 92 iron smelting/refining workshops in Guangdong alone.[45] Steel produced from iron was common.[46] Song China probably produced the highest iron output per capita in the world until *c.* 1750.[47]

Other metals were produced in large quantities, too: copper in Hunan, Jiangxi and Guangdong; tin and lead in Hunan, Jiangxi, Guangdong and Guangxi.[48] From 836 to 1077, the output of copper increased 39-fold; tin, 54-fold; and lead, 467-fold (Table 33).

Song China also reached out in a big way in the maritime world. Large sea-going vessels were designed and constructed. New sea routes, new foreign locations and new markets were explored. In this regard, the Song even outperformed the Ming (see Table 34).

---

[42] Donald B. Wagner, 'The Administration of the Iron Industry in Eleventh-Century China', *Journal of the Economic and Social History of the Orient*, 44/2 (2001), pp. 181–3.

[43] Hartwell, 'Iron and Coal Industries'; also see Patricia B. Ebrey, Anne Walthall, and James Palais, *East Asia: A Cultural, Social, and Political History* (Boston: Houghton Mifflin Company, 2006), p. 158.

[44] Modern chemical analysis has revealed that the high sulpha content in the Song iron products was resulted from the use of coal for smelting; see Hu, *General Economic History of Handicraft Industry*, p. 191.

[45] Tuotuo, *History of the Song*, Vol. 185, in *TFOH*, Vol. 7, p. 5756.

[46] Steel was produced from ion in three ways; see Hu, *General Economic History of Handicraft Industry*, pp. 205–7.

[47] Hartwell, 'A Revolution in the Chinese Iron and Coal Industries', pp. 153–62; his 'A Cycle of Economic Change in Imperial China', *Journal of the Economic and Social History of the Orient*, 10/1 (1967), pp. 102–59; and his *Iron and Early Industrialism in Eleventh-Century China* (Chicago: University of Chicago Press, 1963). Also see Wagner, 'Administration of the Iron Industry', pp. 175–97.

[48] Xue Yaling, 'Zhongguo Lishishang Tong Xi Kuangye Fenbude Bianqian' (Distribution of Copper and Tin Mines and its Changes in China's History), *Zhongguo Jingjishi Yanjiu* (*Research in Chinese Economic History*), 4 (2001), p. 105.

Table 33.   Metal Outputs in the South, 997–1077.

AD	Copper*	Tin*	Lead*
997[†]	4,122,000	269,000	793,000
1077[†]	21,744,750	6,159,300	7,943,350
Annual growth %	2.1	4.0	2.9

Source: Ma, *Historical Records*, Vol. 18, Entry 'Mining'; see also, Du, 'Economic Strength', p. 44. Tang outputs are based on Ouyang, *New History of the Tang Dynasty*, Vol. 54, in *TFOH*, Vol. 6, p. 4277.
Note: * In *catty* = 0.6 kg. [†] Song government procurements only, hence the minimum.

Table 34.   New Geographic Information, 1100–1440.

	S/SE. Asia	Arabian/Red Seas	E. Africa	Total
Song (I)	34	5	3	42
Ming (II)	8	3	4	15
I:II	4.3	1.7	0.8	2.8

Source: Song: based on Zhao Rukuo (Zhao Rushi), *Zhufan Zhi* (*Records of Foreign Peoples*) (Originally published in 1225. Reprint. Beijing: Zhonghua Books, 1956). Translated into English by F. Hirth and W. W. Rockhill (St. Petersburg: Publisher unknown, 1911). Ming: based on Zheng He's voyages (1405–32); Gong Zhen, *Xiyang Fanguo Zhi* (*Journeys to Foreign Countries in the Indian Ocean*) (Originally published in the Ming Period. Reprint. Beijing: Zhonghua Books, 1961); Ma Huan, *Yingya Shenglan* (*Tours to Great Sites Overseas*) (Originally published in 1451. Reprint. Beijing: Zhonghua Books, 1955); Shen Fuwei, 'Zhenghe Baochuanduide Dongfei Hangcheng' (Zheng He's Treasure Fleet and Its Voyages to the Eastern African Coast), in Institute of Maritime History of China (ed.), *Zhenghe Xia Xiyang Lunwen Ji* (*Selected Works on Zheng He's Voyages in the Indian Ocean*) (Beijing: People's Communication Press, 1985), pp. 166–83; Naval Institute of Ocean Cartography and Department of Maritime History, and Dalian Sea Transportation Institute (eds.), *Xinbian Zhenghe Hanghai Tuji* (*A New Compilation of the Navigation Chart of Zheng He's Voyages*) (Beijing: People's Communication Press, 1988), pp. 84–98.
Note: S/SE. = South and Southeast. E. = East.

Consequently, a strong growth in maritime trade yield financial returns for the government (see Table 35). In the end, the maritime duties accounted for an unprecedented 15 percent of the government total revenue.[49]

[49]Chen and Wu, *China's Maritime Trade*, pp. 180–2. For the debate, see Guo, *Commercial and Cash Economy*, pp. 390–405.

Table 35.　Maritime Tax Revenues during the Song Period.

AD	Annual maritime tax (10^6 bronze coins)	Index
1087	416	100
1106	1,110	267
Annual growth %		5.3

Source: Wang Shengduo, *Liangsong Caizheng Shi* (*A Fiscal History of the Northern and Southern Songs*) (Beijing: Zhonghua Books, 1995), pp. 723–4.
Note: On the whole, maritime duties counted for about 15 percent of the government revenue, see Chen Gaohua and Wu Tai, *Songyuan Shiqide Haiwai Maoyi* (*China's Maritime Trade during the Song and Yuan Periods*) (Tianjin: Tianjin People's Press, 1981), pp. 180–2.

Table 36.　Fiscal Shares of Agricultural and Non-Agricultural Sectors.

Year	Total (10^9 bronze coins)	Agricultural share (%)	Non-agricultural share (%)
997	35.6	65	35
1077	70.7	30	70

Sources: Ye Tan, 'Songdai Gongshangye Fazhangde Lishi Tezheng' (Features of Development in Handicrafts and Commerce during the Song Period), *Shanghai Shehui Kexueyuan Xueshu Jikan* (*Academic Quarterly of the Shanghai Academy of Social Sciences*), 2 (1991), p. 108; Bao Weimin, *Songdai Difang Caizhengshi Yanjiu* (*A History of Local Finance during the Song Period*) (Shanghai: Shanghai Classic Press, 2001), pp. 282, 316–9.

From 1021 to 1065, the cash share in the total tax revenue jumped from 17.6 percent to 51.6 percent.[50] The fiscal importance of the agricultural and non-agricultural sectors was reversed (see Table 36).

In contrast to the strong performance in non-agricultural sectors, Song agriculture experienced a relative decline. Government Poll Tax paid in homemade cloth stagnated (see Table 37.1). The Land Tax paid in grain had a similar fate (see Table 37.2).

---

[50] Quan Hansheng, 'Tang Song Zhengfu Suiru Yu Hubi Jingjide Guanxi' (Relationship between Government Revenues and the Cash Economy), in *Academia Sinica* (ed.), *Guoli Zhongyang Yanjiuyuan Lishi Yuyan Yanjiusuo Jikan* (*Bulletin of the Institute of History and Linguistics, Academia Sinica*), 20 (1948), pp. 189–220.

Table 37.1.   Government Poll Tax in Homemade Cloth, 997–1077.

AD	Tax paid in homemade cloth (bolts)
997	2,180,000 (100)
1077	2,672,323 (123)
Annual growth %	0.2

Source: Liang, *Dynastic Data*, pp. 288–9.

Table 37.2.   Land Tax Payments in Grain, 997–1077.

AD	Land tax payments (*shi*)
997	31,707,000 (100)
1077	17,887,257 (56)
Annual growth %	−0.7

Source: Liang, *Dynastic Data*, pp. 288–9; and Bao, *Local Finance*, pp. 282, 316–9.

Unfortunately, the Song growth in wealth and population was brutally interrupted by alien invasions and conquests. In 1128, the Jurgen kingdom of Jin took over North China by force (see Figure 9), destroying the Song industrial centres there,[51] and forcing large numbers of Chinese into slavery.[52] The Mongols conquered North China the second time in 1234 with renewed massacres and arsons against the local population. By 1291, the population across the bygone Northern Song territory dropped by about half.[53] Among those who survived, millions were enslaved (*quding*), including hundreds of thousands of skilled artisans;[54] horses and houses

---

[51] Li Xinchuan, *Jianyan Yilai Xinian Yaolu* (*Annuals of Important Events since 1128*) (Originally published in 1202. Reprint. Beijing: Zhonghua Books, 1956), pp. 87, 744,

[52] Tuotuo, *Jin Shi* (*History of the Jin Dynasty*) (1344 AD), Vols. 46, 73, 80, 82, in *TFOH*, Vol. 9, pp. 7029–30, 7094, 7108, 7113. About half of the Chinese were made slaves; see Han Rulin, *Yuanchao Shi* (*A History of the Yuan Dynasty*) (Beijing: People's Press, 1986), Vol. 2, p. 56. *Note*: Mongols implemented large-scale production slavery on China's soil for the first time since *circa* 100 BC.

[53] Wu, *Demographic* History, Vol. 3, p. 625.

[54] Large numbers of slaves were reported to be used as gifts in Mongol diplomacy; see Han, *History of the Yuan Dynasty*, Vol. 2, pp. 424, 430.

belonging to the Chinese were all confiscated; vast agrarian areas were enclosed either to be used as Mongol grazing land or to become state-owned farms tilled by state serfs.[55] Traditional metal tools were banned as potential weapons; and so were martial arts.[56]

Furthermore, the Mongol taxation burden increased multi-fold: The household tax in cash increased twenty times.[57] In Fujian, the land tax was three *shi* per *mu*, equivalent to the yield level *per se*, meaning that noting was left for the producer after taxation.[58] The Yuan paper-currency-based monetary system was a sham to rip off the population with hyperinflation of 1,450 to 1,650 percent over time.[59] Consequently, the price of rice increased about 40 times; salt, 30 times.[60] Market exchange in China simply went back to barter trade.[61]

In addition, the Mongols made no attempt to accept the Chinese language in the Yuan Court.[62] Of the 11 emperors, only one, Emperor Chengzong (r. 1294–1307), ever made some effort to learn Chinese calligraphy, but unsuccessfully. The Mongol colonisation of China was a fully-fledged apartheid.[63] The Chinese were treated as an outcast.

---

[55] According to the Yuan official record, the forcefully created state farmland through appropriation by the Mongol state from Chinese legal owners amounted for 17.5 million *mu*; about 500,000 households became serfs; see Han, *History of the Yuan Dynasty*, Vol. 1, pp. 362, 374–5. See also Wang, *Imperially Commissioned Continuation of the Comprehensive Study of Literature*, Vol. 1; Perkins, *Agricultural Development in China*, pp. 23–4, 197–9; The Chinese Academy of Agricultural Sciences, *Zhongguo Nongxue Shi* (*History of Chinese Agronomy*) (Beijing: Sciences Press, 1984), Vol. 2, pp. 51–3; Zheng Xuemeng, Jiang Zhaocheng and Zhang Wenqi, *Jianming Zhongguo Jingji Tongshi* (*A Brief Panorama of Chinese Economic History*), Harbin: Heilongjiang People's Press, 1984), pp. 242–4, 254–5; Hu, *General Economic History of Handicraft Industry*, pp. 589–604; Han, *History of the Yuan Dynasty*, Vol. 1, pp. 361–2, 375; Vol. 2, p. 47.

[56] Han, *History of the Yuan Dynasty*, Vol. 1, p. 392; Vol. 2, pp. 44, 45.

[57] *Ibid.*, Vol. 1, pp. 391, 429; Vol. 2, p. 48; Guo Zhengzhong, *Zhongguo Yanye Shi* (*A History of the Salt Sector in China*) (Beijing: People's Press, 1997), Vol. 1, pp. 302, 493.

[58] Han, *History of the Yuan Dynasty*, Vol. 1, pp. 391, 429; Vol. 2, p. 48.

[59] *Ibid.*, Vol. 1, p. 427.

[60] Yu, *History of Prices in China*, pp. 712–3.

[61] Han, *History of the Yuan Dynasty*, Vol. 2, p. 92.

[62] Of all the known travels to the Yuan Empire by outsiders, the languages, both written and spoken, in use by the empire were Mongolian, Persian, Turkish, Arab, and Latin; see Han, *History of the Yuan Dynasty*, Vol. 2, pp. 434–50.

[63] Han, *History of the Yuan Dynasty*, Vol. 1, p. 9; Vol. 2, pp. 54–5.

Politically, Confucianism and Imperial Examinations were both abandoned. China's usual social mobility was terminated. The Confucian literati were ranked at the bottom of society together only with beggars and prostitutes.[64] Official positions were reserved for Mongols and their mercenaries of the 'coloured-eye' race (*semu ren*): Turks, Persians, Arabs, and Europeans who formed a vested interest group.[65] Economically, no Chinese was allowed to organise trade fairs or to engage in large business and long distance trade.[66]

To demonstrate the damage caused by the Mongol destruction: If growth during the Song Period had not been interrupted for the next 200 years, China's population would have reached 800 million by 1300 (based on calculations made in 1970); and its iron output, 8 million metric tons (based on calculations made in 1958).

3. Rise of the Lower Yangzi Delta during the Ming

The Yuan Mongol rule ended violently just as it began. The return to the Chinese rule under the Ming in 1368 has been commonly viewed as a period of conservatism, isolationism, anti-commercialisation, physiocracy, and ruralisation. Such a narrative has now been challenged.

The Ming economy differed from the previous Song or Yuan because of the rise of the Lower Yangzi Delta, or more precisely 'the Lake Tai Economic Community' (TEC), made of eight prefectures (*zhou*), as a new centre of economic gravity of the empire (see Figure 10).

---

[64] Zhao Yi, *Gaiyu Congkao* (*Reading Notes While Looking After Parents*) (Originally published in 1772. Reprint. Beijing: Zhonghua Books, 1963), ch. 'Confucians and Beggars'.

[65] Han, *History of the Yuan Dynasty*, Vol. 1, pp. 6, 430–1; Vol. 2, p. 2. Marco Polo was allegedly appointed as a high ranking official working for the Mongol Imperial Court because of his coloured eyes. It is questionable whether Marco Polo ever spoke Chinese, used chopsticks, drank tea, or saw the Great Wall. If he physically went to China, he lived at best in a non-Chinese circle of Mongols and their cronies; see Frances Wood, *Did Marco Polo Go to China?* (London: Secker & Warburg, 1995). In addition, there is no record on Marco Polo and his services to the Mongols from the known Yuan official documents.

[66] Han, *History of the Yuan Dynasty*, Vol. 2, p. 43.

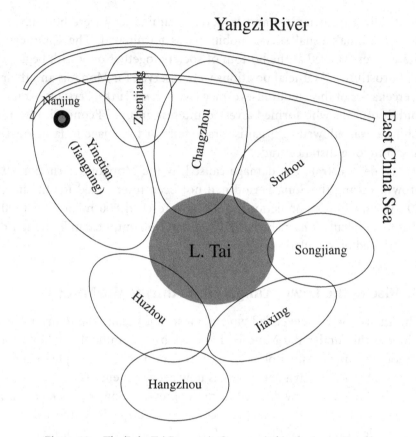

Figure 10.   The 'Lake Tai Economic Community' in the Lower Yangzi.

Source: Based on Guo Hong and Jin Runcheng, *Zhongguo Xingzheng Quhua Tongshi, Ming* (*A General History of Administrative Division in China, the Ming Period*) (Shanghai: Fudan University Press, 2007), p. 152; Feng Xianliang, *Mingqing Jiangnan Diqude Huanjing Biandong Yu Shehui Kongzhi* (*Environmental Changes and Social Control in the Jiangnan Region during the Ming-Qing Period*) (Shanghai: Shanghai People's Press, 2002), pp. 24–7.

Note: Double lines: the Yangzi River. Central circle: Lake Tai. Other circles: Prefectures.

These prefectures counted for 20–40 percent of Jiangsu and Zhejiang's total farmland and 30–50 percent of their total households (see Table 38).

However, the tax burden imposed on the eight prefectures was persistently heavy right from the beginning of the Ming Period (Table 39): 230–310 percent higher than the national par. Suzhou and Songjiang

Table 38. Land and Households of the 'Lake Tai Economic Community', 1290–1829.

Period	Unit	Farmland (*mu*)	Households	No. of counties
Yuan (1290)	TEC	—	2,199,525[67]	34
	Jiangzhe total	—	6,326,423	
	TEC in Jiangszhe	—	34.8%	
Ming (1393)	TEC	47,767,964	1,313,455 (↓)[68]	51
	Nanzhili-Zhejiang	208,332,700	4,050,058	
	TEC in Nanzhili-Zhejiang	22.9%	32.3%	
			Toll tax-payers	
Qing (1820)	TEC	41,804,711 (↓)	24,696,318[69]	60
	Jiangsu-Zhejiang	111,151,100	52,880,370	
	TEC in Jiangsu-Zhejiang	37.6%	46.7%	

Source: Song Lian, *Yuan Shi* (*History of the Yuan Dynasty*), ch. 'Dili Zhi 5', in *TFOH*, Vol. 9, pp. 7409–10; Liang, *Dynastic Data*, pp. 181–2, 211–2, 233–4, 332, 334, 402, 405; Fan Jinmin, *Guoji Minsheng — Mingqing Shehui Jingji Yanjiu* (*The National Economy and People's Life — Selected Essays on Socio-Economic Issues of the Ming–Qing Period*) (Fuzhou: Fujian People's Press, 2008), p. 388.
Note: ↓ = Decline in quantity. The population decline during the Ming was a result of 'voting by foot' of farmers.[70]

prefectures were treated particularly harshly: 520–660 percent higher than that par. In contrast, the Ming state frequently granted tax exemptions elsewhere.[71]

In the previous Mongol Yuan, heavy tax burden applied to North China (Fuli, Henan and Shaanxi). The tax burden on the Lower Yangzi was 20 percent below the national par (Table 40).

---

[67] There were about 11.4 million people, based on the average of 5.2 people per household of the selected prefectures, see Liang, *Dynastic Data*, pp. 181–2.
[68] There were about 4.3 million people, based on the 1462 Ming record of average 3.3 people per household in Songjiang Prefecture; see Liang, *Dynastic Data*, p. 438.
[69] There were about 49.4 million people if on average each household had two eligible tax payers.
[70] Fan Jinmin, *Mingqing Jiangnan Shangyede Fazhan* (*Commercial Development in the Jiangnan Region during the Ming-Qing Period*) (Nanjing: Nanjing University Press, 1998), pp. 334–5.
[71] Li Jiannong, *Song Yuan Ming Jingjishi* (*An Economic History of the Song Yuan and Ming Periods*) (Beijing: Sanlian Books, 1957), p. 279.

Table 39. Tax Burden on the 'Lake Tai Economic Community' during the Ming Period.

AD	Farmland (*mu*)		Tax payment in grain (*shi*)*	
	1395(%)	1578(%)	1395(%)	1578(%)
TEC in China's total	5.6	6.4	23.3	21.3
Suzhou-Songjiang in China's total	1.8	1.9	13.7	11.7

Source: Fan, *National Economy and People's Life*, p. 389.
Note: Figures include actual grain collected as tax payments and 'grain equivalent' (hence 'virtual grain') in the forms of textiles. TEC = Lake Tai Economic Community.

Table 40. Regional Population and Tax Distribution under the Mongol Yuan.

Province	Population (I) Households (% in total)	Tax collected (II) Payment in grain (% in total)	II/I
Fuli	9.8	18.6	1.9
Gansu	0.02	0.5	0.04
Henan	6.5	21.4	3.3
Huguang	19.3	7.0	0.4
Jiangxi	16.9	9.6	0.6
Jiangzhe*	45.6	37.1	0.8
Liaoyang	0.6	0.6	1.0
Shaanxi	0.6	1.9	3.2
Sichuan	0.7	1.0	1.4
Yunnan	—	2.3	—
Total	100	100	1.0

Source: Liang, *Dynastic Data*, pp. 178–84, 303.
Note: * Jiangzhe combined Jiangsu and Zhejiang under the Mongol rule. The Jiangzhe tax burden was 19 percent lower than the national par.

The reason why the TEC was singled out by the Ming authorities for such unprecedented harsh treatment has long been debated with opinions widely divided in six groups.[72] It is essentially a 'chicken-and-egg problem', i.e., which came first: The excessive tax burden or the high productivity. So far, the most reliable source points the decision

[72]See Fan Jinmin, *Guoji Minsheng — Mingqing Shehui Jingji Yanjiu* (*The National Economy and People's Life — Selected Essays on Socio-Economic Issues of the Ming–Qing Period*) (Fuzhou: Fujian People's Press, 2008), pp. 374–7.

Table 41.   Pattern of the Ming Tax Payments, 1391–1520.

Year	Grain payment (*shi*)	Textile payment (bolts)
1391	32,278,983 (100)	646,870 (100)
1414	32,352,244 (100)	1,878,828 (290)
1464	26,348,660 (82)	1,120,724 (173)
1491	26,933,255 (83)	1,330,476 (206)
1520	26,794,024 (83)	1,793,267 (277)
Annual growth %	−0.14	0.79

Source: Liang, *Dynastic Data*, pp. 185–99.

by the first Emperor of the Ming, Zhu Yuanzhang (*r.* 1368–98), who was reported to be furious at people of Suzhou, Songjiang, Jiaxing, and Huzhou who supported Zhu's rivals during the war against the Mongols. The Ming emperor's revenge included confiscation of properties and doubling all taxes.[73] The fact that the early Ming capital Nanjing (1368–1420) was located right inside the TEC made the law reinforcement and tax collections easy.

Meanwhile, the Ming tax payment had a strong preference to cotton goods. In 1376, the Ming grain tax quota allowed grains to be substituted by cotton textiles.[74] The conversion rate was fixed at one bolt of cotton cloth for 1.2 *shi* of rice.[75] At the time inputs in cotton-growing were not much more than rice-farming.[76] Soon, grain payments declined; cotton textiles became the main means of payment to the Ming fiscal state (Table 41).

This tax preference triggered an 'industrious revolution'. The traditional sluggish season after autumn harvest was replaced by full-time weaving. After that, a new growth trajectory appeared. Food production became optional despite its near-perfect conditions for rice-farming in the Delta. In Songjiang Prefecture, 65–80 percent farmland grew cotton during the Qing Period.[77] In the neighbouring prefecture of Jiaxing, dry farmland (for cotton and mulberry trees for silkworms) increased by

---

[73] Li, *Economic History of the Song Yuan and Ming Periods*, p. 279.
[74] *Ibid.*, p. 278.
[75] Fan, *National Economy and People's Life*, pp. 412–3.
[76] Fan, *Commercial Development in the Jiangnan Region*, p. 339.
[77] Fan, *National Economy and People's Life*, p. 319.

Table 42. Export Volumes of the 'Nankin Cloth', 1736–1825.

Year	Export of *nankin*, in bolts
1736	10,374
1786	372,020
1805	1,679,500
1825	1,217,000

Source: Fan, *Commercial Development in the Jiangnan Region*, pp. 123, 125–6.

1.56 million *mu* for better returns (as of the late seventeenth century),[78] while paddies decreased by 1.35 million *mu* in a zero-sum game.[79] On the other face of the same coin, the late Qing grain yield level of per unit of farmland in the TEC dropped by about 10 percent in absolute terms from its Ming level.[80] Higher returns from cash crops pushed land prices up by 500–600 percent, faster then food prices.[81]

The TEC soon became specialised in cotton goods. In 1370, of the 300,000 bolts of cotton cloth for the military, 200,000 bolts came from Songjiang alone.[82] The total output of the weaving sector in the Delta has been estimated as 20 million bolts from a population of 4.3 million people (4.7 bolts per capita) during the early Ming, compared with only 1.6 bolts per capita in later Qing (i.e., 78 million bolts from 49.4 million people).[83] Proto-industrial growth in this region led to the rise of a putting-out system,[84] and the invention of best cotton textiles China ever produced, the *nankin*, for export (see Table 42).

---

[78] *Ibid.*, pp. 298–307.

[79] *Ibid.*, p. 107.

[80] Feng Xianliang, *Mingqing Jiangnan Diqude Huanjing Biandong Yu Shehui Kongzhi* (*Environmental Changes and Social Control in the Jiangnan Region during the Ming–Qing Period*) (Shanghai: Shanghai People's Press, 2002), p. 40; Fan, *National Economy and People's Life*, p. 297.

[81] Chen, *Regional Society and Economy during the Qing Period*, p. 105–6.

[82] Fan, *National Economy and People's Life*, p. 412.

[83] Fan, *Commercial Development in the Jiangnan Region*, pp. 29–30; Wu, *Quantitative Issues of Chinese Economic History*, pp. 379–81.

[84] Fan, *National Economy and People's Life*, p. 483.

Table 43. Food Prices in the Lower Yangzi Delta, 1522–1621.

Year	Price index
1522	100
1567	118
1621	157
Annual growth %	0.46

Source: Yu Yaohua, *Zhongguo Wujia Shi* (*A History of Prices in China*) (Beijing: China's Prices Press, 2000), pp. 771, 786, 801, 802.

One outcome was that the Delta imported 30 percent of its food each year (as during the early eighteenth century).[85] Food prices in the region increased to attract food imports (see Table 43). Fengqiao in Suzhou Prefecture grew to be the largest rice market in the empire.[86] To pay for the large quantities of grain imports, the Delta exported cotton goods produced in TEC (see Figure 11).

This cotton-for-grain trade served the dual purposes of consumption and tax payment for both parties in the trade. During much of the following Qing Period, the total annual rice shipped to TEC (A in Figure 11) from the upstream (B and C) of the Yangzi River was about 10–15 million *shi*,[87] enough to save 3–5 million *mu* land for cash crops and yet feed 4–6 million adults a year. Other foods such as nuts, fruits, legumes and cotton fibre were imported from the Lower Yellow River (D and E in Figure 11); and soybeans and bean cakes from Manchuria (F).[88] Foods coming from the north amounted for about another 10 million *shi* during the nineteenth century.[89] Of all the foods exported from D, E, and F, loose legumes counted for about half of all cargoes, presumably as a source of protein for human consumption.[90] The imported foods from the north

---

[85] Fan, *National Economy and People's Life*, pp. 300, 302.

[86] Fan, *Commercial Development in the Jiangnan Region*, p. 152.

[87] Chen, *Regional Society and Economy during the Qing Period*, p. 110; Fan, *Commercial Development in the Jiangnan Region*, p. 65.

[88] Fan, *Commercial Development in the Jiangnan Region*, pp. 56–7; Wu Chengming, *Zhongguode Xiandaihua: Shichang Yu Shehui* (*China's Modernization: Market and Society*) (Beijing: Sanlian Books, 2001), pp. 153–6.

[89] Fan, *Commercial Development in the Jiangnan Region*, p. 63.

[90] *Ibid.*, p. 58.

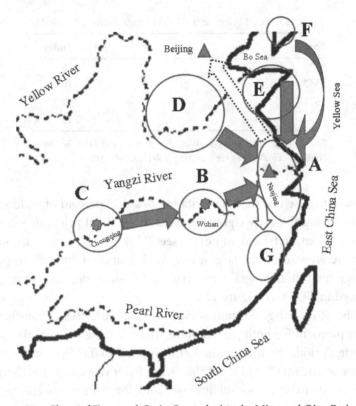

Figure 11.   Flows of Taxes and Grain Cargo during the Ming and Qing Periods.

Source: Based on Guo Hong and Jin Runcheng, *Zhongguo Xingzheng Quhua Tongshi, Ming* (*A General History of Administrative Division in China, the Ming Period*) (Shanghai: Fudan University Press, 2007), p. 152; Feng, *Environmental Changes and Social Control*, pp. 24–7.

Note: Broken lines: Main rivers. Broken arrow: Flow of taxes to the central government. Black arrows: Flows of grain. White arrow: A detour flow of food. Triangles: Capital cities.

A = the Lower Yangzi Delta, B = Hubei of the Middle Reaches of the Yangzi River, C = Sichuan of the Upper Reaches of the Yangzi River, D = the Lower Yellow River, E = Shandong (shipping by sea routes), F = Port Niuzhuang of Manchuria (shipping by sea routes), G = Coastal Fujian. The shipping distance from C to A is 2,400 km.

were able to feed another two million mouths for a year. The remaining half of the cargo from the north was consisted of cotton fibre to meet the shortage of cotton wool (25–38 percent shortfall) in the delta's weaving sector.[91] In the process, the Delta remained an important centre for market exchange as well as the main donor of tax revenues for the empire.

---

[91] *Ibid.*, p. 68.

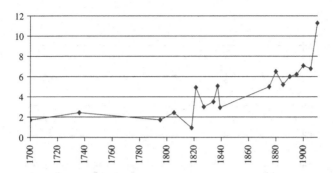

Figure 12. Terms of Trade, Bolts of Cotton Cloth per *Shi* of White Rice.

Source: Huang Miantang, *Zhongguo Lidai Wujia Wenti Kaoshu* (*Study of Prices in China's History over the Long Term*) (Jinan: Qilu Books, 2007), pp. 10, 11–12, 47–9, 52–7, 61–5, 101–7, 109–14, 314, 318–21, 330–3, 336–9; Xu Xinwu, *Jiangnan Tubu Shi* (*A History of Homemade Cotton Cloth in the Lower Yangzi Delta*) (Shanghai: Shanghai Academy of Social Sciences Press, 1989), pp. 176, 201; Yu Yaohua, *Zhongguo Jiage Shi* (*A History of Prices in China*) (Beijing: China's Prices Press, 2000), pp. 805, 921–2, 929.

Note: (1) Here plain cotton (three *zhang* per bolt) was the common homemade type for tax payment and domestic trade, not for export. White rice was husked rice ready to cook. (2) For much lower cotton cloth pries, see Xu, *History of Homemade Cotton Cloth*, pp. 92, 94. For much higher *nankin* cloth prices, see Anben Meixu, *Qingdai Zhongguode Wujia Yu Jingji Bodong* (*Prices and Economic Fluctuations in Qing China*) (Beijing: Social Science Academic Press, 2010), Table 4.8.

The main issue is how much this rural textile production during the Ming Period changed the economy. The answer may be found in Figure 12 where cotton cloth had a decreasing capacity to add value because it took increasingly more cloth to purchase the same amount of rice. So, inside the Delta, either cotton productivity was improved greatly or cotton was produced cheaply by more free labour in low seasons. Or both.

Outside the Delta, there was a decline in the cotton wool prices after the Yellow River region in the north joined the cotton boom. In 1407, one catty of cotton wool exchanged for 105 catties of rice. It dropped to 15 catties, 9.4 catties, and 1.8 catties in 1456, 1573, and 1643, respectively.[92] In comparison, changes appeared much slower in silk textiles during the same period: from about two bolts for one *shi* of rice to one bolt for the same amount of rice (see Figure 13).

---

[92] Yu, *History of Prices*, p. 795.

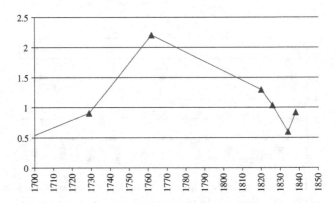

Figure 13.   Terms of Trade, Bolts of Plain Silk Cloth per *Shi* of White Rice.

Source: Huang Miantang, *Zhongguo Lidai Wujia Wenti Kaoshu* (*Study of Prices in China's History over the Long Term*) (Jinan: Qilu Books, 2007), pp. 10, 11–12, 47–9, 52–7, 61–5, 101–7, 109–14, 314, 318–21, 330–3, 336–9; Xu, *History of Homemade Cotton Cloth*, pp. 176, 201; Yu, *History of Prices in China*, pp. 805, 921–2, 929.

4. Territorial and Commercial Growth during the Qing Period

The Qing territorial expansion has been reviewed earlier (see Table 3). This was achieved by merging Manchuria, Mongolia and Xinjiang with China Proper.[93] Such expansion yielded some of the best farming zones including the black-soil region in Manchuria and a natural irrigation system along the Great Bend of the Yellow River in South Mongolia. Efforts were also made to open up the north-western corner (Gansu and Xinjiang) and the south-western corner (Guizhou and Yunnan) to farming.[94] As a result, from 1650 to 1750, an increase in China's farmland moved ahead of the growth of the population (see Figure 14).

China's low and stagnant urbanisation rate during the Qing matched the expansion in farmland very well (Table 44), as the vast majority of the population made their living predominantly from farming.

It is important to note that during the farmland expansion, private ownership of land was entrenched across the empire. The share of the

---

[93] The Qing territorial expansion was associated with policies of Kangxi (*r.* 1662–1722) and Qianlong (*r.* 1736–1795).

[94] By the 1820s, the new farmland in the Balikun and Yili regions of Xinjiang (also known as 'Chinese Turkistan') alone totalled 908,500 *mu* or 121,735 hectares; see Chen, *Regional Socio-Economic Conditions during the Qing Period*, p. 265; see also Jane K. Leonard and John R. Watt, *To Achieve Security and Wealth* (Ithaca: Cornell University Press, 1992), pp. 21–46.

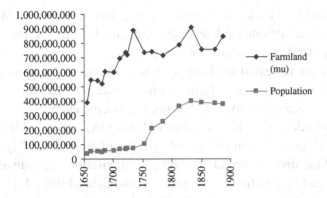

Figure 14. Growth in Farmland and Population, 1650–1900.

Source: Population, based on Deng 2004, Appendix 2; Cao Shuji, *Zhongguo Renkou Shi* (*A Demographic History of China*) (Shanghai, Fudan University Press, 2001), Vol. 5, p. 704. Farmland, based on Liang, *Dynastic Data*, pp. 10, 380, 384, 396, 400, 401.

Table 44. China's Urbanisation Rate, 1776 and 1893.

Region/Province	1776	1893
China-wide	7.4	7.0
North		
Zhili	12.5	8.3
Henan	4.6	5.0
Shandong	4.9	3.4
Anhui	5.0	5.0
Shanxi	10.3	9.3
Shaanxi	5.3	6.6
Gansu	2.7	4.6
Xinjiang	7.0	8.3
South		
Jiangsu (*Jiangnan*)	13.6	14.2
Zhejiang (*Jiangnan*)	10.0	13.7
Hubei	7.0	8.5
Hunan	5.0	4.3
Jiangxi	8.5	7.0
Fujian	6.0	6.8
Guangdong	8.0	8.0
Sichuan	7.0	7.0
Guizhou	4.8	4.8
Yunnan	4.1	4.1
Guangxi	5.0	5.0

Source: Cao, *Demographic History of China*, Vol. 5, pp. 828–9.

state-owned land under the Qing was halved from the previous Ming level of 14 percent.[95] Private landownership warranted strong incentives for the Qing population to produce from agriculture.

With the increased land supply, a new round of internal migration began.[96] Large numbers of farmers left old core regions (such as Hebei, Henan, Shandong, Shanxi, and Shaanxi) to resettle elsewhere.[97] The Qing state responded this with the policy of 'filling the regions of land abundance with people from regions of high population density' (*yi zhai bu kuan*). Measures included 'farming by invitation' (*quannong*), free passage and tax holidays. By 1668, Manchuria absorbed 14 million immigrants from the interior.[98] The scheme continued until 1907.[99] Large-scale immigration also took place in Mongolia. In 1712, Shandong immigrants arrived there in their hundred thousands.[100] During 1743–8, a quarter of a million migrants also moved to Sichuan and beyond.[101] These Qing migrants left permanent genetic, dialectal, and social marks on the recipient regions.[102]

Large-scale supply of new farmlands and large-scale migration benefitted the Qing economy three times: first, it reshuffled resource allocation in China's economy. The population share of advanced farming regions in China's total dropped from 72 percent (as of 1787) to 55 percent (as of 1933), while the farmland share of the same regions dropped from 74 percent (as of 1787) to 49 percent (as of 1933). The population and farmland in migrant recipient regions increased 17 percent and 26 percent in

[95] Liang, *Dynastic Data*, pp. 351, 384.
[96] For a spatial survey, see Wang, *Late Taxation*, p. 85.
[97] For the eighteenth century, see Will, *Bureaucracy and Famine*, pt. 2. See also Myers and Wang, 'Economic Developments', p. 567.
[98] Anon., *Veritable Records of Emperor Gaozong*, Vol. 311, Entry 'Shisannian Sanyue' (The Third Month of the Thirteenth Year under the Gaozong Reign); Zhang, 'Advancing to Manchuria', pp. 57–64.
[99] Tian and Chen, *Brief History of Migration in China*, pp. 110–2.
[100] The Qing state imposed a ban on permanent immigration to Manchuria (1668–1860) and Mongolia (1740–1897). But there was little control over seasonal migrants to both regions. Moreover, by the time the restriction was introduced, a large number of immigrants had already settled in; see Zhao, *History of the Qing Dynasty*, Vol. 120, Entry 'Economy', in *TFOH*, Vol. 11, p. 9253.
[101] Lee, 'Population Growth in Southwest China'.
[102] Yuan Yida and Zhang Cheng, *Zhongguo Xingshi: Qunti Yichuan He Renko Fenbu* (*Chinese Surnames: Group Genetics and Demographic Distribution*) (Shanghai: East China Normal University Press, 2002), pp. 6–57.

China's total, respectively.[103] Such changes in man-to-land ratios effectively delayed the onset of a Malthusian crisis. Second, farming yield level increased. By 1760, the Yangzi–Han Plain had doubled its food output capacity from the Ming level and, as a result, exported 2.2 million tons of grain a year,[104] as well as large quantities of silk and cotton goods.[105] The total output and marginal product of labour of that region increased simultaneously. Third, a new type of regional specialisation emerged upon which intra-regional trade thrived. From 1750 on, Manchuria supplied the Yangzi Delta with millions *shi* of wheat, rice and soya bean products (as fodder and fertilizers) a year.[106] In return, the Yangzi Delta supplied Manchuria with cotton goods.[107] The market economy expanded.

On the technological front, rice farming and its improvement remained on the agenda of the state and literati as the most desirable crop. The best practice was actively promoted (Table 45).

During the Qing, double-cropping 'winter wheat with rice' spread across most southern regions.[108] In contrast, the double cropping of 'rice with rice' (meaning sowing rice seed twice within the same calendar year) remained less popular. By the 1930s, China-wide, double-cropped winter wheat with rice claimed a share five times of that of its rice counterpart.[109] The double cropping of 'rice with rice' counted for merely four percent of China's total farmland.[110]

---

[103] Wang, *Late Taxation*, p. 90.

[104] Zhang Jiayan, 'Mingqing Jianghan Pingyuande Nongye Kaifa Dui Shangren Huodong He Shizhen Fazhande Yingxiang' (Impact of Agricultural Development in the Yangzi–Han Plain on Commercial Activities and Urbanization during the Ming–Qing Period), *Zhongguo Nongshi (Agricultural History of China)*, 4 (1995), p. 42.

[105] Chen, *Regional Socio-Economic Conditions*, ch. 4.

[106] See Wu, *China's Modernisation*, pp. 154–6; see also Elvin, *Pattern*, p. 214; Pomeranz, *Great Divergence*, p. 226; cf. Perkins, *Agricultural Development*, p. 210, fn 1.

[107] See Zhang Haiying, *Mingqing Jiangnan Shangpin Liutong Yu Shichang Tixi (Commodity Flows and Market Structure in the Jiangnan Region during the Ming–Qing Period)* (Shanghai: East China Normal University Press, 2001), pp. 198–206. See also Myers and Wang, 'Economic Developments', p. 613.

[108] E.g., Li, 'Rengen Shimu'. According to the British East India Company's Hamilton H. Lindsay who travelled in 1832 to Shanghai on the *Amherst*, 'Upon our arrival, wheat was just harvested in. That was immediately followed by ploughing, sowing and irrigation to grow rice in the same plots. Rice ripens in the Ninth Month.' See Hu, 'A-meishide', p. 277.

[109] Cited in Perkins, *Agricultural Development*, p. 46. Perkin's own figure for the 1930s was 18.6 percent of China's farmland subject to the 'winter-wheat plus rice regime'; see his *Agricultural Development*, pp. 16, 46.

[110] Perkins, *Agricultural Development*, pp. 16, 44.

Table 45. Writings on Rice Cultivation Technology.

Number of writings		A	B	C
Song	50	10	2	2
Ming	42	12	16	3
Qing	91	39	47	1

Source: Chen Zugui, *Dao* (*Rice*) (Beijing: Zhonghua Books, 1958).
Note: A = New rice varieties, B = New places for rice growing, C = New methods of rice growing.

The New World crops — sweet potato, white potato, and maize introduced to China between the end of the Ming and early Qing Periods — made inroads in China's farming choices but did not completely take over traditional crops.[111] According to John Buck's data for the 1920s, maize was mainly grown along a narrow corridor across Yunnan, Guangxi, Sichuan, Shanxi and Shaanxi. This corridor accounted for about 14.5 percent of China's total farmland.[112] Within this corridor, the main crop was still wheat and rice. The area under maize was barely 25 percent.[113] The spread of sweet potatoes was even less extensive: only in three enclaves in central Sichuan (about one-third of the province), southern Guangdong (one-fifth of the province), and central Fujian (one-eighth of the province). The aggregate acreage of these enclaves was about four percent of China's total agricultural land.[114] Within the enclaves, the acreage under sweet potatoes also was about 25 per cent of the local farmland.[115] It did not challenge rice.[116] In essence, the total volume of New World crops grown in concentration used less than five percent of China's farmland (see Table 46).

Overall, China's traditional food stuff — rice, wheat, millet and legumes — still dominated the Qing farming landscape.

---

[111] Sweet potato vines (*fanshu, Ipomoea batatas*) were smuggled to China from Luzon in 1593. Maize (*yumi, Zea mays*) was first mentioned in Xu Guangqi's *Nongzheng Quanshu* (*Complete Treatise on Agricultural Administration*) (Originally published in 1628. Reprint. Shanghai: Shanghai Classics Press, 1979). White potato (*malingshu, Solanum tuberosum*) was first introduced to Taiwan around 1650. See Guo Wentao, *Zhongguo Nongye Keji Fazhan Shilue* (*A Brief History of Development of Agricultural Science and Technology in China*) (Beijing: Chinese Science and Technology Press, 1988), pp. 383–4.
[112] Buck, *Land Utilization in China: Atlas*, pp. 62–3.
[113] *Ibid.*, pp. 72–6.
[114] *Ibid.*, p. 82.
[115] *Ibid.*, pp. 82–3.
[116] Buck, *Land Utilization in China: Atlas*, pp. 64, 77, 78, 94.

Table 46. Proportion of New World Crops Grown in the 1920s (%).

	Maize	Sweet potatoes	Total
Sown area in adopting regions	<25.0	<25.0	<25.0
Share in China's total	<3.6	<1.0	<4.6

Source: Buck, *Land Utilization in China: Atlas*, pp. 64, 77, 78, 94.

Table 47. China's Annual Intra-regional/International Exports in the 1830s.

	Value (in tons of silver)	% in total
'Exportables', maximum	5,910.0 (157.6)	39.6
Cotton cloth	3,547.5 (94.6)	23.8
Tea	1,196.3 (31.9)	8.0
Silk textiles	547.5 (14.6)	3.7
Raw silk	450.0 (12.0)	3.0
Porcelain	168.8 (4.5)	1.1
'Non-Exportables'	9,026.3 (240.7)	60.4
Grain[117]	6,123.8 (163.3)	41.0
Salt	2,197.5 (58.6)	14.7
Raw cotton fibre	480.0 (12.8)	3.2
Metals	225.0 (6.0)	1.5
Total trade	14,936.3 (398.3)	100.0
China's total GDP	104,298.8–131,568.8	
Foreign trade in total GDP		4.5–5.7

Source: Market values, based on Wu Cengming, *Zhongguode Xiandaihua: Shichang Yu Shehui* (*China's Modernization: Market and Society*) (Beijing: Sanlian Books, 2001), pp. 148–9. China's total GDP, based on Chung-li Chang, *The Income of the Chinese Gentry* (Seattle: University of Washington Press, 1962), p. 296; Albert Feuerwerker, *The Chinese Economy, 1870–1949* (Ann Arbor: Center for Chinese Studies of the University of Michigan, 1995), p. 16; Liu Foding, Wang Yuru and Zhao Jin, *Zhongguo Jindai Jingji Fazhang Shi* (*A History of Economic Development in Early Modern China*) (Beijing: Tertiary Education Press, 1999), p. 66.
Note: Figures in parentheses are in million *taels*.

Against this backdrop, the Qing economy was by and large a close one: until the 1830s, China exported no more than 6 percent of its GDP (Table 47).

By the end of the Ming Period, China's own silver deposits were exhausted. China needed to sell its products to obtain silver from

---

[117]This is more optimistic than Wang's estimates of 30–40 million *shi* of un-husked rice for the same period (Wang, 'Chinese Monetary System'). Given that the period price was 2.0–2.4 *taels* of silver per *shi* for un-husked rice, the total value of the grain would be 80 million *taels*. This is half of Wu's value.

Table 48.   Estimated Silver Imports to China from Japan (in Metric Tons), 1550–1644.

Period	Total	Average per year
1550–1645 (1)	2,716.5–2,851.5*	28.6–30.0 (7.6–8.0)
1560–1640 (2)	5,512.5–7,087.5*	68.9–88.6 (18.4–23.6)
1560–1640 (3)	9,448	118.1 (31.5)
1571–1644 (4)	1,987.5	27.2 (7.3)

Source: Figures (1) are based on Richard von Glahn, *Fountain of Fortune, Money and Monetary Policy in China, 1000–1700* (Berkeley: University of California Press, 1996), p. 140; Brian Moloughney and Xia Weizhong, 'Silver and the Fall of the Ming: A Reassessment', *Papers on Far Eastern History*, 40 (1989), pp. 65, 68. Figures (2), based on J. F. Richards (ed.), *Precious Metals in the Late Medieval and Early Modern Worlds* (Durham [NC]: Carolina Academic Press, 1983), pp. 350–2. Figure (3), D. O. Flynn, Arturo Giráldez and Richard von Glahn (eds.), *Global Connections and Monetary History, 1470–1800* (Aldershot: Ashgate, 2003), p. 174. Figure (4), Liang Fangzhong, *Liang Fangzhong Jingjishi Lunwen Ji* (*Collected Works by Liang Fangzhong in Economic History*) (Beijing: Zhonghua Books, 1989), pp. 178–9.
Note: * Converted to pure silver from the original ingots of lower silver contents. Figures in parentheses are in 10,000 *taels*.

overseas. China's main silver supplier was first Japan and then the Spanish New World (the 'Manila Galleon Trade'). China's exports were overwhelmingly manufactures (such as porcelain, stationeries, silk textiles and tools), not farming products (with the exception of processed luxury foods such as sugar).[118]

The amount of silver imported from Japan was small for the size of China's economy. At its peak, it was about 118 tons a year (see Table 48), or 1.2 grams (or 0.03 *taels*) per capita.

Silver imported from the non-Japanese sources was less than from Japan, but lasting much longer (see Table 49).[119] If China received two-thirds of the 'New World sliver' coming to Asia,[120] towards the end of the Ming Period, the annual amount was likely to be another 70 tons, 0.7 grams per head (0.018 *taels*).

[118] Sun, *Nautical History of Premodern China*, ch. 6.
[119] D. O. Flynn and Arturo Giráldez, 'China and the Spanish Empire', *Revista de Historia Econimica* (*Journal of Economic History*), 14/2 (1996), pp. 309–38; Frank, *ReOrient*; Deng, 'Miracle or Mirage?'; Francois Gipouloux, *The Asian Mediterranean, Port Cities and Trading Networks in China, Japan and Southeast Asia, 13th–21st Century* (Cheltenham: Edward Elgar, 2011).
[120] No one knows exactly how much silver from the Spanish New World came to Asia. Gunder Frank's estimate was a third of that landed in Asia; see Frank, *ReOrient*, p. 143.

Table 49.   New World Silver for Asia, 1550–1800.

Period	Silver output*	Export to Asia*	Annual to Asia*
1550–99	5,728.1 (245 mln RD)[†,121]	3,436.9 (147.0 mln RD)	70.1 (3.0 miln RD)
1600–49	16,038.7 (686)	5,040.7 (215.6)	102.9 (4.4)
1650–99	14,893.1 (637)	6,873.7 (294.0)	140.3 (6.0)
1700–49	13,747.4 (588)	9,737.8 (416.5)	198.7 (8.5)
1750–79	13,560.4 (580)	8,271.8 (353.8)	168.8 (7.2)
1780–99	9,772.8 (418)	6,530.0 (279.3)	133.3 (5.7)
1800	701.4 (30)	420.8 (18.0)	420.8 (18.0)
Total	74,441.9	40,311.7	161.2 (6.9)

Source: Based on Arthur Attman, *American Bullion in the European World Trade 1600–1800*, translated by Eva and Allan Green (Göteborg: Kungl, 1986), p. 33.
Note: * In metric tons. [†] RD = Rix-Dollars which were medieval silver coins, containing a maximum of 23.38 grams of pure silver each, see Attman, *American Bullion*, p. 101.

Overtime, China's cumulative intake amounted for about 20,000 metric tons, or 530 million *taels*, just over one *tael* (37.5 grams) per head by 1900 (see Figure 15).

China's foreign trade really took off after the 1840 Opium War (see Table 50) when all the commercial restrictions were removed by the external force. Meanwhile, large quantities of silver left China in exchange for foreign imports, including opium (Table 51).

Meanwhile, the opening of China by the Opium War in 1840 for more trade ushered in an era of volatile silver account (see Figure 16).

It is important to note that China's silver importation were unregulated and handled almost entirely by the private sector. The government access to the silver pool in the economy only via taxation: About 50 million *taels* a year (30–40 million *taels* as Land-Poll tax revenue and another 10 million as Salt Tax). During the Qing, to pay taxes in silver were more common than in the previous Ming. The government silver revenue then went back to the economy through government spending on wages, salaries, and procurements of

---

[121] Noted, this 5,728.1 tons for 49 years makes an annual average of 116.9 tons which does not agree with E. J. Hamilton who suggested that Spain was able to shipped 322.2 tons of silver a year from the New World to Seville during the heydays of 1591–1600, see his *American Treasure and the Price Revolution in Spain, 1501–1650* (Cambridge: Harvard University Press, 1934), pp. 1–42.

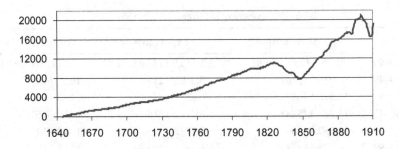

Figure 15.   China's Cumulative Silver Intake from Overseas Trade, 1644–1910.

Source: Based on Li Longsheng, 'Qingdai (1644–1911) Meinian Liuru Zhongguo Baiyin Shulangde Chubu Guji' (Preliminary Estimates of Annual Silver Inflow to China during the Qing Period (1644–1911), *Journal of Humanities and Social Sciences* (Taiwan), 5/2 (2009), pp. 45–56; *cf.* Peng Xinwei, *Zhongguo Huobi Shi* (*A History of Currencies in China*) (Shanghai: Shanghai People's Press, 1965), pp. 855, 868.

Note: In metric tons.

Table 50.   Total Value of China's Foreign Trade (in Million *Taels*), 1801–1891.

Year	Customs duty revenue	Total value	Index
1801	—	15.3* (15.5)	100
1821	—	16.3* (16.6)	107
1831	—	17.3* (17.5)	113
1841	—	30.0[†] (30.0)	194
1851	—	51.4[†] (51.4)	332
1861	4.3 [4.4]	86.9[§] (87.8)	566
1871	7.0 [7.0]	140.4[§] (141.0)	910
1881	11.1 [9.5]	222.3[§] (190.0)	1,226
1891	12.2 [9.2]	243.4[§] (181.6)	1,172

Source: Data for 1801–31, based on Yan Zhongping, *Zhongguo Jindai Jingjishi Ziliao Xuanji* (*Selected Statistical Materials of Economic History of Early Modern China*) (Beijing: Sciences Press, 1955), p. 3; data for 1839, based on Yan, *Selected Statistical Materials of Economic History* , pp. 3–5; Morse, *Chronicles of the East India Company*, Vols. 4–5 and Wu, *China's Modernization*, p. 286; data for 1861–91, based on Tang Xianglong, *Zhongguo Jindai Haiguan Shuishou He Fenpei Tongji* (*Data for Customs Revenue and Its Distribution in Modern China*) (Beijing: Zhonghua Books, 1992), pp. 63–6. The silver-gold exchange rates are based on Yu, *A History of Prices in China*, p. 865 and Liu Foding and Wang Yuru, *Zhongguo Jindaide Shichang Fayu Yu Jingji Zengzhang* (*Market Development and Economic Growth in Early Modern China*) (Beijing: Tertiary Education Press, 1996), pp. 178–9.

Note: Figures in parentheses indicate the constant price of 1839. Indices and annual growth rates are calculated by the 1839 price. *Only the 1800's silver-gold exchange ratio is available and hence is applied as a proxy. [†] No datum available, estimates are made by linear growth between 1831 and 1861. [§] Conversion based on 5 percent duty rate (Tang, *Data for Customs Revenue*, p. 14).

Table 51.   China's Annual Opium Imports, 1800–35.

Years	Chests*	Weight (*catties*)	Value in peso	Pesos [*taels*]/*catty*
1800–5	3,562	401,960	2,009,800† (47.9)	5.0 [3.2]
1805–10	4,281	484,580	—	—
1810–5	4,713	534,980	—	—
1815–20	4,633	519,740	—	—
1820–5	6,774	729,320	33,502,440 (799.0)	45.9 [29.4][122]
1825–30	12,108	1,312,440	56,930,593 (1,357.8)	43.4 [27.8]
1830–5	20,546[123]	2,217,260	63,866,684 (1,523.3)	28.8 [18.5]
1836–7	21,505	2,312,000	14,454,193 (344.7)	6.3 [4.0]
1838	50,000	6,000,000	15,000,000§ (357.8)	2.5 [1.6]

Source: Morse, *Chronicles of the East India Company*, Vols. 3–5; Timothy Brook and B. T. Wakabayashi (eds.), *Opium Regimes* (Berkeley: University of California Press, 2000), p. 204 (for the 1838 figure); *cf.* Hao, *Commercial Revolution*, p. 117; Gong Yingyan, *Yapiande Chuanbo Yu Duihua Yapian Maoyi* (*Spread of Opium Consumption and Opium Imports to China*) (Beijing: East Press, 1999), pp. 284–90, 292.

Note: Figures in parentheses are in metric tons. All the figures may double if smuggling is included.[124] Figures in brackets are in *taels*. Chest–weight conversion is based on Gong 1999: 281, 284–90, 292. * A chest contained 40 opium balls (the same size as a cannon ball, 15 cm in diameter, 3 *catties* each) of 100–120 *catties* (133.3–140 lb) in total,[125] † Maximum price based on 2,000 chests for 1,200,000 pesos,[126] § Based on Article IV of The Treaty of Nanking regarding six million silver dollars for the seized 20,000 chests of opium (1839 price).

goods and services. Even so, the weight of silver tax payment in the economy remained tiny, a fraction of China's total GDP (see Table 52).

In this context, the commonly circulated notion of 'silverisation' of the Ming-Qing currency and economy is a myth. All the time, China ran its

---

[122]One Qing *catty* was made of 16 *liang*. So, the average opium price per *catty* was higher than silver in weight.

[123]Chinese sources often put a figure of 25,000 to 35,500 chests a year for the late 1830s due to the factor of smuggling. Morse's data here are taken as the minimum.

[124]This is based on a comparison between Morse and Wu. The former has China's annual purchase of opium in the 1830s as worth 22.2 million *liang* (832.5 tons) a year on the book; see H. B. Morse, *The Chronicles of the East India Company Trading to China, 1635–1834* (Oxford: Oxford University Press, 1926–9), Vols. 4–5, while the latter has an estimate of 43.4 million *liang* (1,627.5 tons) including smuggling; Wu, *China's Modernization: Market*, p. 286.

[125]Booth, *Opium*, ch. 1.

[126]E. H. Pritchard, *Anglo-Chinese Relations during the Seventeenth and Eighteenth Centuries* (Urbana: The University of Illinois Press, 1929), p. 160.

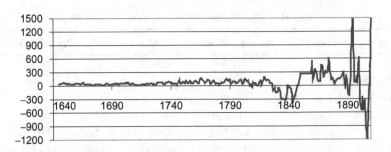

Figure 16. Annual Inflow of Silver to China, 1644–1910.

Source: Based on Li, 'Preliminary Estimates of Annual Silver Inflow to China', pp. 45–56.
Note: In metric tons. Minus amounts are trade deficits paid for by silver from China.

Table 52. Pattern of Tax Payments during the Qing Period.

Year	Grain payment (*shi*)	Silver payment (*taels*)
1661	6,479,465	21,576,006
1685	4,331,131	24,449,724
1724	4,731,400	26,362,541
1753	8,406,422	29,611,201
1784	4,820,067	29,637,014
1820	8,971,681	30,206,144
1885	—	32,356,768
1894	—	32,669,086
1903	112,966	35,116,387

Source: Liang, *Dynastic Data*, pp. 391–418.

own fully functional legal tender of bronze currency.[127] Silver served at best as an auxiliary. Silver (and gold) thus commanded a premium.[128] Such a premium is shown in Figure 17.

---

[127] Among monetary historians of China, there has been a long debate on (1) whether China had a parallel bimetallic system consisting of traditional bronze coins and imported silver, and (2) whether silver was taking over China's monetary market and hence becoming the dominant form of currency; see von Glahn, *Fountain of Fortune*, pp. 253–5. Opinions are divided. China's increased silver stock in itself supports the notion of silverisation of the economy, while China's own records and anecdotes endorse a different view that the role of bronze coins never diminished; see Wang 'Evolution of the Chinese Monetary System', pp. 469–96; Kuroda, 'Copper Coins Chosen and Silver Differentiated'. However, the issue of bronze currency goes beyond the capacity of this chapter and hence will not be elaborated further.

[128] Peng, *History of Currencies in China*, p. 850.

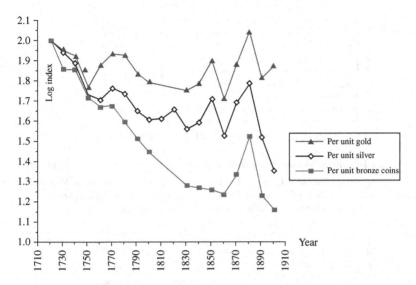

Figure 17. Purchasing Power of Three Currencies for per Unit of Rice, 1710–1910.

Source: Yu, *History of Prices*, pp. 903–4. Gold price is derived from silver-gold exchange rates; see Liu and Wang, *Market Development and Economic Growth*, pp. 178–9.

Table 53.   Growth in Silver Premium, South and North Compared.

Bronze currency price index (I)	Silver price index (II)	Premium index (I:II)
Southern rice price: Suzhou		
1707 100	100	100
1785 286	179	160
1823 471	204	230
1850 329	90	370
Northern retail price: Zhili		
1800 100	100	100
1820 118	85	140
1843 118	63	190

Source: Based on Lin, 'Over-supply of Inferior Currency', pp. 370–2.

Over time, the silver premium increased, particularly fast in the south where the economy was most open to foreign trade (see Table 53).

Consequently, the rice price measured by silver was more stable than that by bronze coins (see Figures 17, 18 and 19).

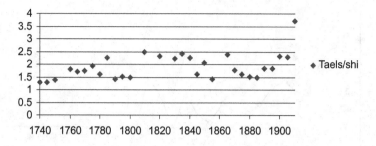

Figure 18.   Rice Prices in Silver in Jiangsu during the Harvest Season, 1740–1910.

Source: Wang Yejian, *The Database of Grain Prices in the Qing Dynasty* (Institute of Modern History, *Academia Sinica*, 2013, available on line at: http://ccts.ascc.net/integration.php?lang=en).
Note: Current prices in *taels* per *shi* during the Ninth Month of the year.

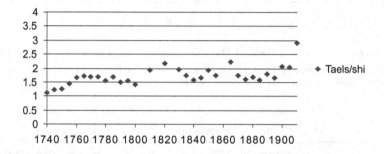

Figure 19.   Rice Prices in Silver in Zhejiang during the Harvest Season, 1740–1910.

Source: Wang Yejian, *The database of grain prices in the Qing Dynasty* (Institute of Modern History, *Academia Sinica*, 2013, available on line at: http://ccts.ascc.net/integration.php?lang=en).
Note: Current prices in *taels* per *shi* during the Ninth Month of the year.

5. A Proto-Welfare State of the Qing and Population Growth

What made the Qing Period stand out in China's long-term history was its proto-welfare state in line with Confucian benevolence.

To begin with, the Ming population remained stubbornly stagnant from 1393 to 1542 at an annual rate of mere 0.02 percent.[129] From 1550 to 1600, China's population may have recovered from 60 million to the previous Northern Song level of 100 million (at an annual rate of 0.9 percent)

---

[129] Cao, *Demographic History of China*, Vol. 4, p. 199; also Liang, *Dynastic Data*, pp. 9–10.

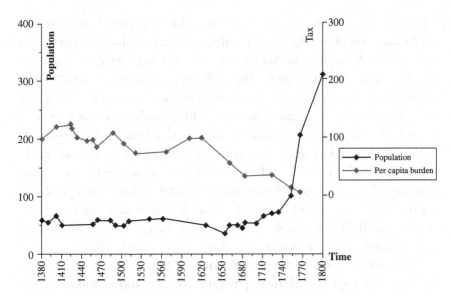

Figure 20.   Ming–Qing Direct-Tax Burden, 1380–1800.

Source: Liang, *Dynastic Data*, p. 428; Deng, 'Official Census Data', Appendix 2.

before dropping back to 50–60 million again.[130] A sustained growth in China's population took place after 1700. By 1900, China's population reached the level of 400 million with an average annual rate of 1.07 percent over three centuries, the same rate as that of the Northern Song. What was unusual about the Qing was that the state decided not to take the advantage of China's population growth in tax collection. In the end, the Qing per capita tax burden (direct tax of Land-Poll, *diding*) was about half of the previous Ming (see Figure 20).

This new fiscal approach was the result of Emperor Kangxi's 1715 policy of 'freezing the tax revenue' (*yongbu jiafu*) at the level of 30 million *taels* of silver (1,125 metric tons).[131] The policy lasted for over one century until 1840 and benefited about 80 percent of the population — the peasantry.

On top of the Land-Poll Tax, there was the 'silver wear and tear surcharge' (*haoxian*) of 12 percent.[132] This made the land-related direct tax

---

[130] Cao, *Demographic History of China*, Vol. 4, p. 201. Note, China's official census indicates that its population reached 100 million again only in the 1730s, see Deng, 'Unveiling China's True Population Statistics', Appendix 2.

[131] Zhao, *History of the Qing Dynasty*, Vol. 121, Entry 'Economy', in *TFOH*, Vol. 11, p. 9261.

[132] See Liang, *Dynastic Data*, p. 419; Wang, *Late Taxation in Imperial China*, p. 70.

a total of 33.7 million *taels* of silver (1,263.8 tons). In per capita terms, the tax burden was about 0.08 *taels* (or three grams) of silver per year (as of the 1880s). According to Sidney Gamble, the average daily wage for unskilled labourers in Beijing in the 1850s was 80 copper coins (0.05–0.08 *taels* of silver) for the sluggish season and 150 copper coins (0.09–0.15 *taels* of silver) for the busy season. The annual direct tax burden was about one to two day wage for an unskilled worker.[133] In addition, the amount of Stipen Rice (*caomi, caoliang*) to pay bureaucrats and soldiers stationed in the north was fixed at four million *shi* (289,960 metric tons) a year.[134] This was about 5 grams of grain (worth about 0.00001 *taels* of silver) per capita for the country as a whole. Whichever way one looks at it, the Qing taxation was so light that people 'barely noticed the tax system, almost as if they suffered no tax burden at all'.[135] Such observation is valid.

However, China's farming sector did not always have good harvests. For example, a quarter of the population living in North China was subject to the notorious flooding of the Yellow River.[136] From the best available data for 1821 to 1910, 30 percent of all the counties of the Qing Empire suffered crop failures, 54 percent broke even; and only 16 percent had bumper harvests.[137] The state could have left the market or migration to do the resource re-allocation. Instead, the Qing state performed the most effective disaster relief schemes ever seen in China's long-term history.

The Qing relief system included an empire-wide disaster monitoring network, an annual budget for disaster-aid, and state 'ever-even granaries' (*changping cang*), and local communal 'charity granaries' (*yicang*).

---

[133] For the wage data see Gamble, 'Daily Wages', p. 62. For the money exchange rate, see Yu, *History of Prices*, p. 860.

[134] He Changling and Wei Yuan (eds.), *Huangchao Jingshi Wenbian* (*Collection of Documents of the Qing Administration*) (N.d. Reprint, Beijing: Zhonghua Books, 1992), p. 1087; also see Liang, *Dynastic Data*, pp. 366–73. One *shi* of dry rice is 72.49 kilograms, according to Liang, *Dynastic Data*, p. 545; and also Chao, *Man and Land*, p. 209. This amount is enough to feed 1.5 million adults a year at the subsistence level, while one million was roughly the size of the population in Beijing during Ming and Qing times. Another source cites 5–8 million *shi* per year; see Zhou, *Financial History of China*, pp. 419–21, 426. See also Wang, *Late Taxation*, p. 70. But, the inflated amount is trivial regarding all the 'extras' associated with the rice.

[135] Mann, *Local Merchants and the Chinese Bureaucracy*, p. 16.

[136] See Perkins, *Agricultural Development*, p. 172.

[137] This is based on Fairbank and Liu, *Cambridge History of China*, Vol. 11, pt. 2, p. 7; also Buck, *Land Utilization in China: Atlas*, pp. 30–1.

Table 54. Government Aid Recipients (Counties), 1674–1911.

Year	Tax exemptions	Aid hand-outs	Total
1674–1723	3,281	—	3,281
1724–1773	9,784	6,082	15,866
1774–1823	8,850	1,889	10,739
1824–1873	7,295	3,004	10,299
1874–1911	6,278	2,465	8,743
Total	35,488	13,440	48,928
Ten-year average	1,479	560	2,039

Source: Zhao Erxun, *Qingshi Gao* (*Draft of the History of the Qing Dynasty*), Vols. 4–25 'Benji' (Biographies of the Qing Emperors), in *TFOH*, Vol. 11, pp. 8827–8937.

According to Pierre-Étienne Will, Roy Bin Wong, Myers and Wang, the Qing granary system had a stockpile of 30–45 million *shi* of unhusked rice (2.2–3.3 million metric tons) ready to be sent off when disasters struck. This system remained active until the 1860s.[138] The Qing state also provided 'cash aid' which often accounted for 50 percent of an aid package. This type of aid took advantage of the market of staple food where about 30 percent of China's grain output was sold annually.[139] There were also tax exemptions (*chu, huan, jian,* and *mian*).[140] The Qing had in all 1,672–2,074 counties.[141] The empire was covered by aid schemes many times over (see Table 54).

About 75 percent of the beneficiaries were in the old core farming zones where the population densities were the highest (see Figure 21).

The scale and scope of the Qing disaster relief were remarkable: By the end the Qing, the disaster relief efforts saved in all 166.6–251.3 million

---

[138] Pierre-Etienne Will and R. B. Wong, *Nourish the People: the State Civilian Granary System in China, 1650–1850* (Ann Arbor: University of Michigan Center for Chinese Studies, 1991), pp. 21, 482–3; W. J. Peterson (ed.), *The Cambridge History of China* (Cambridge: Cambridge University Press, 2002), Vol. 9, p. 602.

[139] See Li Wenzhi, 'Lun Mingqing Shidai Nongmin Jingji Shangpinlü' (Marketing Rates of the Peasant Products in Ming–Qing Times), *Zhongguo Jingjishi Yanjiu* (*Study of Chinese Economic History*), 1 (1993), pp. 21–42.

[140] Myers and Wang, 'Economic Developments', p. 603.

[141] Normally, the Qing had 1,672. If all the 402 county equivalent units are counted, the total number is 2,074; see Zhao, *History of the Qing Dynasty*, Vols. 54–81, 'Administrative Geography', in *TFOH*, Vol. 11, pp. 9071–9131.

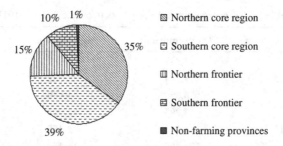

Figure 21.   Regional Distribution of Aid Recipients, 1644–1911.

Source: Zhao, *History of the Qing Dynasty*, Vols. 4–25 'Benji' (Biographies of the Qing Emperors), Vols. 54–81 'Dili Zhi', in *TFOH*, Vol. 11, pp. 8827–8937, 9071–9131. Late Qing provincial population, based on Liang, *Dynastic Data*, pp. 401–11.

Note: Northern core region (5 provinces): Zhili, Henan, Shandong, Shanxi and Shaanxi. Southern core region (8 provinces): Anhui, Jiangsu, Zhejiang, Hubei, Hunan, Jiangxi, Fujian, and Guangdong. Northern frontier (5 provinces): Fengtian, Jilin, Heilongjiang, Gansu, and Xinjiang. Southern frontier (5 provinces): Sichuan, Guizhou, Guangxi, Yunnan, and Taiwan. Non-farming regions (4 units): Tibet, Qinghai, Chahar, and Outer Mongolia.

Table 55.   Qing Government Aid Schemes and Its Impact, 1666–1911.

Period	Food aid (rice *shi*)	Cash aid (silver *tael*)
1. Pre-Opium War (1666–1836)	11,130,000	15,315,000
Million lives rescued[†]	60.8–90.5	52.8–80.6*
2. Post-Opium War (1847–1911)	3,457,500	9,900,000
Million lives rescued[†]	18.9–28.1	34.1–52.1*
3. Total	14,587,500	25,215,000
Million lives rescued[†]	79.7–118.6	86.9–132.7*
Million lives rescued in total		166.6–251.3

Source: Zhao, *History of the Qing Dynasty*, Vols. 4–25, 'Biographies of the Qing Emperors', in *TFOH*, Vol. 11, pp. 8827–8937.

Note: * Converted to amount of food by the mean price at 1.56 *taels* of silver per *shi* of rice derived from the rice price range of 0.94 to 2.18 *taels* of silver per *shi* in the Yangzi and Pearl deltas of the seventeenth and eighteenth centuries; see R. B. Marks, 'Rice Prices, Food Supply, and Market Structure in Eighteenth-Century South China', *Late Imperial China* 12/2 (1991), p. 102; Yeh-chien Wang, 'Secular Trends of Rice Prices in the Yangtze Delta, 1638–1935', in T. G. Rawski and L. M. Li (eds.), *Chinese History in Economic Perspective* (Berkeley: University of California Press, 1992), pp. 40–7. [†] Estimation is made by the Ming standard: 20–30 *sheng* per head (12.4–18.6 kilograms of unhusked rice for an adult to last 18–37 days) to survive a famine, not trivial.[142]

lives (see Table 55), equivalent to about one third to one half of China's standing population in the nineteenth century, not trivial.

---

[142] Zhang, *History of the Ming*, Vol. 2, Entry 'Hongwu Shinian' (Tenth Year of the Hongwu Reign), and Vol. 16, Entry 'Hongzhi Shisannian' (Thirteenth Year of the Hongzhi Reign), in *TFOH*, Vol. 10, pp. 7791, 7807.

With more farmland, less taxes, and persistent disaster relief, it is not entirely surprising that in the 1750s, a century after the Manchu takeover, China's average family size increased by 20 percent (one extra person in a family of five).[143] In the following century, China's population jumped from about 200 million to about 400 million.[144]

6. Legacies of the Qing Rule

The first legacy of the Qing Period was China's weakness in internal and external security. This was inevitable given the size of the Qing government — too small both in manpower and in budget. China's ability to resist external shocks was in shambles (losing all wars: two wars over opium in 1839–40 and 1856–60; wars with France in 1883–5, with Japan in 1894, and a war against eight powers during the Battle of Peking in 1900); and so was its capacity to cope with internal unrest (the White Lotus riot in 1796–1805, the Taiping-Nian-Mao-Muslim unrest in 1850–70, the Boxer Rebellion in 1900, and the Republican Revolution of 1911). It is very easy to see Qing China a case of state failure.[145] Such a conclusion seems justifiable if one compares Qing China with Meiji Japan (1868–1912) and Chulalongkorn's Siam (Thailand, 1868–1910) in Asia. One tends to forget, however, that Japan and Siam were exceptions of the time. The rest of Asia crumbled under Western colonialism and imperialism.

The second legacy was the development of a robust private economy. China's imports and exports were unregulated by the state, and dictated by the world market. So much so, China's traditional exports of manufactures — metals, paper, porcelain, and textiles — were later replaced by primary products. By the eve of the First Opium War, tea had dominated China's exports: 78 percent of the total value of exports to Britain and 72 percent of that to the Netherlands.[146] Consequently, in

---

[143] See James Lee and Wang Feng, *One Quarter of Humanity: Malthusian Mythology and Chinese Realities, 1700–2000* (Cambridge: Harvard University Press, 1999), pp. 34–5, 38.

[144] Deng, 'Official Census Data', Appendix 2.

[145] J. K. Fairbank (ed.), *The Cambridge History of China, Late Ch'ing, 1800–1911, Part I* (Cambridge: Cambridge University Press, 1978), Vol. 10; J. K. Fairbank and Kwang-ching Liu (eds.), *The Cambridge History of China, Late Ch'ing, 1800–1911* (Cambridge: Cambridge University Press, 1980), Vol. 11; Spence, *Search for Modern China.*

[146] Morse, *The Chronicles of the East India Company*, Vols. 2–4; E. H. Pritchard, *The Crucial Years of Early Anglo-Chinese Relations, 1750–1800* (Washington: Pullman, 1936), pp. 395–6; K. N. Chaudhuri, *The Trading World of Asia and the English East India Company* (Cambridge: Cambridge University Press, 1978), p. 538; Jörg, *Porcelain*, pp. 217–20.

1800–1900, China's share of industrial production in the world declined by about 80 percent.[147] China's downgrade to a primary exporter made China more vulnerable. In the latter half of nineteenth century, the share of tea in the total value of China's exports decreased from 58.3 percent to 17.4 percent.[148] In 1895, for the first time, the combined tea export in the world market from India, Ceylon, and Japan surpassed that from China. In 1910, India alone led China by 28.1 percent in tea export.[149] On the silk front, Japan had a rapid increase of 600 percent in output between 1886 and 1911.[150] By 1915, Japan became the Number One raw silk exporter in Asia.[151] China resorted to soybeans in which China still maintained absolute advantage. In 1913, the total value of China's soybean exports surpassed that of tea. In 1928, it overtook that of raw silk.[152] It is however important to note that exports accounted for a tiny proportion of China's total GDP. The impact of China's decline from an industrial-goods exporter to a primary-goods exporter on the economy should not be exaggerated.[153]

The third legacy was the emergence of a new attitude around the time of the First Opium War. In 1839, Lin Zexu (1785–1850), the Imperial Commissioner in charge of the opium ban, instructed his officials to collect and translate European knowledge and information into Chinese, including newspapers and magazines published in Portuguese-controlled

[147] Paul Kennedy, *The Rise and Fall of the Great Powers* (New York: Random House, 1987), p. 149.
[148] Chen Ciyu, 'Yi Zhong Yin Ying Sanjiao Maoyi Wei Jizhou Tantao Shijiu Shiji Zhongguode Duiwai Maoyi' (Study of Nineteenth Century Sino-foreign Trade Based on the Trade Triangle of China, India, and Britain), in Editing Committee for *Maritime History of China* (ed.), *Zhongguo Haiyang Fazhanshi Lunwenji* (*Selected Essays on the Maritime History of China*) (Taipei: Academia Sinica, 1984), Vol. 1, pp. 156–7.
[149] Lin Renchuan, *Fujian Duiwai Maoyi Yu Haiguan Shi* (*A History of Fujian's Foreign Trade and Customs*) (Xiamen: Lujiang Press, 1991), p. 244.
[150] Kunio Yoshihara, *Japanese Economic Development: A Short Introduction* (Tokyo: Oxford University Press, 1979), p. 10.
[151] L. M. Li, 'Silk by Sea: Trade, Technology, and Enterprise in China and Japan', *Business History Review*, 2 (1982), pp. 196–7.
[152] Soybean oil was exported to the West for soap-making. Soybean cakes were exported to Japan as fodder and fertiliser. See Chen Zhengping, 'Shixi 1895–1930 Nian Zhongguo Jinchukou Shangpin Jieguode Bianhua' (A Structural Change in China's Imports and Exports in 1895–1930), *Zhongguo Jingjishi Yanjiu* (*Research into Chinese Economic History*), 3 (1997), p. 52.
[153] Deng, *Chinese Maritime Activities and Socioeconomic Development*, ch. 5.

Macao,[154] Emericide Vattel's *Law of Nations* written in *c.* 1758, Hugh Murray's *Encyclopaedia of Geography* published in 1834, and Algernon S. Thelwall's 1834 moralising essay *The Iniquities of the Opium Trade with China*. Immediately after the Opium War, there was a surge of information about Europe, published in Chinese for the public consumption, such as Wei Yuan's *A Comprehensive Survey of Off-shore Countries* written in 1841,[155] Chen Fengheng's *A Brief History of England* written in 1841, Wang Wentai's *A Study of England of Red-haired Barbarians* (*Hongmaofan Yingjili Kaolue*) written in 1842, Liang Tingnan's *Four Essays on Off-shore Countries* in 1846, Xu Jishe's *Records of Lands and Peoples Overseas* in 1848, and Xia Xie's *Main Events between China and the West* in 1850. Compared with the early works of the Jesuits, the new trend covered a wider range of tangible information concerning Europe, especially customs, values, institutions, and social conditions.

By the time of the Second Opium War in 1856, the Qing elite began to understand the Social Darwinian principle of 'the survival of the fittest'. The new attitude was crystallised in the new slogan of 'Chinese knowledge as the foundation and Western knowledge for utility' (*zhongxue weiti, xixue weiyong*). High ranking officials like Zeng Guofan (1811–72), Zeng Guoquan (1824–90), Zuo Zongtang (1812–85), Shen Baozhen (1820–79), Li Hongzhang (1823–1901), Zhang Zhidong (1837–1909), and Sheng Xuanhuai (1844–1916) emerged as 'Westernisers' (*yangwu pai*) to push for a three-decade long 'Westernisation Movement' (*yangwu yundong*) and 'Self-strengthening Movement' (*zhiqiang yundong*) with the mission of adopting and adapting Western technology in China. These movements finally involved the Qing monarch during the radical and short-lived '1898 Reform', or the '100-Day Reform', endorsed by the young (27 years old) Emperor Guangxu (*r.* 1875–1908). The emperor's edict was as follows:

> *Our country needs to adopt Western ways to develop all businesses vigorously …*
> *I, the Emperor, have been contemplating reforms day and night to improve*

---

[154] They included *Aomen Yuebao* (*The Chinese Repository*), *Aomen Xinwenzhi* (*The Canton Press*), and *Guangzhou Jishi Bao* (*The Canton Register*).
[155] The main body of text was Lin Zexu's *Sizhou Zhi* (*Encyclopaedia of Geography*) (Publishers unknown). It was introduced to Japan in 1854 and became an instant best seller.

[China] in all areas ... Let us be united across society to implement the reforms and to strengthen China.[156]

The 1898 Reform was radical and wide-ranging. Over 100 Imperial edicts were issued, including abolishing 'eight-legged essays' (*bagu*) in the Imperial Examinations, ending Bannermen military tenure, trimming government departments, establishing a state-run post and a central bank, promoting modern textiles, shipbuilding, mining and railways, and re-building naval defence.

The need to deal with the West led to some changes in Qing institutions. A new government organ, the Foreign Affairs Department (*Zongli Geguo Shiwu Yamen*), was established in 1861. Apart from diplomacy, the department ran the Capital Foreign Language Academy (*Jingshi Tongwen Guan*). William A. Martin (Ting Weiliang, 1827–1916), a Yale-educated missionary, was hired as Dean for 25 years. In Shanghai, another translation centre, the Translation Division of the Jiangnan (Kiangnan) Arsenal (*Jiangnan Zhizaoju Fanyi Guan*) was established in 1868 and hired John Fryer (Fu Lanya, 1839–1928), a Briton, as Translator-in-Chief. By 1896, 352 Western books were translated by these two centers.[157] Moreover, from 1862 to 1895, 22 modern military academies were established.[158] The Northern Sea Fleet's sailor-training centre (*Lianyong Xuetang*) adapted the British standard.[159] Naval cadets were also sent to Britain and France to learn the latest technology and crafts.[160]

In 1861, China's first modern factory, the Anqing Arsenal (*Anqing Neijunxiesuo*), began to produce European–style firearms. In 1865, the factory launched China's first steam ship.[161] Two other modern factories, the Jinling

---

[156] Zhao, *History of the Qing Dynasty*, Vol. 24, Entry 'Biography of Emperor Dezong', in *TFOH*, Vol. 11, p. 8926.

[157] Liang Qichao, *Yinbingshi Heji* (*Readings for Ice Drinkers' Hut*) (Originally published in 1896. Reprint. Beijing: Zhonghua Books, 1989), Vol. 1, pp. 122–5.

[158] Hao Peiyun, *Zhongguo Haijun Shi* (*A Naval History of Modern China*) (Beiping: Xuewu Books, 1929), pp. 17, 65, 71, 167.

[159] Anon., *Beiyang Haijun Zhangcheng* (*Regulations of the Northern Sea Fleet*) (Originally published in 1890. Reprint. Taipei: Wenhai Press, 1968), pp. 199–204.

[160] Anon., *Northern Sea Fleet*, pp. 13, 20, 45, 159, 170–1.

[161] The ship was 18 metres' long (55 *chi*) with a 25-ton displacement. It travelled at a speed of about 10 kilometres (20 *li*) per hour powered by a single cylinder.

Machinery Bureau (*Jinling Jiqiju*) and the Jiangnan (or Kiangnan) Arsenal (*Jiangnan Zhizaoju*), followed suit. The Jiangnan Arsenal was largest in East Asia of that time.[162] In 1879, the quality of its workforce was recognised as close to its European counterparts.[163] In all, 25 arsenals in 14 provinces supplied provincial forces with modern weapons. In addition, in 1888, on the eve of the Sino–Japanese War, China had three modern naval fleets with 65 large warships and 43 torpedo boats. In the world league table for navies, China was ranked the eighth, ahead of Japan's eleventh place ranking.[164]

Changes occurred within society too. In the post-Opium War era, the first group of modern entrepreneurs, the compradors (*maiban*), emerged as new commercial agents.[165] They lived on 2–3 percent commission in a competitive market,[166] and were active in a wide range of commercial ventures such as modern banking, manufacturing, transport and communication.[167] By the end of the nineteenth century, China had over 10,000 compradors (compared with no more than 100 chartered merchants in Canton in pre-1840) with the aggregate wealth of 18,500–19,900 tons of silver (493–530 million *taels*), richer than any other private merchant group.[168] By 1900, over one-third of China's bourgeoisies had this comprador background.[169]

Furthermore, in the 1890s, China began to have a modern industrial workforce of about 92,000, hired by three groups (see Table 56).

---

[162] M. C. Wright, *The Last Stand of Chinese Conservatism* (Stanford: Stanford University Press, 1957), p. 212.

[163] Sun Yutang, *Zhongguo Jindai Gongyeshi Ziliao* (*Materials of Early Modern Industries in China*) (Beijing: Sciences Press, 1957), Vol. 1, p. 1224.

[164] Tang, *Last Seventy Years*, p. 191; Xu Tailai, *Yangwu Yundong Xinlun* (Re-examination of the Westernisation Movement) (Changsha: Hunan People's Press, 1986), p. 40; J. L. Rawlinson, *China's Struggle for Naval Development* (Cambridge: Harvard University Press, 1967), pp. 168–9.

[165] Yen-P'ing Hao, *The Comprador in Nineteenth-Century China: Bridge between East and West* (Cambridge [MA]: Harvard University Press, 1970); Hao, *Commercial Revolution*, Chs. 8–9.

[166] Yan Zhongping, 'Shilun Zhongguo Maiban Zichanjiejide Fasheng' (Emergence of the Comprador Class in China), *Zhongguo Jingjishi Yanjiu* (*Research into Chinese Economic History*), 1 (1986), pp. 85–7, 89, 90, 93.

[167] Hao, *Comprador*, ch. 4.

[168] *Ibid.*, p. 105; Huang Qichen, 'Mingqing Guangdong Shangbang' (The Guangdong Merchant Group during the Ming–Qing Period), *Zhongguo Shehui Jingjishi Yanjiu* (*Study of Chinese Socio-Economic History*), 4 (1992), pp. 31–8.

[169] Sun, *Early Modern Industries*, p. 1166–72.

Table 56.   China's Modern Industrial Workforce, the 1890s.

	Workers	% in total
Foreign enterprises	34,000	37.0
Government-run enterprises	30,600	33.3
Chinese private enterprises	27,250	29.7

Source: Sun, *Early Modern Industries*, p. 1201.

Table 57.   Investment and Investors in China's Railways, 1888–1946.

	Total	Foreign	China (private)	China (state)
Projects	90	76	10	4
Investment*	1,398.2	1,078.9	299.7	19.6
% in Total	100.0	77.2	21.4	1.4

Source: Based on Research Centre of History of Railways in China (ed.), *Zhongguo Tielu Dashiji, 1876–1995* (*Main Events in the History of Chinese Railways, 1876–1995*) (Beijing: China's Railway Press, 1996); Yang Yonggang, *Zhongguo Jindai Tielu Shi* (*A History of Railways in Modern China*) (Shanghai: Shanghai Books, 1997).
Note: * In million *taels* of silver, converted at current rates of exchange.

The number of modern workers grew to 600,000 in 1914, one million in the 1920s, and three million in the 1930s.[170] This was an annual increase of 9.1 percent over 40 years.[171] At this rate, it would take another 37 years (hence in the 1970s) for China's modern industrial workforce to claim half of China's labour market.

Modern infrastructure also began to take roots in China. By 1887, all provincial capital cities and strategic locations were linked up by a telegraphic network of over 23,000 kilometres (46,450 *li*),[172] which yielded business profit.[173] Railway construction also grew (see Table 57).

---

[170] Fairbank, *Cambridge History of China*, Vol. 12, p. 36; Xiao Xiaoqin and Li Liangzhi, *Zhongguo Geming Shi* (*A History of Revolutions in China*) (Beijing: Red Flag Press, 1983), p. 29; Shi Tanjin, *Laodong Fa* (*Labour Law*) (Beijing: Economic Sciences Press, 1990), pp. 25–6.

[171] Anon., *Mao Zedong Sixiang Wansui* (*Long Live Mao Zedong's Thought*) (Beijing: Peking University, August 1969, SOAS Library Copy), p. 70.

[172] Institute of Modern History, *Academia Sinica* (Taiwan) (ed.), *Haifang Dang* (*Archival Materials on Naval Defence*), Entry 'Dianxian' (Telegraphic Lines) (Taipei: Yiwen Press, 1957), Vol. 4.

[173] Xu, *Westernisation Movement*, pp. 89–93.

Table 58.   Structure and Distribution of Investment in New Industries, *c.* 1900.

	Firms	Weight (%)	Costs (Million *taels*)	Weight (%)
Heavy industry	17	10.2	0.6	3.1
Mining	37	22.1	8.5	44.2
Utility	2	1.2	0.02	0.1
Transport and communication	3	1.8	5.8	30.2
Light industry	108	64.7	4.3	22.4
Total	167	100.0	19.2	100.0

Source: Based on Xu, *Westernisation Movement*, pp. 76–84. All the silver *yuan* figures are converted at one *yuan* = 0.637 *taels* of pure silver.

However, only about 20 million *taels* of silver were invested in the modern sector accumulatively — which accounted for less than one percent of China's annual GDP of the time (see Table 58). The scale and scope of modern industry were hence trivial. Nevertheless, the seed of changes was planted.[174]

The last legacy of the Qing rule involved living standards. The elastic supply of farmland, private property rights, social mobility, regional and local autonomy, low tax burden, and disaster relief not only fuelled a

---

[174]Numerous works explore this: e.g., J. R. Pusey, *China and Charles Darwin* (Cambridge [MA]: Harvard University Press, 1983); J. A. Fogel and P. G. Zarrow, *Imaging the People, Chinese Intellectuals and the Concept of Citizenship, 1890–1902* (Armonk: M. E. Sharpe, 1997), p. 15; Aihwa Ong and Donald Nonini, *Ungrounded Empires: The Cultural Politics of Modern Chinese Transnationalism* (New York and London: Routledge, 1997), p. 46; Kewen Wang, *Modern China, An Encyclopedia of History, Culture and Nationalism* (New York: Garland Press, 1998), p. 321; E. S. Rawski, *The Last Emperors: A Social History of Qing Imperial institutions* (Berkeley: University of California Press, 1998), p. 2; Spence, *Modern China*, pp. 290–4; Brook and Wakabayashi, *Opium Regimes*, p. 71; Henrietta Harrison, *China* (London: Arnold, 2001), p. 73; Kai-Wing Chow, K. M. Doak, and Poshek Fu, *Constructing Nationhood in Modern East Asia* (Ann Arbor: University of Michigan Press, 2001), pp. 53–4; C. X. G. Wei and Xiaoyuan Liu, *Exploring Nationalisms of China: Themes and Conflicts* (London and West Port: Greenwood Press, 2002), p. 12; S. L. Glosser, *Chinese Visions of Family and State, 1915–1953* (Berkley: University of California Press, 2003), p. 2; Giovanni Arrighi, Takeshi Hamashita and Mark Selden, *The Resurgence of East Asia: 500, 150 and 50 Year Perspectives* (London and New York: Routledge, 2003), p. 54; A. D. Voskressenski, *Russia and China: A Theory of Inter-State Relations* (London: Routledge Curzon, 2003), p. 91; Kwang-Ching Liu and Richard Shek, *Heterodoxy in Late Imperial China* (Honolulu: University of Hawaii Press, 2004), p. 17; P. F. Williams and Yenna Wu, *The Great Wall of Confinement: The Chinese Prison Camp through Contemporary Fiction and Reportage* (Berkeley: University of California Press, 2004), p. 13.

Table 59.　Wage-Workers' Calorie Intake across China.

	Daily calorie intake	2,100 calories = 100
China-wide average	2,537	121
Beijing wage-workers	2,670	127
Shanghai wage-workers	3,008	143
Wuhan wage-workers	3,500	167
Changsha wage-worker	3,008	143

Source: Ta-chung Liu and Kung-chia Yeh, *The Economy of the Chinese Mainland: National Income and Economic Development, 1933–1959* (Princeton: Princeton University Press, 1965), p. 31; Li *et al.*, *Social Surveys*, Vol. 1, pp. 35, 47, 276, 386; Vol. 2, p. 829; Zhang, 'Dietary Structure and Nutrition Structure', p. 15.

Note: * Subsistence calorie intake.

strong momentum in population growth but also supported respectable standards of living. In the rural sector, the average food intake across 21 provinces was 3,295 kilocalories per day.[175] In urban China, it was 2,537 (as of the 1930s) (see Table 59). Other nutrients intakes were also reasonable.

In 1900, Marshall Alfred Graf von Waldersee (1832–1904) carried out a physical examination scheme at 13 city gates of Beijing — 95 percent of Chinese males aged 18 to 60 years old passed the standard for the German army recruits of the time.[176] In addition, in the 1920s and 1930s, China's national average Engel Coefficient was 0.47;[177] in large cities like Tianjin, Shanghai, and Wuhan the reading was below 0.6.[178] Such a level was

[175] Zhang Donggang, 'Shipin Jiegou He Yingyang Jiegou: 20 Shiji Er-sanshi Niandai Yige Zhongguo Guomin Shehui Shenghuode Shizheng Fenxi' (Dietary Structure and Nutrition Structure: Analysis of Social Life in China in the 1920s and 30s), *Zhongguo Jingjishi Yanjiu* (*Research into Chinese Economic History*), 4 (2007), p. 15.

[176] Ding Shiyuan, *Meileng Zhangjing Biji* (*Witness Account of the 1911 Revolution*) (Originally published in 1942. Reprint. Beijing: Zhonghua Books, 2007), p. 284.

[177] Bureau of Social Affairs of Shanghai, *The Cost of Living Index Numbers of Laborers, Great Shanghai, January 1926–December 1931* (Shanghai: Bureau of Social Affairs of Shanghai, 1932), p. 18; Li *et al.*, *Social Surveys*, Vol. 1, pp. 25, 26, 358; Vol. 2, pp. 758, 827, 1225.

[178] Wu Baosan, *Zhongguo Guomin Suode 1933* (*China's National Income, 1933*) (Shanghai: Zhonghua Books, 1947), pp. 160–70.

comparable with Britain, Japan and India at the time.[179] In 1933, China's import of cosmetics alone was worth 1.4 million silver *yuan* (33.4 metric tones).[180] All the evidence in this chapter therefore challenges the 'China-in-poverty' view expressed by many historians.

---

[179]Li *et al.*, *Social Surveys*, Vol. 1, pp. 273, 359. Zhang, 'Dietary Structure and Nutrition Structure', pp. 13–22. For Meiji Japan's Engel Coefficient see Hanley, *Everyday Things in Premodern Japan*, p. 171.

[180]Chen *et al.*, *Counter-Japanese Invasion*, p. 73.

Chapter Seven

Growth after the Empire

In the twentieth century, the Westernisation Movement continued to grow under the Republican rule on the mainland until 1949. It was replaced by what essentially was 'Soviet/Russian learning as the foundation and Soviet/Russian knowledge for utility' under Mao Zedong, and then by 'Soviet/Russian learning as the foundation with Chinese characteristics' under Deng Xiaoping. In offshore Taiwan, the same 'Chinese learning as the foundation and Western knowledge for utility' perpetuated, while in Hong Kong the model was 'Western learning as the foundation and Western knowledge for utility'. China thus ran three system after 1949.

1. Changes and Growth Performance in the Republican Era (1912–49)

The ending of the Qing monarch was swift and bloodless after the 1911 Mutiny in Wuchang, where a few hundred army cadets rebelled. It was a poorly organised event. The mutineers had a total of 50 live rounds and no real leader until they succeeded in overthrowing their local governor.[1]

A lesser known factor which has not been discussed much is the economic cause of this munity of the time. Beijing's economic policy to nationalise China's railways was announced in May 1911 and it allowed the rights to be granted to foreigners. This agitated China's indigenous

---

[1] Sun Zhongshan (Yat-sen), *Sun Zhongshan Quanji* (*Complete Selection of Works by Sun Zhongshan*) (Beijing: Zhonghua Books, 1981), Vol. 10, pp. 294–5.

investors who organised the 'Anti-Nationalisation Movement' (*baolu yundong*).[2] The situation turned ugly in the upper stream of the Yangzi River, Chengdu (Sichuan), in September that year. Confrontation between provincial officials and railway investors spread downstream along the river to Wuchang (Hubei) in October where Republican sympathisers of the New Hubei Army (*Hubei Xinjun*) mutinied on 10 October and formed the 'Grand Hubei Military Government of the Nation of the Han Chinese'.

What followed next was the development of a provincial independence movement. Armed strong men, already well entrenched in provinces as a result of the Westernisation Movement, soon stopped taking orders from Beijing and carved China in pieces. The Qing administration, which was very small and weak to begin with, crumbled and vanished at a frightening speed. Earlier, in the 1900s, the Western idea of a republic had already taken root among China's political class after decades of Westernisation.[3] China was in fact ready to end the Imperial rule before 1911. In 1908–9, new legislations regarding elections were drafted. The new law specified that all males of the age 30 and above were entitled to be elected. All males above the age of 25 had the right to vote provided they met certain criteria.[4] This was not yet a universal franchise but it was a reasonable start. In the same year, 1,677 members of the Consultative Bureau were elected and they were ready to form a provisional parliament.[5] Finally, in 1910, the first parliament was formed with a total of 196 members — a half by selection, and the other half by election. It was a young parliament, with an average age of 40.[6] Ethnic Han counted for 70 percent of all members. In April 1913, two ex-Qing generals, Yuan Shikai (1859–1916) and Li Yuanhong (1864–1928), won China's first national

---

[2] For more details on the background of the movement, see Lee En-han, *China's Quest for Railway Autonomy, 1904–1911* (Singapore: Singapore University Press, 1977).

[3] Latin: *res publica* meaning that the state power resides in the people and leaders are elected and responsible for the voters.

[4] One of the following: (1) Holder of the Cultivated Talent Degree or higher, (2) holder of a modern schooling at the medium level, (3) a civilian official at the Seventh Grade or above or as an army officer at the Fifth Grade or above, (4) owner of assets locally of 5,000 *yuan* (about 3,000 *taels*) or more, and (5) worker in local affairs and charities for three years or longer.

[5] Zhang Yufa, *Qingjide Lixian Tuanti* (*Societies for Constitutional Changes during the Qing*) (Taipei: Academia Sinica, 1971), pp. 386–9.

[6] *Ibid.*, pp. 420–35.

election with 62 and 20 percent votes, respectively.[7] Despite some inevitable defects comman in any young democracy, the experience with a republic was by and large a success.

However, the genie of Social Darwinism, introduced to China as 'Western knowledge' in the late nineteenth century, was already out of the bottle. Modern arms were readily available across China. Provinces had already become mini-states. Civil wars followed despite the election and the new republic: A total of 140 battles were fought between provincial warlords from 1916 to 1928. Another war between the Republicans (the Guomindang) and the northern warlords broke out in 1926–27; and another two between the Republicans and Communists between 1931–34 and 1946–49, respectively. These civil wars were further complicated by the Japanese invasion and conquest of northern and eastern parts of China in 1928–45. China's political landscape was again complicated with the emergence of four Japanese puppets regimes: (1) The 'Manchukuo' (*Manzhou Guo*, 1932–45) in Manchuria, (2) the 'Interim Government of the Republic of China' (*Zhonghua Minguo Linshi Zhengfu*, 1937–40) in Hebei, Henan, Shanxi, and Shandong, (3) the 'Inner-Mongolian Regional Coalition Autonomous Government' (*Mengjiang Lianhe Zizhi Zhengfu*, 1938–45),[8] and (4) Wang Jingwei's 'Nanjing Citizens' Government' (*Nanjing Guomin Zhengfu*, 1940–5), controlling Anhui, Jiangsu, Zhejiang, Hubei, Hunan and Jiangxi, and Guangdong. China was a mess.

The Republicans and Communists also faced internal splits. The Republicans ran two parallel governments, one in Wuhan under Wang Jingwei (1883–1944), Sun Ke (Sun Yat-sen's son, 1891–1973) and Song Ziwen (1894–1971); and the other in Nanjing under Chiang Kai-shek (1887–1975). During the Second World War (1940–45), the Republicans split into two governments again, one in Chongqing in China's deep west, led by Chiang Kai-shek; and the other, the Chinese *Régime de Vichy*, in Nanjing, headed by Wang Jingwei. In the Communist camp, there was an open rift and deadly power struggle between Zhang Guotao (1897–1979) and Mao Zedong in 1936.

---

[7] Li Jie, *Wenwu Beiyang* (*Achievements of the 'Northern Modern' Elite*) (Nanning: Guangxi Normal University Press, 2004), p. 109.

[8] Liu Jingzhong, *Huabei Riwei Zhengquan Yanjiu* (*The Japanese Puppet Regime in North China*) (Beijing: People's Press, 2007).

Consequently, during the first half of the twentieth century, China ran a war economy in which resource allocation was drastically and continuously distorted. Inflation and heavy taxation were common among all mini-states and belligerent parties without any exception. Despite harsh conditions for the economy, there was a silver lining: A strong growth was achieved in China's infrastructure in particular. From 1900 to 1927, China's railway lines increased 13-fold at a rate of 10 percent *per annum.*[9] China's 15 sample industrial items had year-by-year unbroken growth in value from 1912 to 1936,[10] and 16 main agricultural products held their yield records unbroken until 1957.[11] China's urban population doubled from 20.2 million (1911) to 41.2 million (1936); and China's urbanisation rate increased from 5.5 percent (1905) to 8.6 percent (1938).[12] The economy remained open. From 1919 to 1933 a total of 5.3 million Chinese went overseas to join the international labour market.[13]

The best performance occurred during the 'Nanjing Decade' from 1927/8 to 1937. China's GDP grew at nine percent a year,[14] not too far behind Japan at that time. Such a growth was partly state-led. The newly emerged Republican leader Chiang Kai-shek, who triumphed over all his rivals in the civil war, had ambitious long-term targets for agricultural and industrial outputs, modern education, and infrastructure. For example, technical degree courses were set to have 2.7 million graduates; rice, 756 million *shi*; wheat, 882 million *shi*; steel output, 28.5 million tons; coal, 515.9 million tons; cement, 70.7 million tons; and highways, 1.5 million kilometres.[15] The state role was most prominent in capital

---

[9] Wang Jingyu, *Zhongguo Jindai Jingjishi, 1895–1927* (*An Economic History of Early Modern China, 1895–1927*) (Beijing: People's Press, 2000), Vol. 3, pp. 2021–2.

[10] J. K. Chang, *Industrial Development in Pre-Communist China, A Quantitative Analysis* (Edinburg: University of Edinburg Press, 1969), pp. 60–1.

[11] Perkins, *Agricultural Development*, pp. 266–89.

[12] Cao, *History of Migration*, Vol. 6, p. 606.

[13] Li Changfu, *Zhongguo Zhimin Shi* (*A History of Chinese Settlement*) (Shanghai: Shanghai Books, 1984), pp. 323, 326.

[14] Chang, *Industrial Development*, p. 71; T. G. Rawski, *Economic Growth in Prewar China* (Berkeley: University of California Press, 1989), p. 274.

[15] Chiang Kai-shek, *China's Destiny and Chinese Economic Theory*, translated by Philip Jaffe (New York: Roy Publishers, 1947), pp. 174–8.

Table 60. Distribution of Outputs in Industrial GDP (%), 1921 and 1936.

	1921	1936
Consumer products	44.1	30.7
Mining	41.5	32.3
Metals	7.7	8.5
Electricity	5.4	22.1
Other	1.3	6.4
Total	100.0	100.0

Source: Liu Foding and Wang Yuru, *Zhongguo Jindaide Shichang Fayu Yu Jingji Zengzhang* (*Market Development and Economic Growth in Early Modern China*) (Beijing: Tertiary Education Press, 1996), p. 294.

formation and capital accumulation with 10 state-run banks (the 'Big Four' and six associated banks), which controlled over 70 percent of all assets in the banking sector.[16] Heavy industry was given the national priority, (see Table 60).

By 1936, China had had a total rail length of 21,800 kilometres, thanks to optimism among foreign investors.[17] China's locomotives and freight cars also grew by a factor of three.[18] Additionally, China's motor-road length tripled from 1927 to 1936, reaching 111,000 kilometres. Its overland transport system totalled 132,800 kilometres.[19] By 1936, the country also had 100,000 kilometre long telegraphic lines (as in 1932) and 2.7 million kilometre air links.[20] All these figures were comparable with India at that time.

---

[16] P. M. Coble, *The Shanghai Capitalists and the Nationalist Government* (Cambridge [MA]: Harvard University Press, 1980), p. 198.

[17] By the 1930s, foreign investors had poured a total of 943.5 million *yuan* in China's railway system in comparison with China's domestic investors' 180.2 million *yuan* capital stock (by 1927); see Wang, *Early Modern China*, Vol. 3, p. 2025; *cf.* Yang Yonggang, *Zhongguo Jindai Tielu Shi* (*A History of Railways in Early Modern China*) (Shanghai: Shanghai Books, 1997), pp. 3, 4.

[18] Chang, *Industrial Development*, p. 110; see also Tim Wright (ed.), *The Chinese Economy in the Early Twentieth Century* (New York: St Martin's Press, 1992), pp. 32, 67.

[19] Rawski, *Economic Growth in Prewar China*, pp. 209, 214, 217.

[20] Zheng Yukui, *Zhongguo Duiwai Maoyi He Gongye Fazhan* (*Growth in China's Foreign Trade and Industry*) (Shanghai: Shanghai Social Sciences Press, 1984), p. 39.

This period has also been dubbed as 'the Golden Age of the Chinese Bourgeoisie', who led strong growth in light industries especially textiles and food processing.[21]

The increasing industrial strength and competitiveness of coastal China was the key reason for the Japanese Army to attack China Proper in 1937 to stop China from becoming Japan's market rival in East Asia.[22]

However, the modern sector of the economy still claimed a small share of China's total output in value in the 1930s.[23] Modern banks had a market share of merely 2.4 percent in rural China where the traditional credit-providers were still dominated by pawnshops, native banks, and money lenders.[24] Within the manufacturing sector, modern factories claimed just 16 percent of the sectoral output value in the 1920s.[25] China's traditional agriculture still employed 75 percent of the country's total workforce (as of 1946).[26] China's GDP structure was as distinctively traditional as ever, with modern sector producing 7.4 percent of the country's total GDP.[27]

In this context, treaty ports like Shanghai were mere enclaves of modernity in a vast traditional rural economy despite the fact that in the 1930s, Shanghai housed 40 percent of China's modern industrial capital, 46 percent of China's modern industrial workers,[28] and 50 percent of China's modern industrial output (as in 1934).[29] After all, Shanghai's share in China's GDP was about 2–5 percent.[30] Moreover, Shanghai's 223,000 factory workers among its three million residents counted for less than

---

[21] Marie-Claire Bergere, *The Golden Age of the Chinese Bourgeoisie, 1911–1937* (Cambridge: Cambridge University Press, 1982).

[22] Kaoru Sugihara, 'Intra-Asian Trade and East Asia's Industrialisation, 1919–1939', *Working Papers in Economic History*, 44 (1998), London School of Economics and Political Sciences, pp. 25–57.

[23] Wright, *Chinese Economy*, p. 116; Mao came up with 10 percent; see Mao, 'Democratic Dictatorship', p. 1484. N. R. Lardy only accepted three percent; see Lardy, *Agriculture*, p. 7.

[24] Fairbank, *Cambridge History of China*, Vol. 12, p. 88.

[25] Wang, *Early Modern China*, Vol. 3, p. 1843.

[26] See Anon., *Mao Zedong's Thought*, p. 70; D. K. Lieu and Ta Cheun Liu, *China's Economic Stabilization and Reconstruction* (New Brunswick: Rutgers University Press, 1948), p. 5.

[27] National Bureau of Statistics, *Zhongguo Tongji Nianjian, 2002* (*China's Statistical Year Book, 2002*) (Beijing: China's Statistics Press, 2002), p. 51.

[28] Sun, *Early Modern Industries*, p. 1202.

[29] Huntley Dupre, 'Review of Robert W. Barnett's *Economic Shanghai: Hostage to Politics, 1937–1941*', *Journal of Farm Economics*, 24/4 (1942), p. 919.

[30] Derived from $Q/(1-Q) \cdot (1-P)/P$; where Q = Shanghai's GDP share, and P = Shanghai's population share.

8 percent of the city's total (as of the 1930s).[31] These workers were employed mainly to produce wage goods.[32] The majority of them were women and children who were almost certainly illiterate with handicapped labour productivity.

On the other hand, China's rural sector showed its extreme resiliency. A nation-wide survey shows that only 4.8 percent rural households migrated to other parts of the country. The rate of emigration in the north (5.5 percent) was slightly higher than that its southern counterparts (3.9 percent). Population pressure on farmland attributed 3.6 percent to all emigration cases; civil wars, 14.3 percent; disasters and income, 69.2 percent.[33] As the disaster and income problems hit everyone, emigration became a choice of landlords (17 percent of all cases), owner-farmers (29 percent), as well as tenants (35 percent).[34] This confirms how important the Qing disaster relief was regarding China's social stability.

2. Changes and Growth Disasters during the Maoist Era, 1949–76

Unlike the Republican Era when the late Qing approach of 'Chinese learning as the foundation and Western knowledge for utility' remained unchanged among the ruling elite, Mao's attitude was both anti-traditional and anti-Western. His solution for China's future growth and development was distinctively 'Soviet/Russian learning as both the foundation and for utility'. Stalin and Comintern's heavy involvement in the formation, financing, and development of the Communist Movement in China from 1918 onwards played a continuous and decisive role in Mao's choice (or no choice).[35]

---

[31] Based on Xu Xuejun, *Shanghai Jindai Shehui Jingji Fazhan Gaikuang, 1882–1931* (*A Survey of Shanghai's Socio-economic Development in Early Modern Times, 1882–1931*) (Shanghai: Shanghai Social Sciences Press, 1985), p. 275.

[32] *Ibid.*, p. 275.

[33] Lu Xiqi, 'Zhongguo Jindai Nongmin Litu Xianxiang Qianxi' (Causes for Rural Emigration in Early Modern China), *Zhongguo Jingjishi Yanjiu* (*Research into Chinese Economic History*), 3 (1995), pp. 91–101.

[34] *Ibid.*, p. 95.

[35] It all begun with two Soviet agents sent to China in 1918, identified as A. A. Ivanov and S. A. Polevoi (or А. А. Иванов and С. А. Полевой); see Institute of Modern History of the Chinese Academy of Social Sciences (ed.), *Wusi Yundong Huiyilu* (*Memoirs of the May Fourth Movement*) (Beijing: China's Social Sciences Press, 1979), Vol. 1, p. 340.

The Soviet/Russian approach was (1) to replace an existing regime (be it a monarchy or a republic) with a dictatorship ('proletarian dictatorship') of a party-state (or 'the rule of a single party') whose interests overrules that of society if the latter does not agree,[36] (2) to substitute private ownership with state and 'collective' ownerships, (3) to abandon the market and establish economic planning for resource allocation in the economy, and (4) to remove individual autonomy and incentives in order to impose uniformity in thought and behaviour regarding production, consumption, and distribution. The Soviet/Russian model was completely incompatible with either 'Chinese learning as the foundation and Chinese knowledge for utility' or 'Chinese learning as the foundation and Western knowledge for utility' with which private ownership, market exchange, and individual incentives were all functional. Such changes were said to be imperative for a new China of industrialisation/modernity, egalitarianism, and universal affluence.[37]

Despite its mass movement appearance, the Soviet/Russian model was operated by a tiny minority from the top, as openly admitted by Mao himself in 1958,

Among China's 600 million population and 12 million party members, only a tiny minority of a few million really believe in the socialist route that we have decided to take.[38]

In 1959, he went on to say that,

The truth was often not in the hands of the majority but in the hands of minority ... But we represented the truth and China's final destination.[39]

---

[36] Ideologically, the party-state automatically represents people's interests. Thus, the party-state often pretends to represent nationalism. The party-state is always right in an alleged 'party *vis-à-vis* individual dichotomy'. Any other interests that are different from that of the party-state are overruled. This Soviet/Russian 'state as the foundation of the ruler' (*guoben*) is the antithesis of the Confucian 'people as the foundation of the ruler' (*minben*).

[37] In 1964, Zhou Enlai, Mao's Premier, announced at the Third National People's Congress 'four modernisations' (*sige xiandaihua*) in agriculture, industry, military, and science and technology. The same plan was announced again at the Fourth and Fifth National People's Congresses in 1975 and 1978, respectively.

[38] Anon., *Mao Zedong's Thought*, p. 170.

[39] Institute of Documents of the Chinese Communist Party Central Committee (ed.), *Mao Zedong Wenxuan* (*Collected Works of Mao Zedong*) (Beijing: People's Press, 1999), Vol. 8, p. 338.

The minority nature of the Soviet/Russian model required inevitably personal cult to ensure its acceptance by the general public. Also, without the market there is no need for reliable and objective feedback for economic decision-makers. The personal cult of Mao was confirmed by Peter Vladimirov (Chinese name 'Sun Ping', 1905–53), Mao's key liaison with Moscow in 1942–5:

Mao Tse-tung's 'erudition' makes him almost a prophet.[40]

Mao Tse-tung is being identified with the revolution, and truth in general. For party members Mao Tse-tung is the apostle of their revolutionary belief; he is infallible ... They believe without understanding because it comes from Mao Tse-tung.[41]

Compatible with the personal cult was a top–down party machine for social control. Unlike the Qing state, which was small, cheap, weak, and tolerant, the Maoist government was larger, expensive, strong and intrusive. It reached all villages and urban streets alike. Mao's bureaucracy had one million functionaries in 1949, 10 million in 1958, and 15 million upon his death in 1976.[42] Mao's bureaucrats amounted to three percent of China's total population,[43] about 450 times that of the Qing. Its annual growth rate of was 10.6 percent, about five times of China's population growth rate during the same period.

The short–term efficiency of the Soviet/Russian approach was demonstrated by its military victory over the Republicans during the 1946–9 Civil War. Decisions — even irrational ones — were able to be implemented swiftly be they on wars, foreign debts and political purges. Typically, Mao decided to join 'someone else's' war in Korea one year after the establishment of the Communist regime, a decision that resulted in China's heavy debt to the Soviet Union (6.6 billion Roubles).

---

[40] Vladimirov, *Diaries*, p. 99.
[41] Peter Vladimirov, *The Vladimirov Diaries, Yenan, China: 1942–1945* (New York: Doubleday, 1975), p. 483.
[42] Li Yi, *The Structure and Evolution of Chinese Social Stratification* (Lanham [Maryland]: University Press of America, 2005), pp. 66, 83.
[43] *Ibid.*, p. 65; Hongyung Lee, *From Revolutionary Cadres to Party Technocrats in Socialist China* (Berkeley: University of California Press, 1991), pp. 207–9.

It took the country 15 years to repay it.[44] Mao was also notorious for his intolerance towards any resistance against his dictatorship (e.g., the '1951–2 Three-Anti and Five-Anti Movement', the '1950–3 Suppression of Anti-revolutionaries', the '1957 Anti-Rightist Movement', and 'Destroying Four Olds' during the '1966–76 Great Proletarian Cultural Revolution') and against his party and bureaucracy (e.g., the '1955 Purge of the Hu Feng Anti-Party Clique', the '1957 Internal Rectification Purge', the '1959 Lushan Purge against the Party Right-Wingers', the '1964 Four Cleansings', and 'Overthrowing Capitalist Routers inside the Party' during the '1966–76 Great Proletarian Cultural Revolution'). These were very effective self-inflicted destructions of China's human capital, on an industrial scale and lasting for years.

The rational implementation, impact, and externalities of the Soviet/Russian system have been controversial between pro-Mao and anti-Mao camps simply because Mao's regime developed the unclear weapon (1964) on the one hand; and on the other not only closed all the high schools and universities (1966–76), but also starved 30–40 million ordinary peasants to death (1959–61), known as 'the Great Leap Famine'. Both were done 'efficiently'.

To transcend the on-going debate, one can examine the three promises — industrialisation/modernity, egalitarianism, and universal affluence — to assess the performance of Maoism. First, at best, Mao's regime achieved anything but industrialisation. The main evidence comes from China's official data for employment. With 77–84 percent of China's workforce working in the primary (mainly agricultural) sector (see Table 61),[45] the Maoist economy was as rural as that of the Republican Era when 75 percent of China's workforce was employed by the agricultural sector (as of 1946).

A real structural change occurred only after Deng Xiaoping's reforms. In 1997, the share of rural employment dropped to 50 percent of China's total

---

[44] It has been revealed that Mao's regime raised 6.6 billion Roubles (1.7 billion US Dollars) debt from the Soviet Union (about 15 Roubles per head of China's population of the time). Ninety-five percent of the debt was for the military; see Shen Zhihua, 'Guanyu 20 Shiji 50 Niandai Sulian Yuanhua Daikuande Lishi Kaocha' (Soviet Loans to China in the 1950s), *Zhongguo Jingjishi Yanjiu* (*Research into Chinese Economic History*), 3 (2002), pp. 83–93.
[45] Ling, *No More Hesitation*, p. 102; National Bureau of Statistics, *Statistical Year Book, 2003*, p. 34.

Table 61.   China's Employment Structures, 1952–75.

	1952	1957	1962	1965	1970	1975
Total workforce*	207.3	237.7	259.1	286.7	344.3	381.7
Primary sector[†] (% in total)	83.5	81.2	82.1	81.6	80.8	77.2
Secondary sector[†] (% in total)	7.4	9.0	8.0	8.4	10.2	13.5
Tertiary sector[†] (% in total)	9.1	9.8	9.9	10.0	9.0	9.3

Source: National Bureau of Statistics, *Zhongguo Laodong Tongji Nianjian, 2004* (*China's Labour Primary sector Statistical Year Book, 2004*) (Beijing: China's Statistics Press, 2004), p. 7.
Note: *Workers in million. [†]The three sectors are proxies for agriculture, industry and services.

Table 62.   Slow Growth in Industrial Workforce, 1959–74.

Year	Industrial workforce (I)	Total population (II)	I/II
1959	45.5	672.1	6.8%
1964	36.4	705.0	5.2
1969	40.9	806.7	5.1
1974	59.1	908.6	6.5
Annual growth (%)	1.76	2.03	0.87

Source: Data for the industrial workforce is based National Bureau of Statistics, *Zhongguo Laodong Tongji Nianjian, 1998* (*China's Labour Statistical Year Book, 1998*) (Beijing: China's Statistics Press, 1998), p. 81. Data for China's population figures are based on National Bureau of Statistics, *Statistical Year Book, 1986*, p. 91.

workforce.[46] China finally showed some signs of moving towards industrialisation and modernity. But that happened only after Mao and Maoism.

Meanwhile, Mao's industrial workforce was frozen below seven percent of China's total population. The increase in the industrial workforce (1.76 percent per year) was even lower than China's population growth (2.03 percent per year), suggesting that China's industrialisation process stalled (Table 62).

Worse still, among those who were employed in the industrial sector, a considerable proportion was technically redundant:

From the early years of Mao's regime, China practised a policy of low pay with over-employment called 'three jobs to be shared by five workers' in order to

---

[46]National Bureau of Statistics, *Zhongguo Tongji Nianjian, 2003* (*China's Statistical Year Book, 2003*) (Beijing: China's Statistics Press, 2003), p. 34.

reduce unemployment. This was accompanied by the 'iron rice-bowel' system. ...
A great many enterprises allowed workers to idle and efficiency to decline.[47]

Towards the end of Mao's era, about 30 percent of China's urban workforce was made redundant that way.[48] If one discounts the redundant share of the workforce, the affective industrial workforce was in the region of only 40 million in a total population of 900 million.

Even so, urban unemployment was very high: In 1977, the urban sector had as many as 15 million young people waiting for jobs, or an over-supply of labour by a quarter.[49] By 1979, it rose up to 20 million, or an over-supply of labour by a third.[50] In 1980, the number of unemployed young people reached 30 million or an over-supply of labour by a half.[51]

Yet, we have been told that the aforementioned 40–60 million industrial workers were responsible for 60 to 70 percent of China's total GDP.[52] If this was true, Mao's urban industrial workforce had to be the most productive one in the world.

The lack of industrial progress is also reflected by stagnation in urbanisation under Mao's rule. Officially, China's urban residents accounted for 18 percent of China's total population (as of 1978).[53] This represents a growth at only 0.3 percent a year from 1949, slower than that of the general population.[54] This was a result of a deliberate anti-urbanisation approach, announced in *the 1956 to 1957 Guideline for National Agricultural Development*.

---

[47] *Ibid.*, p. 479.
[48] Based on the situation in the mid-1990s as a proxy; see Gu Xin, 'Danwei Fuli Shehui Zhuyi Yu Zhongguode Zhiduxing Shiye' (Enterprise-based Welfare Socialism and China's Structural Unemployment), *Xinhua Wenzhai* (*Xinhua Compilation*), 11 (1998), p. 61; Niu Renliang, 'Lun Zai Jiuye' (Re-Employment), *Xinhua Wenzhai* (*Xinhua Compilation*), 2 (1998), p. 56.
[49] Yu Guangyuan (ed.), *China's Socialist Modernization* (Beijing: Foreign Language Press, 1984), p. 584.
[50] Xue Muqiao, *Xue Muqiao Huiyilu* (*Memoir of Xue Muqiao*) (Tianjin: Tianjin People's Press, 1996), p. 348.
[51] *Ibid.*, p. 478.
[52] National Bureau of Statistics, *Zhongguo Jingji Nianjian, 2002* (*China Statistical Year Book, 2002*) (Beijing: China Statistics Press, 2002), pp. 51–2.
[53] Elisabeth Croll, *The Family Rice Bowl, Food and the Domestic Economy in China* (Geneva: UNRISD, 1983), p. 111; National Bureau of Statistics, *Statistical Year Book, 2003*, p. 97.
[54] Based on Liu and Yeh, *Economy of the Chinese Mainland*, p. 212; Zhong Dajun, *Guomin Daiyu Bupingdeng Shenshi* (*Assessment of Unequal Entitlement amongst Citizens*) (Beijing: China's Workers' Press, 2002), pp. 224, 242.

All secondary and primary school graduates in cities must answer the state's call to go to rural regions to partake in agricultural production. ... To work in the countryside is extremely necessary and exceptionally glorious.[55]

The man-made ceiling for urbanisation was temporarily broken in 1958 during the 'Great Leap Forward' when 20 million workers were hastily recruited from rural China. But by 1965 not only were all of them sent back to their villages, but two million urban students were also re-settled in the rural sector.[56] Between 1967 and 1977, Mao's government sent another 16 million urban students to the countryside.[57] Clearly, Mao's state was incapable of creating urban jobs. Real progress occurred only after Deng Xiaoping's reforms. From 1980 to 2000, China's urban population increased at 3.2 percent a year, over 10 times faster than Mao's record.[58]

In the agriculture sector, very little progress was made towards modernity, as official documents have admitted that,

[Under Mao] for more than 20 years, there was virtually no progress in labour productivity. The enormous waste of labour power presents agriculture a serious problem.[59]

And,

Changes in the agricultural output clearly reveal that People's Communes performed worse than rural co-operatives; ... co-operatives performed worse than mutual aid groups; and mutual aid groups performed worse than private farmers.[60]

---

[55] Chinese Communist Party Central Committee, *1956 Nian Dao 1957 Nian Quanguao Nongye Fazhan Gangyao* (*The 1956 to 1957 Guideline for National Agricultural Development*) (Nanjing: Jiangsu People's Press, 1956), Entry 38. This guideline was drafted by Mao himself.

[56] Zhang Hua and Su Caiqing (eds.), *Huizhou Wedge, Zhongguo Simian Wedge Benxi Yu Fans* (*Recollection of the Decade of Cultural Revolution, Analyses and Soul-Researching*) (Beijing: Chinese Communist Party History Press, 2000), Vol. 2, p. 889.

[57] *Ibid.,* Vol. 2, p. 890.

[58] National Bureau of Statistics, *Statistical Year Book, 2003*, p. 97.

[59] Yu, *China's Socialist Modernization*, pp. 264–5.

[60] Li Honglin, 'Wode Lilun Gongzuozhe Jingli' (My Experience as a Party Theorist), *Yanhuang Chunqiu* (*History of Chinese*), 11 (2008), p. 21.

Table 63.   China's Food Exports (in 10,000 Tons).

Time period	South China	North China	China's total
Pre-collectivisation			
1953–5	688.5	204.3	892.8
Post-collectivisation			
1956–60	1,950.5	−472.0*	1,478.5
1961–5	669.5	−2,013.5	−1,344.0
1966–70	942.0	−796.5	145.5
1971–5	952.5	−1,159.0	−206.5
1976–8	−22.8	−1,106.4	−1,129.2

Source: Based on Contemporary Agricultural History Study Group, Rural Economy Institute, Ministry of Agriculture (ed.), *Dangdai Zhongguo Nongye Biange Yu Fazhan Yanjiu* (*A Study of Agricultural Reforms and Development in Contemporary China*) (Beijing: China's Agriculture Press, 1998), p. 251.
Note: *Negative value means food imports due to food deficits.

As a result, food supply was tight under Mao's rule. After collectivisation, North China stopped food exports. At the end of the Cultural Revolution, South China followed suit (Table 63).

In the industrial sector — the 'darling' of the Maoist economy — modernity moved very slowly. It seemed promising between 1953 and 1957, when the 'first five-year plan' was implemented: Mao's government contracted 156 projects to the Soviet Union to modernise China's industry, mainly for the military. But in the wake of Mao's rift with Nikita Khrushchev, Soviet Union terminated all the projects in 1960.[61] Earlier, Mao's involvement in the Korean War closed China's doors to the West. Mao turned to 'self reliance' whose performance record was poor due to a lack of understanding of economic growth in general and modernity in particular.

---

[61] Earlier in 1950, the Soviets provided Mao's government with a US$ 300 million loan with one percent annual interest plus US$ 30 million annual capital repayment for 13 years; see Zhao Xuezhang (ed.), *Yong Baozhi Xie Lishi, Jiefanghou* (*History Seen on Newspapers, pre-1949*) (Taipei: Seadove Publishing Co., 2007), pp. 70–1.

First of all, basic economic laws such as the economies of scale were ignored. Mao favoured small enterprises in iron and steel, coal mines, cement, electricity and chemical fertilizers.[62] By 1975, a third of all counties had some sort of iron and steel plants; and 90 percent of all counties built farming machines such as tractors and water pumps.[63] Often than not these plants produced either low quality products or nothing at all.[64] During the 1970s, a third of China's tractors were reported to have broken down permanently, another third suffered technical defects, and only a third worked properly.[65] These percentages were similar to the state-owned enterprises: Only a third functioned properly and made money. If this was not enough, during the 1960s and 1970s Mao pushed hard to re-locate China's heavy and military industries from the coastal regions to the mountainous interior. The strategy disintegrated factories whose divisions were spread out miles apart in the most difficult terrain.[66] By 1971, less than a third of such projects had been completed, and less than eight percent of production targets were met.[67] Growth in heavy industry in particular was poorly understood, planned and executed. The whole process was marred by 'false reports on costs and profits' and 'reckless spending once money was allotted by the state';[68] and 'factories produced for inventories'.[69] In 1971, China's total steel inventory amounted to 8.8 million tons, accounting for 52 percent of China home output and imported quantity put together.[70] These inventories were routinely included in China's industrial GDP to boost the number.

---

[62] *Ibid.*, Vol. 1, pp. 437–8.
[63] *Ibid.*, p. 418.
[64] *Ibid.*, p. 442.
[65] *Ibid.*, p. 441.
[66] *Ibid.*, p. 11.
[67] *Ibid.*, p. 442.
[68] Yu, *China's Socialist Modernization*, pp. 471–2.
[69] Zong Fengming, *Zhao Ziyang Ruanjinzhongde Tanhua* (*Conversations with Zhao Ziyang under House Arrest*) (Hong Kong: Open Press, 2007), p. 243.
[70] Zhang and Su, *Decade of Cultural Revolution*, Vol. 1, p. 446.

Secondly, Mao did not seem to understand the role of human capital and technology. He systematically persecuted intellectuals to the point of closing down schools and universities and sending down professors and students to the countryside for manual labour during the time when China's modernisation desperately needed the educated stratum. As a result, technology contributed negatively at −1.2 percent per year to China's growth under Mao.[71] In comparison, in the post-Mao's era, technology contributed on average 38 percent to China's industrial GDP growth.[72] Similarly, China's capital productivity from 1952 to 1978 increased −3.1 percent a year; and China's total factor productivity, −1.4 percent a year.[73] Mao's economic planners and allocators depended heavily on capital input to generate growth: 70 percent of the growth came from capital input.[74] Therefore, a quarter of China's annual GDP was reinvested annually. It is known that one *yuan* investment normally produced one *yuan* GDP after 1957.[75] So, after each round of re-investment China's GDP would increase a quarter, *ceteris paribus*. After 25 years (1952–1977), China's capital stock should have grown to a factor of 265 from its starting size (24.1 billion *yuan* in 1952, constant price) to a total of 6,379.3 billion *yuan*.[76] In reality, however, the registered state-owned fixed capital assets (*guding zichan*) in 1978 were mere 448.2 billion *yuan* (constant prices).[77] The amount was seven percent of the expected total. The rest had been wasted investment. The aggregate compounded waste was about 19 years' total GDP of China at the starting level (1952), a judgement that the official view agreed:

> A high rate of accumulation and large-scale capital construction alone cannot bring about sustained fast growth and good economic result.[78]

---

[71] *Ibid.*, p. 448.

[72] *Ibid.*, p. 449.

[73] Liu Xin and Liu Gang, *Zhongguo Jingjixue Sanshinian* (*Economics in China in the Past Thirty Years*) (Beijing: China's Finance and Economy Press, 2008), p. 115.

[74] Gu Shutang, *Shehuizhuyi Shichang Jingji Lilun Yanjiu* (*A Model for Socialist Market Economy*) (Beijing: China's Audit Press, 2001), p. 448.

[75] Ministry of Finance, *Zhongguo Caizheng Nianjian, 1997* (*China's Financial Year Book, 1997*) (Beijing: China's Finance Magazine Press, 1997), p. 479; National Bureau of Statistics, *Statistical Year Book, 2002*, p. 51.

[76] National Bureau of Statistics, *Statistical Year Book, 2002*, p. 51.

[77] Ministry of Finance, *Financial Year Book, 1997*, p. 479.

[78] Yu, *China's Socialist Modernization*, p. 458.

Similarly, if one believes in the official figures of nine percent a year in GDP growth during Mao's era,[79] the economy in 1978 should have been 12 times as large as 1949. This was however not the reality.

In the rural sector, capital accumulation and investment were commonly wasteful just like in the state sector:

> *The utilization rate of our farm machinery is very low, about 70 percent. Approximately 100,000 to 200,000 tractors and 40 to 50 million hp [horsepower] of machinery are not used. Chemical fertilizers are not available in full variety or adequate proportion. ... There is, of course, poor management, plus astonishing waste in capital construction.*[80]

The combination of a redundant workforce and wasted capital investment became ever apparent after Deng Xiaoping's reforms. In 2004, foreign-invested enterprises employed just three percent of China's total workforce (24 million), but were responsible for about a third of China's total GDP.[81] Theoretically, with Western efficiency, China would only need 40 percent of its capital investment and 10 percent of its workforce to support Mao's economy. The waste under Maoism was thus 60 percent of the capital investment and 90 percent of the workforce. Whichever way one looks at it, the Soviet/Russian system was highly counter-productive. Hence, the first aspect of this alien system failed in China.

---

[79] National Bureau of Statistics, *Zhongguo Tongji Nianjian, 1987* (*China's Statistical Year Book, 1987*) (Beijing: China's Statistics Press, 1987), pp. 36, 38. Also se Mark Selden and Patti Eggleston (eds.), *The People's Republic of China: A Documentary History of Revolutionary Change* (New York: Monthly Review Press, 1979), p. 135.

[80] Yu, *China's Socialist Modernization*, p. 267.

[81] John Whalley and Xian Xin, 'China's FDI and Non-FDI Economies and the Sustainability of Future High Chinese Growth', *Working Paper No. 12249* (Cambridge [MA]: National Bureau of Economic Research, 2006); K. H. Zhang, 'Foreign Direct Investment and Economic Growth in China: A Panel Data Study for 1992–2004', A Paper for 'WTO, China and Asian Economies Conference', the University of International Business and Economies, Beijing, June, 2006; James Laurenceson and Kam Ki Tang, 'The FDI-Income Growth Nexus: A Review of the Chinese Experience', *Discussion Paper No. 9* (March 2007), School of Economics, the University of Queensland.

Table 64.   Inequality in China, 1952–1978.

Year	Gini coefficient	Index
1952	0.25	100
1958	0.37	148
1978	0.31	124

Source: Zhang Daoge, 'Bufen Xianfude Gaige Xiaoying' (Effect of 'Allowing a Few to Become Rich First'), *Xinhua Wenzhai* (*Xinhua Compilation*), 4 (1994), p. 41.

Table 65.   Income Differences within Bureaucracies, 1935–1983.

Eras	Ratio between the top and bottom ranks
Chiang's Republic (1935)	14.5:1
Chiang's Republic (1946)	12.0:1
Mao's People's Republic (1956)	28.0:1
Deng's People's Republic (1983)	15.1:1

Source: R. M. Marsh, *The Mandarin: The Circulation of Elite in China, 1600–1900* (London: The Free Press, 1980), p. 63; Li, *Chinese Social Stratification*, pp. 49, 61–2, 107–8; Cui, *Changes in Political and Social Structures*, Vol. 3, p. 1483; and Li, *Chinese Social Stratification*, pp. 106–8.

The second aspect, egalitarianism, did not perform that well either. Firstly, 'omniparity in income' during Mao's rule is a myth. Measured by Gini Coefficients, China's was increasingly unequal (see Table 64).

Within the bureaucracy, income gap increased under Mao's rule (see Table 65). Across the communist ranks, the greatest income differential was 88 times.[82] In the rural sector, 60 million local bureaucrats and functionaries (about seven percent of China's rural population) earned about 30 percent of the total income, four times over the sectoral par.[83]

There was a hidden and institutionalised inequality in the form of 'scissors pricing differentiation' (*jiandao cha*) with state-run arbitrage (*tonggou tongxiao*) between monopsonic procurement of agricultural

---

[82] Chen Mingyuan, *Zhishifenzi Yu Renminbi Shidai* (*Intellectuals and the Age of People's Currency*) (Shanghai: Wenhui Press, 2006), pp. 58, 61.
[83] Ling Zhijun, *Lishi Buzi Paihuai* (*History, No More Hesitation*) (Beijing: People's Press, 1997), p. 332.

outputs at a low price and monopolistic sale of industrial goods and services at a high price. This adopted Soviet system began in 1950 with a list of 230 rural products subject to government monopsony,[84] staple food being the main item with top priority.[85] The total gain from this scissors pricing under Mao's rule has been estimated between 428.3 and 800 billion *yuan*.[86] From 1952 to 1978, the net increase in the Maoist state-owned capital stock was 424.1 billion *yuan* (or 448.2 billion yuan in constant prices).[87] Given that China did not receive foreign direct investment during this period, most of the increase in state assets almost certainly came from the peasantry with institutionalised unequal exchange.

Secondly, there was a strong city-bias in public goods provision of health care, pensions, scientific research, education, and disaster relief. The beneficiaries of Mao's showcase of 'iron rice-bowl' were no more than a quarter of China's total population. To make sure that the rural sector did not dip into the urban bowl, the Maoist state implemented a strict economic apartheid to shield off peasants from going into cities. The policy was embodied by the 'domicile registrations' (*hukou*) under the 1958 *Decree of Domicile Registration* to ban on people's social mobility.

China's scientists and technicians under Mao were in general poorly funded and in low quality: The government spending on research

---

[84] Ling, *No More Hesitation*, p. 137.

[85] Croll, *Family Rice Bowl*, p. 78.

[86] Wen Tiejun, *Zhongguo Nongcun Jiben Jingji Zhidu Yanjiu* (*Basic Institutions in Rural China*) (Beijing: China's Economy Press, 2000), p. 177; Li Wei, *Nongye Shengyu Yu Gongyehua Ziben Jilei* (*Agricultural Surpluses and Capital Accumulation for Industrialisation*) (Kunming: Yunnan People's Press, 1993), pp. 302–3; Wang Gengjin and Zhang Xuansan, *Woguo Nongye Xiandaihua Yu Jilei Wenti Yanjiu* (*Agricultural Modernisation and Capital Accumulation*) (Taiyuan: Shanxi Economy Press, 1993), pp. 75–6; Cui Xiaoli, 'Tongguo Tongxiao Yu Gongye Jilei' (Government Monopsonic Procurement and Monopolistic Sale and Industrial Capital Accumulation), *Zhongguo Jingjishi Yanjiu* (*Research into Chinese Economic History*), 4 (1988), p. 144; Zhang Xiangshu, Zhou Wenbin, and Zhou Wenbiao, *Zhongguo Nongye Jubian Yu Zhanlue Xuanze* (*Huge Changes in and Strategic Choices for China's Agriculture*) (Beijing: China's Price Press, 1993), p. 47.

[87] Wu Li, '1949–1978 Nian Zhongguo Jiandaocha Cha-e Bianzheng' (Assessment of the Gain from Scissors Pricing in 1949–1978), *Zhongguo Jingjishi Yanjiu* (*Research into Chinese Economic History*), 4 (2001), pp. 3–12.

(including that of military technology) was normally below five percent of the government annual budget; and over half of scientists and technicians only received polytechnic education or lower.[88] Meanwhile, professionals were not considered trustworthy politically and were the easy and reper toire targets for Mao's purges.

In terms of education, the best record of Mao's education provision was a literacy rate of 64 percent in 1964. A third of Mao's population remained illiterate. A government survey in the 1980s reveals Mao's legacy in rural education: A great many rural schools made of dark class-rooms, earth tables and dirty kids; and teachers receiving irregular pay.[89] Only in 2000, were over 90 percent of the rural Chinese able to read and write.[90] This was simply because rural schools were all sponsored by local communities collectively. The state provision was but a lip service.

Moreover, there was no earmarked fund for citizens' health care during Mao's era. Modern medicine was all produced by state-run pharmaceutical firms and monopolistically priced. In 1981, entire China had just two million hospital beds and 1.2 million registered medical doctors for a population of over one billion.[91] On average, there were merely five hos-pital beds and three doctors for every 10,000 people, which places Mao's China together with current developing countries such as Afghanistan (as of 2001), Cambodia (2004), Guatemala (2003), Myanmar (2000), and Yemen (2003).[92] Empirically, a large sample from the World Health Organization reveals that to reach a life expectancy level of over 60 years, a country needs an average of 26 hospital beds per 10,000 people.

---

[88] National Bureau of Statistics, *Zhongguo Keji Tongji Nianjian, 1991* (*China's Statistical Year Book of Science and Technology, 1991*) (Beijing: China's Statistics Press, 1992), p. 24; Ma Hong (ed.), *2000 Niande Zhongguo Kexue Jishu* (*China's Science and Technology in 2000*) (Beijing: Social Sciences Press, 1988), p. 5.

[89] Hu Qili, 'Zhonggong Zhongyang Guanyu Jiaoyu Tizhi Gaigede Jueding Chutai Qianhou' (How Was Educational Reform Decided by the Chinese Communist Party Central Committee), *Yanhuang Chunqiu* (*History of Chinese*), 12 (2008), p. 3.

[90] National Bureau of Statistics, *Zhongguo Nongcun Zhuhu Diancha Nianjian, 2002* (*China's Rural Households Survey Year Books, 2002*) (Beijing: China's Statistics Press, 2002), p. 11; National Bureau of Statistics, *Statistical Year Book, 2003*, p. 99.

[91] Yu, *China's Socialist Modernization*, p. 740.

[92] World Health Organization, *World Health Statistics 2006* (Geneva: WHO, 2006), pp. 59–61.

To reach a life expectancy level of 70 years, a country needs an average of 40.6 hospital beds per 10,000 people.[93] China's official life expectancy figures for Mao's era are hence dubious. In a 2006 report, the United Nations re-figured the life expectancy under Mao to around 54 years, and not 65.[94]

The rural population had no medical cover from the state. This was openly admitted by Mao himself in 1965:

The Ministry of Health serves only 15 percent of China's population, most of who are 'aristocrats' [laoye]. All the peasants are not served. They have no doctor or medicine.[95]

His simple solution was described as:

Primary school graduates will be good enough to receive three-year medical training. ... They will be affordable by peasants.[96]

After 1966, a large number of 'barefoot doctors' were produced. The peasantry still had to pay for these barefoot doctors no matter how cheap they became.

As a result, Mao's China had very high infant mortality rate. In 1965, the rate was 165 per 1,000.[97] The same level of infant mortality in the 2000s' was applicable to only the poorest countries such as Afghanistan, Angola, Liberia, Niger, Sierra Leone, and Somalia, where life expectancy levels were around 40 years.[98] China's infant mortality rate also only declined sharply after 1977. By 1987, it reached the level of 40 per 1,000 births.[99]

---

[93] *Ibid.*, p. 28.
[94] United Nations' Population Division, *World Population Prospects: The 2006 Revision*, available on line at: http://www.un.org/esa/population/publications/wpp2006/wpp2006.htm.
[95] Anon., *Mao Zedong's Thought*, p. 615.
[96] *Ibid.*, p. 616.
[97] D. H. Perkins, 'Reforming China's Economic System', *Journal of Economic Literature*, 26/2 (1988), pp. 638, 640.
[98] World Health Organization, *World Health Statistics 2006*, pp. 22–6.
[99] Joint Committee of Congress of the United States, *China's Economic Dilemma in the 1990s* (New York: M. E. Sharp, 1993), p. 236.

Table 66. Disaster Relief Funds in Government Budget, 1952–75 (in Billion *Yuan*, Constant Prices).

Year	Relief expenses (I)	Total expenditure (II)	I/II %
1952	0.1	17.6	0.6
1957	0.2	30.4	0.7
1960	0.4	65.4	0.6
1965	0.6	46.6	1.3
1970	—	64.9	—
1975	0.6	82.0	0.7

Source: Ministry of Finance, *Financial Year Book*, 2000, pp. 392–3, 402, 416–7.

Table 67. Nominal and Real Wages in the State Sector, 1957–78.

Year	Nominal wage (annual)	Index	Real wage (1957 Price)*	Index
1957	637	100	637	100
1961	537	71	493	77
1965	652	93	539	85
1970	609	88	429	67
1976	605	86	327	51
1978	644	88	310	49

Source: Based on V. D. Lippit, *The Economic Development of China* (Armonk, New York and New York: M. E. Sharpe, 1987), p. 150.

Note: * Conversion is based on the average inflation rate of 2.01% per year for the period of 1950 to 1978, based on Li, 'Macro Control', pp. 49–50.

Furthermore, the rural population had no state pension. The elderly depended on their families for support. The Maoist disaster relief took just 0.6–1.3 percent of the state expenditure (see Table 66). There is no evidence that Mao's state provided any sizeable famine relief during the '1959–62 Great Leap Famine'.

Finally, Mao's regime failed spectacularly the third aspect of universal affluence, too. By 1978, half of China's population had lived either on or below the official poverty line.[100] In the privileged urban sector, workers' wages were halved under Mao's rule (see Tables 67 and 68).

---

[100] Chen Zongsheng, *Shouru Chabie Pinkun Ji Shiye (Income Differentiation, Poverty and Unemployment* (Tianjin: Nankai University Press, 2000), pp. 132–3.

Table 68. Decline in Dependent-Supporting Capacity per Wage Worker, 1957–77.

Year	Average family (persons)	Dependents (persons)
Pre-1949	6.9 (100)	4.0 (100)
1957	4.5 (65)	3.3 (83)
1964	5.8 (84)	3.4 (85)
1970	—	2.5 (63)
1977	4.5 (65)	2.1 (53)

Source: For pre-1949, see Cao, *Demographic History*, Vol. 6, p. 516. For 1989 and 2000, see National Bureau of Statistics, *Statistical Year Book, 2003*, pp. 341, 345. For other stated years, see Cui Xiaoli, 'Xinzhongguo Chengxiang Guanxide Jingji Jichu Yu Chengshihua Xianxiang' (The Economic Basis of the Urban–Rural Relationship and Urbanisation in New China), *Zhongguo Jinjishi Yanjiu* (*Study of Chinese Economic History*), 4 (1997), pp. 17–18.

In the rural sector, it was very common for individual peasants to come out empty-handed even in a good year with a bumper harvest, known as 'no income increase after output increase' (*zengchan bu zengshou*).[101] In a 1978 survey, of 803.2 million collective farmers, 97 percent had a cash income between 0.1 and 0.2 *yuan* per day, only enough for a candle or a visit to a public bath.[102] In another account, two-third of the peasantry had their living standards lowered from the 1950s' level and one-third even lowered than the 1930s.[103] Nation-wide, there was tyranny of austerity with foods and housing (see Table 69). Not until Mao's death did availability of basic items for ordinary citizens in China improve.[104]

In 1978, China-wide urban benchmark daily calorie intake was 2,009 kilocalories of which 1,750 kilocalories came from cereals (83 percent of all calories).[105] This food intake level was the equivalent to 57 percent and 67 percent of the calorie intakes of wage workers during the 1930s in Wuhan and Shanghai, respectively.[106] The dietary structure (i.e., the share

[101] Gao, *Quiet Rebellion*, p. 73.
[102] Ling, *No More Hesitation*, pp. 102–3.
[103] *Ibid.*, p. 103.
[104] Joint Committee of Congress of the United States, *China's Economic Dilemma*, pp. 396–8.
[105] Croll, *Family Rice Bowl*, p. 211.
[106] Liu and Yeh, *Economy of the Chinese Mainland*, p. 31; Li *et al.*, *Social Surveys*, Vol. 1, pp. 35, 47, 276, 386; Vol. 2, p. 829.

Table 69. Basic Consumption per Capita, 1937 vs. 1952–78.

Year	Grain*	Oil*	Meat*	Fish*	Housing (U)	Housing (R)
1937	307.0	—	13.6	—	—	—
1957	203.1	2.4	1.6	4.3	4.5	11.3
1966	190.5	1.8	7.1	—	—	—
1978	195.5	1.6	1.2	3.4	3.6	8.1

Source: Based on Yu Guangyan (ed.), *China's Socialist Modernization* (Beijing: Foreign Language Press, 1984), p. 12; Zhao Deqin, 'Zhongguo Jingji Wushinian Fazhande Lujing Jieduan Yu Jiben Jingyan' (Path, Stages and Main Lessons from the 50-year Long Growth of the Chinese Economy), *Zhongguo Jingjishi Yanjiu* (*Study of Chinese Economic History*), 1 (2000), pp. 73–86. Data for 1937 and 1965 are based on Cao, *Demographic History*, Vol. 6, p. 561; and World Bank, *China, Socialist Economic Development* (Washington, D.C.: World Bank, 1983), Vol. 1, p. 108. For housing, see Zhong Dajun, *Guomin Daiyu Bupingdeng Shenshi* (*Assessment of Unequal Entitlement amongst Citizens*) (Beijing: China's Workers' Press, 2002), p. 169. Data for 2000, National Bureau of Statistics, *Zhongguo Tongji Nianjian, 2003* (*China's Statistical Year Book, 2003*) (Beijing: China's Statistics Press, 2003), pp. 40, 378.

Note: *Annual total in kilograms. U = Urban, in square meters. R = Rural, in square meters.

of cereals) under Mao resembles that of the poorest stratum in the 1920s and 1930s.[107] According to a survey conducted in the 1930s, a Chinese male adult needed a minimum of 1,886 kilocalories (if idle) and 2,486 kilocalories (if working 12 hours) per day.[108] Mao's provision clearly fell short of that. Deng Xiaoping's criterion for 'reasonably comfortable life' (*xiaokang*) includes 2,600 kilocalories and 80 grams of protein *per diem*.[109] The Maoist 2,009 kilocalories thus represents at best a famine diet.

The legacy of Mao's rule has been debated since Mao's death. Undoubtedly, Maoism meant first and foremost a model from the Soviet Union that was utterly alien to both China's tradition and to the post-1840 Westernisation Movement. For the first time in China's history, all labour, land, and capital in the economy was subject to control from one centre that obeyed one man. Secondly, Mao's economic track record was littered with economic waste and self-destruction, as announced in February 1978 at the Fifth People's Congress by Premier Hua Guofeng (1921–2008),

---

[107] Zhang, 'Dietary Structure and Nutrition Structure', p. 14.
[108] *Ibid.*, p. 15.
[109] Ma and Sun, *China's Economic Situation and Prospect*, p. 263.

At the end of Mao's rule, our entire economy was on the brink of collapse.[110]

Deng Xiaoping also pointed out that:

The decade-long Cultural Revolution caused us even more hardships and greater disasters,[111]

It is now agreed that the Cultural Revolution, the monster created by Mao at the pinnacle of his political career, cost China 800 billion *yuan,*[112] equivalent to the total capital stock of the state-owned enterprises in 1979.[113] The third legacy was 'utopia fatigue'. Ordinary citizens lost faith in empty promises made by the party leadership. In 1978, in one of the poorest provinces Anhui, 18 farmers in Fengyang Village decided to break free from their collective farming which made them poor. This was illegal but offered individuals some hope.[114] These farmers were prepared to go to prison should their experiment go wrong.[115] What these farmers wanted were fixed-rent tenancy and economic freedom, common in late Qing China. It allowed the tenant to decide what to farm, how to farm, whom to farm, what to retain and what to sell at the market price. Against all the odds, the experiment was endorsed by liberal officials from the ruling party. The new system that followed is known as the output-*cum*-tenure (*lianchan chengbao zerenzhi*, literarily 'output responsibility tenure') between state agents (often disguised as the manager of a rural commune) and family farmers. But land

---

[110] Hua Guofeng, 'Tuanjie Qilai, Wei Jianshe Shehuizhuyide Xiandaihua Qianguo Er Fendou' (United to Build a Socialist Modern Power), *Renmin Ribao* (*People's Daily*), 27 February, 1978, p. 1.

[111] Deng Xiaoping, *Deng Xiaoping Wenxuan* (*Selected Works of Deng Xiaoping*) (Beijing: People's Press, 1994), Vol. 2, p. 249.

[112] Jiang Yuanming, *Wangshi 1966 Xiezhen* (*Memory of 1966*) (Tianjin: Hundred-Flower Art Press, 1998), p. 3.

[113] For China's 1953 GDP, see National Bureau of Statistics, *Statistical Year Book, 2002*, p. 51. For the state assets, see Xi and Jin, *Great Cultural Revolution*, pp. 349, 352.

[114] Ma Licheng, *Jiaofeng Sanshi Nian* (*Thirty Years of Confrontation*) (Nanjing: Jiangsu People's Press, 2008), p. 38.

[115] Li Li-an and Zheng Keyang (eds.), *Deng Xiaoping Yu Gaige Kaifang Shisi Nian* (*Deng Xiaoping and Fourteen Years of Reforms and Opening Up*) (Beijing: Beijing Normal University Press, 1993), p. 7. For a replica, see Ling, *No More Hesitation*, p. 7.

alienation was not permitted.[116] Even so, China's age old 'permanent lease-holding rights' (*yongdian*) were revived.[117] The tenure on the state land was set for 30 years, according to Clause 20 of the 2002 'Rural Land Contract Law' (*Nongcun Tudi Chengbao Fa*). The Soviet/Russian system to control land welt down. The re-building of family farms spread like a wild fire. In North China, the new tenancy increased labour productivity by 50 percent; and land yield level 200–300 percent.[118] What followed was the collapse of rural Maoist communes like a house of cards. By 1985, people's communes had disappeared on China's soil without a trace.[119] Mao's rent-seeking scissors pricing also ended. The government agency had to purchase rural products by market negotiation.[120]

Researchers have indicated that de-collectivisation was by far the single greatest contributor to the revitalising of China's agricultural productivity — up to 87 percent.[121] Technology contributed up to 40 percent; and the ending of the scissors pricing, about 20 percent.[122] The gamble by the 18 peasants in 1978 paid off.

3. Exit from Maoism, 1978 to 2010

The comprehensive failure in Maoist industrialisation/modernity, egalitarianism and universal affluence led to an exit strategy for the ruling party. The 1976 denouncement of Mao's trusted aides Jiang Qing (1914–91, also Mao's wife), Zhang Chunqiao (1917–2005), Yao Wenyuan (1931–2005) and Wang Hongwen (1935–1992) was a *coup* to end the devastating Cultural Revolution while saving Mao's 'face' as the leader who led the Communists to military victory in a civil war in 1949. Deng Xiaoping's reforms immediately followed in 1978.

---

[116] Li and Zheng, *Fourteen Years of Reforms*, p. 21.
[117] Deng, *Premodern Chinese Economy*, pp. 56–60.
[118] Ling, *No More Hesitation*, pp. 297, 303, 305.
[119] *Ibid.*, p. 335.
[120] Xue, *Memoir*, p. 482.
[121] J. Y. Lin, 'Rural Reforms and Agricultural Growth in China', *The American Economic Review*, 82/1 (1992), pp. 34–51; Chris Bramall, *Sources of Chinese Economic Growth, 1978–1996* (New York: Oxford University Press, 2000), p. 334.
[122] Jikun Huang and Scott Rozelle, 'Technological Change: Rediscovering the Engine of Productivity Growth in China's Rural Economy', *Journal of Development Economics*, 49/2 (1996), pp. 337–69; John McMillan, John Whalley and Lijing Zhu, 'The Impact of China's Economic Reforms on Agricultural Productivity Growth', *The Journal of Political Economy*, 97/4 (1989), p. 800.

Table 70. Differences between Policies under Mao and Deng.

	Mao	Deng
Consumer revolution	No	Yes
Economic freedom	No	Yes
Efficient resource allocation	No	Yes
Fast technological change	No	Yes
Fast urbanisation	No	Yes
Firms and workers' incentives	No	Yes
Freeing from excessive and wide poverty	No	Yes
Freeing from man-made famine	No	Yes
Freeing from negative GDP growth	No	Yes
Higher income for ordinary people	No	Yes
Modern economic structure	No	Yes
Private property rights (*de facto*)	No	Yes

Source: Author's own analysis.

Statistically, China's GDP growth rate was 5.9 percent a year in 1980–90 and then 8.2 percent in 1990–9.[123] So, in the beginning, Deng's growth rate appeared lower than Mao's (6.2–6.4 percent).[124] But the quality of the new growth was very different in 12 areas (see Table 70).

First of all, the Soviet/Russian model was abandoned. Deng Xiaoping declared in 1979 that his new goal was to build socialism with 'Chinese characteristics',

We want the realisation of four modernisations. They are modernisations of the Chinese style ... It means 'reasonably comfortable material life'.[125]

In the final analysis, our economic policies are judged by the growth in productivity and people's income.[126]

We allow some people to live a better life first.[127]

---

[123] World Bank, *World Development Report 2000/2001* (New York: Oxford University Press, 2001), p. 294.
[124] National Bureau of Statistics, *China's Statistical Year Book*, 1987, pp. 36, 38; National Bureau of Statistics, *Statistical Year Book, 1989*, pp. 29, 31; National Bureau of Statistics, *Statistical Year Book, 2002*, p. 51.
[125] Deng, *Selected Works of Deng Xiaoping*, Vol. 2, p. 237.
[126] *Ibid.*, Vol. 2, p. 314.
[127] *Ibid.*, Vol. 2, p. 152.

174 Mapping China's Growth and Development

Deng's 'new policies' were in fact not that new. Historically, 'Chinese characteristics' in Deng's context of a descent living standard meant a system prior to the Soviet/Russian model; and 'modernisation' meant industrialisation coming from the West, which had been highlighted by the catchy phrase of 'Chinese learning as the foundation and Western knowledge for utility'. Hence, to emphasise 'Chinese characteristics' singled a sharp departure from the Soviet/Russian trap.

Deng's approach caused earthquakes in following areas:[128]

1. Pedagogically: Unlike Mao's dogmatic preference to European terminologies such as 'dialectics', 'materialism', 'superstructure', 'force of production', 'relations of production', 'class struggle', 'proletarian dictatorship', and so forth, Deng famously cited Chinese utilitarian savvy metaphors of 'a good cat catching mice' and 'groping for rocks to cross a river',[129] something that even the illiterate are able to understand.

2. Socially: To re-build law and order and social harmony (compatible with the Confucian social order) that Maoism destroyed, and to resume supply of the well educated to the bureaucracy (similar to the Imperial Examinations for Recruiting Bureaucrats) that Mao abandoned.

3. Economically: To resume economic rights, incentives and freedom for ordinary people (compatible with the old Confucian order), and to re-aim at 'comfortable material life for all' (*xiaokang shehui*) (similar to the late Qing policies)

4. Diplomatically: To ease the tension with foreign powers (similar to the late Qing tactic), and to promote foreign trade and FDI in order to ride on globalisation with more jobs and more economic growth for China (similar to the late Qing and Republican policies).

In sharp contrast to Mao and Maoism, Deng's 'socialism with Chinese characteristics' had the following goals:

1. To re-build law and order and social harmony (to end man–made 'class struggle').

---

[128] For the Confucian *minben* ideology, see Deng, *Premodern Chinese Economy*, ch. 2.
[129] Li and Zheng, *Fourteen Years of Reforms*, p. 31; Ling, *No More Hesitation*, p. 131.

2. To resume supply of the well-educated bureaucrats (to end the supply of low-quality human capital to administration).
3. To resume economic rights, incentives and freedom for ordinary people (to end state monopoly over land, capital and labour).
4. To ease the tension with foreign powers (to end China's cold war with the capitalist world).
5. To promote FDI and exports to create more jobs and more economic growth (to end the wasteful and unsustainable 'self-reliance').
6. To build 'comfortable material life for all' (*xiaokang shehui*) in exchange for party's legitimacy to rule (to redeem Mao's damage to the economy and society).[130]

Deng's successors Jiang Zemin (General Secretary of CCP, 1989–2002 and President of PRC, 1993–2003) and Hu Jintao (General Secretary of CCP, 2002–12 and President of PRC, 2003–2013) inherited Deng's reforms. The signature slogan of Jiang was 'three represents' (*sange daibiao*), put forward in 2000, to re-define the Communist Party as a party now stands for an 'advanced culture', the 'advanced productive power', and the 'interests of the general population'.[131] These three components are obvious at present in all industrialised democracies. Jiang's manifesto was hailed as a new beginning of the party's history:

> From now on, the [Marxian] criterion of productive forces has finally prevailed in our party's thought; and the old [Maoist] tradition that public ownership is what communism is all about has been totally abandoned.[132]

As result of the new ideology, by 2000, 13,900 private entrepreneurs (i.e. capitalists) entered local parliaments (called "people's congresses") and local think-tanks (called "people's political consultative conferences"); and eight of them even managed to join the National People's Congress.[133]

---

[130] For the Confucian *minben* ideology, see Deng, *Premodern Chinese Economy*, ch. 2.

[131] Jiang Zemin, *Lun Senge Daibiao* (*Three Represents*) (Beijing: Central Documents Press, 2001).

[132] Liu and Liu, *Economics in China*, p. 59.

[133] He Qinglian, *Women Rengzai Yangwang Xingkong* (*We Are Still Praying*) (Guilin: Lijiang Press, 2001), p. 14.

Hu's addition to the party ideology was 'scientific development outlook' (*kexue fazhang guan*) which emphasised 'people as the foundation' (*yi ren wei ben*) and 'harmonious society' (*hexie shehui*), a clear move towards a renaissance of Confucianism. It was announced at the Seventeenth Congress of the Party in October 2007 that:

> The theoretical system of socialism with China's characteristics is a scientific one which includes important strategic points of Deng Xiaoping's theory, the 'Three Represents' and a scientific development outlook.[134]

Here, for the very first time since 1934, Maoism was openly omitted from the party ideology. This was a major progress from the party's previous position that Maoism was 70 percent right and 30 percent wrong (*sanqi kai*), which stripped the halo off Mao as a god.[135]

What was pivotal in Deng's reforms was to rebuild the market to allocate resources and resume people's incentives to produce. In the 1980s, over 400 pieces of anti-market laws and regulations were abolished,[136] including the rent-seeking 'scissors pricing'; collective farming was replaced by household farming; artificial planning gave way to resource allocation by the market; universal poverty was replaced by 'allowing some people to live a better life first'; profit-making was no longer a crime; conformity was replaced by economic autonomy and incentives of individuals were encouraged; autarky was replaced by opening up for foreign trade and investment.

With the revival of 'Chinese characteristics', China's economy exited from the *cul de sac* of the Soviet/Russian model. The first sector to take off was agriculture, affecting the vast majority in society (see Table 71).

China's chronic food scarcity was replaced by modest plenty. In 1990, food rationing finally came to an end in all cities.[137] Ordinary Chinese were

---

[134] Hu Jintao, *Gaoju Zhongguo Tese Shehuizhuyi Weida Qizhi Wai Duoqu Quanmian Xiaokang Shehui Xin Shengli Er Fendou* (*Upholding the Great Banner of Socialism with China's Characteristics and Striving for a New Victory in Building a Comprehensive Well-off Society*) (Beijing: People's Press, 2007), pp. 7, 11.

[135] John Pomfret, *Chinese Lessons* (New York: Henry Holt, 2007), p. 68.

[136] Ma, *Confrontation*, p. 163.

[137] Ma, *Confrontation*, p. 171.

Table 71. Outputs and Sales of Agricultural Goods, 1980 and 2000.

Type of good	Increase in output (%)	Increase in sales per household (%)
Staples (cereals)	144	214
Oilseeds	477	128
Cotton	163	137
Tea	225	—
Fruits	916	672
Meats	—	214

Source: National Bureau of Statistics, *Statistical Year Book, 2003*, pp. 430–2, 442–3.
Note: Data for 2000, 1980 = 100.

able to eat as much as their wallets allowed for the first time since 1957. The Chinese physical stature began to improve from the 1980s onwards. In addition, for the first time since 1930, obesity, not malnutrition, became headline news in the media. In other words, ordinary Chinese began to taste economic affluence.

Peasant new incomes pushed up the aggregate demand for manufactures and services (such as transport and catering) that the peasantry were unable to afford under Mao. But the Maoist state-owned urban sector, still with command-economy shackles and heavy industry bias, responded to that the peasant demand too slowly during much of the 1980s. This created opportunities for the rural sector to produce its own manufactures and services, and hence a rise in village and township enterprises to exploit the new market fortune.[138] These enterprises were the first completely market-oriented businesses on China's soil since 1957.

Meanwhile, further changes occured in the rural sector. In 1988, the share of collective production dropped to a quarter of all rural household income. The rest was attributed to private undertakings.[139]

---

[138] Andrew Walder, 'Local Government as Industrial Firm: An Organizational Analysis of China's Transitional Economy', *American Journal of Sociology*, 101/2 (1995), p. 266; J. C. Oi, *Rural China Takes Off: Institutional Foundations of Economic Reform* (Berkeley: University of California Press, 1999), pp. 193–6.

[139] Yu Dechang, *Nonghu Jingji Xingwei Ji Laodong Shijian Liyong Tiaocha Ziliaoji (Survey Data for Rural Households' Economic Behaviour and Labour Input Patterns)* (Beijing: China's Statistical Press, 1992), p. 331.

What followed was a boom in private capital investment. From 1978 to 2000, irrigation acreage was doubled;[140] there was a seven-fold growth in the total machine power in farming;[141] inputs of chemical fertilizers also increased nearly 10-fold.[142]

A knock-on effect followed. Some provinces as a whole were privatised. For example, in 2000 the private sector in Zhejiang controlled 80 percent of all assets, provided over 90 percent of all jobs, and commanded 90 percent sales and profits.[143] The private economy made Zhejiang the second wealthiest province in China (only three percent lower in total GDP than Guangdong).[144]

Moreover, in 1988 the share of non-farming activities reached 58 percent of all rural household income.[145] A decade later, in 2000, the share increased to 70 percent.[146] According to the same survey, 30 percent of the rural households no longer farmed at all.[147]

Farmers were even given the choice to quit farming altogether.[148] The period of 1980 to 2000 was marked by rapid 'rural industrialisation'.[149]

---

[140] National Bureau of Statistics, *Statistical Year Book, 2003*, pp. 417, 419, 425.

[141] National Bureau of Statistics, *Zhongguo Tongji Nianjian, 1981* (*China's Statistical Year Book, 1981*) (Beijing: China's Statistics Press, 1981), p. 171; National Bureau of Statistics, *Statistical Year Book, 2002*, p. 387. The figure for 1978 is discounted by 30 percent due to the constant break down of one-third of farming machines in Maoist communes. After the production responsibility system such a wasteful practice stopped.

[142] National Bureau of Statistics, *Statistical Year Book, 1981*, p. 182; National Bureau of Statistics, *Statistical Year Book, 2002*, p. 389. The figure for 1978 is discounted by 50 percent due to the constant problem of data unavailability under Mao's rule.

[143] Lu Xueyi, *Dangdai Zhongguo Shehui Jiecen Yanjiu Baogao* (*Survey of Social Strata in Contemporary China*) (Beijing: Social Science Literature Press, 2002), p. 238.

[144] National Bureau of Statistics, *Statistical Year Book, 2003*, p. 72.

[145] *Ibid.*, p. 331.

[146] National Bureau of Statistics, *Zhongguo Shichang Tongji Nianjian, 2001* (*China's Market Statistical Year Book, 2001*) (Beijing: China's Statistics Press, 2001), p. 29.

[147] Yu, *Survey Data*, pp. 325–6.

[148] Ashwani Saith, 'From Collectives to Markets: Restructured Agriculture-Industry Linkages in Rural China: Some Micro-Level Evidence', *Journal of Peasant Studies*, 22/2 (1995), pp. 212–7.

[149] This is known as the 'Fei Xiaotong process of rural manufacturing'. The British trained sociologist Fei Xiaotong (1910–2005) established a modernisation model for rural China by the way of rural industrialisation without a high degree of urbanisation; see Fei Xiaotong, *Fei Xiaotong Lun Xiaochengzhen Jianshe* (*Fei Xiaotong on Development of Small Cities and Towns*) (Beijing: Qunyan Press, 2000).

The number of township and village enterprises expanded 14-fold (14.4 percent increase a year) to 21.1 million; the number of workers hired by these enterprises was more than trebled (6.2 percent increase a year) to 128.2 million. Rural Jiangsu took the lead: in 1988 rural manufacturing and services contributed 83 percent of the local GDP and 63 percent of the jobs.[150] The engine of such a growth was profit. From 1980 to 2000, the total revenue of rural enterprises grew 18 times (29.7 percent a year, current prices) to 1,078.3 billion *yuan*; and the net profit, six times (22.2 percent a year, current prices) to 648.2 billion *yuan*.[151] Business profit also lured these rural enterprises beyond China's domestic market. The total value of their exports was worth 887.0 billion *yuan* in 2000, over 18 times of the 1990 level.[152]

Meanwhile, the relaxation of the 'domicile registrations' (*hukou*) for the rural workers and the strong growth in China's urban manufacturing and infrastructure in the 1990s created the surge of wage workers who migrated from rural regions to urban centres in a textbook fashion of Arthur Lewis' dualism.[153] According to the 2000 national census, conservatively a quarter of the rural workforce or 88 million people had moved to cities.[154] The real figure was likely to be 40 percent higher.[155] Consequently, by 1997 wages had overtaken other earnings and become the main type of income in the rural sector (see Figure 22).

Finally, by 2000 China's urban population share in China's total had doubled its 1978 level to a historical 36.2 percent.[156] The annual growth rate was 3.2 percent, over 10 times faster than Mao's record. Now, for the first time after 1949 living standard improvement, industrialisation and urbanisation synchronised in China. It is no exaggeration that Deng's reforms saved China from Maoist ruins.

---

[150] National Bureau of Statistics, *Statistical Year Book, 2003*, p. 352.

[151] *Ibid.*, pp. 447, 448, 450, 451.

[152] *Ibid.*, p. 452.

[153] A. W. Lewis, 'Economic Development with Unlimited Supplies of Labour', *Manchester School*, 22/2 (1954), pp. 139–91.

[154] Lu, *Survey of Social Strata*, p. 180; National Bureau of Statistics, *Statistical Year Book, 2003*, pp. 99, 123.

[155] Li, *Chinese Social Stratification*, p. 219.

[156] National Bureau of Statistics, *China's Statistical Year Book, 2003*, p. 97.

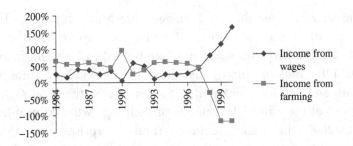

Figure 22. Changes in Income Structure in the Rural Sector, 1985–2000.

Source: National Bureau of Statistics, *Zhongguo Nongcun Zhuhu Diaocha Nianjian 2000* (*Yearbook of National Survey of Rural Households, 2000*) (Beijing: China's Statistics Press, 2000), pp. 14–17.

In addition, the ruling party, the CCP, has changed almost beyond recognition. A new breed of 'party capitalists' emerged. According to China's 2003 official statistics, about 30 percent capitalists in China were party members prior to their business success. The real figure could be 70 percent.[157] Often, they became capitalists because of their party membership.[158] And, their main source of capital was from the state sector and *via* state-private sectoral arbitrage.[159] A 1999 survey also revealed that the vast majority (over 80 percent) of China's newly emerged private proprietors and entrepreneurs after the 1978 reforms had a family background of poor workers and peasants back in 1949. Descendants of the previous landlords and bourgeoisie were negligible, indicating that these old 'undesirable classes' had long been 'liquidated' under Mao's rule.[160] So, this is

---

[157] Li, *Chinese Social Stratification*, p. 202.

[158] Communist bureaucrats have unrivalled advantage to benefit from market-based reform and are most desirable candidates for the new bourgeoisies. For the Hungarian case, see Akos Rona-Tas, 'The First Shall Be Last? Entrepreneurship and Communist Cadres in the Transition from Socialism', *American Journal of Sociology*, 100/1 (1994), pp. 40–69.

[159] He Zengke, *Fanfu Xinlu* (*New Path to Combat Corruption*) (Beijing: Central Translation Services Press, 2002), pp. 109–12, 229–35; Li Peilin, Li Qiang and Sun Liping, *Zhongguo Shehui Fenceng* (*Social Stratification in Contemporary China*) (Beijing: Social Science Literature Press, 2004), p. 342.

[160] Lu, *Survey of Social Strata*, p. 225; Li *et al.*, *Social Stratification*, p. 318.

genuinely a new class in the making. Now these capitalists can legally stay on in the party as 'red-hat capitalists,' or simply 'capitalist roaders', despite their obvious political mismatch with the Marxist fundamentals.[161] By 2003, over 9,000 of them entered parliaments at various levels, (*renda*), and 32,000 served as policy consultants in Political Consultative Conferences (*zhengxie*).[162]

Meanwhile, the party is no longer what it claims to be. A state-run China-wide survey reads:[163]

> *[Our survey indicates that] the number of Communist Party members has visibly increased among the class of private entrepreneurs. ... This is the result of large numbers of party officials and state-owned enterprise managers joining in the private sector since 1992. This in a way reflects an improved political status of the private sector.*
>
> *On the other hand, the number of Communist Party members has noticeably decline among industrial workers ... This shows that a deteriorating political status of the working class and its alienation from the party.*

4. Growth Performance and Achievements, 1978–2010

When they started, Deng's reforms had a number of mundane and pressing social and economic issues to deal with due to the landslide economic disaster of Maoism. For Deng Xiaoping, the top priority was to rejuvenate China's economic through new institutions that were able to improve economic efficiency. Economic equality came the remote second or third in his thinking. Undoubtedly, China's economic efficiency took off after Deng's reforms.

To map out China's growth and yet to keep free from the common problem of an arbitrary choice of base years, we can establish a long-term counter-factual GDP benchmark. It is known that the Qing economy grew

---

[161] Data show that about half of China's post-1978 entrepreneurs had 'red hats'; see Li *et al.*, *Social Stratification*, pp. 323–4.
[162] Ma Ling and Li Ming, *Wen Jiabao Xinzhuan* (*New Biography of Wen Jiabao*), 8th edition (Hong Kong: Mingpao Press, 2003), p. 232.
[163] Lu, *Survey of Social Strata*, pp. 36–7.

at 0.9 percent a year from 1750 to 1830, and 1.2 percent a year from 1887 to 1936, averaging at 1.05 percent a year.[164] Meanwhile, China's population growth rate from 1766 to 1812 was 1.2 percent a year; it slowed to 0.5 percent a year from 1812 to 1833 (before the heavy population losses caused by the empire-wide unrest).[165] The average rate is 0.85 percent. If so, China's benchmark annual average per capita GPD growth rate can be set at 1.23 percent. This is a premodern and very achievable rate. China's actual per capita GDP can be compared with this slow premodern benchmark.[166]

The results are revelatory: (1) China's per capita GDP matched its potential (i.e., the Qing growth benchmark) only three times in 1911, 1936, and after 1982, and (2) only after 1982 the growth in China's per capita GDP seems accelerating (Table 72).

Given that Deng Xiaoping's leadership was willing to abandon Maoism fully, other conditions also played vital parts in China's sudden economic take-off after 1982. First of all, China's fast industrialisation can partly be attributed to the new wave of globalisation after the Second World War. As an indicator, the international community collectively reduced and removed the tariff wall against international trade in nine rounds of negotiations from 1947 (23 member countries in Geneva) to 2001 (159 member countries in Doha). As a result, the tariff rate of the United States declined steadily from 7.3 percent in 1960 to 2.6 percent in 1995 and then to 1.3 percent in 2010.[167] The unprecedented high degree of global market

---

[164] A GDP estimate for the 1830s is 3,603 million *taels*; see Liu Ti, '1600–1840 Nian Zhongguo Guonei Shengchan Zongzhide Gusuan' (Estimation of China's GDP between 1600 and 1840), *Jingji Yanjiu* (*Economic Study*), 10 (2009), pp. 144–55. A GDP estimate for 1750, at 1,713 million *taels* is based on Albert Feuerwerker, 'The State and the Economy in Late Imperial China', *Theory and Society*, 13/3 (1984), pp. 297–326. A GDP estimate for 1880 at 3,500 million *taels* is based on Liu Foding, Wang Yuru and Zhao Jin, *Zhongguo Jindai Jingji Fazhan Shi* (*A History of Economic Development in Early Modern China*) (Beijing: Tertiary Education Press, 1999), p. 66. Figures for 1914 and 1936 are based on Liu and Wang, *Market Development and Economic Growth*, p. 44.

[165] Cao, *Demographic History*, Vol. 6, pp. 236, 257, 266, 274, 281, 298.

[166] Data for 1952 to 2000 are based on National Bureau of Statistics, *China's Statistical Year Book, 2002*, p. 51. Data for 1982 to 2010 in a constant price are based on China's National Bureau of Statistics website, available on line at: www.stats.gov.cn/tjsj/ndsj/2012/indexch. htm; *cf.* GDP in current prices from the World Bank, 'GDP per Capita', available on line at: http://data.worldbank.org/indicator/NY.GDP.PCAP.CD.

[167] See Office of Management and Budget, the US Government, 'Historical Tables', Table 1.1 and Table 2-5 (www.whitehouse.gov/omb/budget/Historicals).

Table 72. China's per Capita GDP Performance, 1830–2010.

Year	Actual GDP/head (I)	Benchmark GDP/head (II)	I/II*
1830	1.00	1.00	1.00
1887	0.98	1.15	0.85
1911	1.32	1.24	1.06
1936	1.39	1.27	1.09
1946	0.67	1.29	0.52
1952	1.16	1.31	0.89
1962	1.12	1.33	0.84
1972	1.15	1.36	0.84
1977	1.20	1.36	0.88
1982	1.26	1.39	0.91
1992	5.34	1.41	3.79
2000	10.70	1.44	7.43
2010	27.38	1.43	19.15

Source: The benchmark is based on Albert Feuerwerker, 'The State and the Economy in Late Imperial China', *Theory and Society*, 13/3 (1984), pp. 297–326; Liu Ti, '1600–1840 Nian Zhongguo Guonei Shengchan Zongzhide Gusuan' (Estimation of China's GDP between 1600 and 1840), *Jingji Yanjiu* (*Economic Study*), 10 (2009), pp. 144–55. The actual growth, based Liu and Wang, *Market Development and Economic Growth*, p. 44; Liu Foding, Wang Yuru and Zhao Jin, *Zhongguo Jindai Jingji Fazhan Shi* (*A History of Economic Development in Early Modern China*) (Beijing: Tertiary Education Press, 1999), p. 66; National Bureau of Statistics, *China's Statistical Year Book, 2002*, p. 51. Data for 1982 to 2010 in a constant price are based on China's National Bureau of Statistics, '2–3 Bubianjia Guonei Shengchan Zhongzhi' (GDP in Constant Prices) (China's National Bureau of Statistics website, available on line at: www.stats.gov.cn/tjsj/ndsj/2012/indexch.htm).

Note: * I/II = 1 means the per capita GDP grew at the same speed as the benchmark of 1.23 percent per year; I/II < 1 means that the per capita GDP grew slower than the benchmark; I/II > 1 means that the per capita GDP grew faster than the benchmark.

openness allowed a country like China to free ride on the international demand for manufactures whereby export earnings financed the country's industrial growth. This is commonly known as the 'export-oriented industrialisation' (EOI), which contrasts the Maoist model of 'self reliance' (also known as 'import substitution industrialisation', or ISI). The EOI model clearly associates with the global capitalist system with which capital, labour, and technology are allocated in such a way that profits can be maximised in favour of the owner of capital and technology. If globalisation had been absent, China would have no opportunity to ride on other countries' demand for China's cheap manufactures.

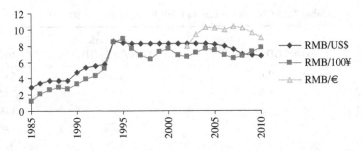

Figure 23.   Renminbi Exchange Rates, 1985–2010.

Source: China's National Bureau of Statistics, '6-2 Renminbi Huilü' (Renminbi Exchange Rates) (China's National Bureau of Statistics website, available on line at www.stats.gov.cn/tjsj/ndsj/2012/ indexch.htm).

Secondly, the Beijing administration clearly understood the mechanisms of EOI in a globalised world. Apart from Deng's open-door policy to lure foreign trade and foreign investment, the Chinese government deliberately manipulated the *renminbi* exchange rates with the main Western currencies to make China's already cheap labour and goods even cheaper on the one hand and foreign investment worth more on the other (see Figure 23). Cheap infrastructure in special economic zones functioned along the same line.

Once the global demand for China's cheap manufactures and China's supply of cheap labour and infrastructure met together, several things happened simultaneously. First, export growth went hand in hand with and GDP growth (see Figure 24).

Moreover, China became an open economy that exports a large proportion of its GDP, mainly in the form of manufactures (see Figure 25). Meanwhile, the dependency of China's national economy on exports increased from zero in 1978 to 67 percent in 2006, which was higher than any G7 countries. After the global financial crisis of 2008, such dependency still remained at 47 percent.[168]

Furthermore, China's comparative advantage in international trade led to the country reaping in huge foreign trade surpluses and foreign reserves (see Figure 26), which was similar to where China was during

[168] Gu Haibing, Sun Ting and Chen Fangfang, *Zhongguo Jingji Anquan Niandu Baogao 2014: Jiance Yujing* (*Annual Report on China's Economic Security: Monitoring and Early Warning, 2014* (Beijing: China's People's University Press, 2014), pp. 28, 32.

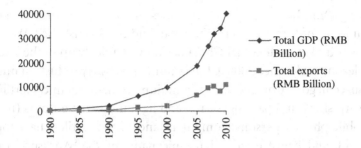

Figure 24. China's Export Growth and GDP Growth, 1980–2010.

Source: China's National Bureau of Statistics, '2-1 Guonei Shangchan Zongzhi' (Total GDP and GNP), and '6-3 Huowu Jinchukou Zong-e' (Aggregate Imports and Exports of Goods) (China's National Bureau of Statistics website, available on line at: www.stats.gov.cn/tjsj/ndsj/2012/indexch.htm).

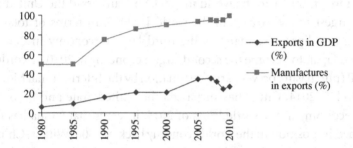

Figure 25. Weight and Pattern of Exports in China's Economy, 1980–2010.

Source: China's National Bureau of Statistics, '2-1 'Guonei Shangchan Zongzhi) (Total GDP and GNP), and '6-4 Linian Chukou Huwu Fenlei Jin-e' (Value of Exports over Time) (China's National Bureau of Statistics website, available on line at: www.stats.gov.cn/tjsj/ndsj/2012/indexch.htm).

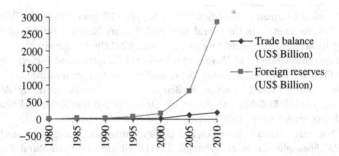

Figure 26. Foreign Trade Balance and Foreign Reserves, 1985–2010.

Source: China's National Bureau of Statistics, '6-3 Huowu Jinchukou Zong-e' (Aggregate Imports and Exports of Goods), and '19-7 Huangjin He Waihui Zhubei (Gold and Foreign Reserves) (China's National Bureau of Statistics website, available on line at: www.stats.gov.cn/tjsj/ndsj/2012/indexch.htm).

the Ming-Qing Era when large quantities of Chinese exports bought in large amount of foreign silver from Japan and the Spanish New World.

It was in this context that China has moved quickly up in the international league table since 2000. China's numerous heavy industrial outputs (like oil, coal, gold, iron and steel, aluminium, cement, chemical fertilizers, electricity, ships, and passenger cars) and light industrial outputs (including mobile phones, personal computers, and cotton textiles) have topped the world, and hence earned it the nickname of the 'Workshop of the World'.[169] In 2004, with over US$ 60 billion of incoming foreign capital investments, China surpassed the United States and became the largest FDI recipient in the world. In the same year, China also eclipsed Japan as the third largest foreign trader in the world. It overtook Germany as the second largest foreign trader in the world in 2009, and surpassed the United States as the largest foreign trader in the world in 2013. In terms of total GDP, China also eclipsed Germany as the third largest economy in 2007, and bypassed Japan to become the second largest economy in 2010. According to the PPP (purchasing power parity) estimation by the International Monetary Fund in late 2014, China has surpassed the United State and become the largest economy in the world.[170] As of 2015, it seems that China has finally reclaimed its position in the world economy back in 1800. With it, China has now returned to the core of the World-Systems, *a la* Immanuel Wallerstein.

The compounded impact of China's rapid EOI was modernity in China's economic structure. The country's urbanisation rate increased for the first time in China's long-term history to 51 percent in 2011,[171] with which the workforce

---

[169] China's National Bureau of Statistics, '2-14 Zhongguo Zhuyao Zhibiao Ju Shijie Weici' (China's Main Parameters in the World Ranking' (China's National Bureau of Statistics website, available on line at: www.stats.gov.cn/tjsj/ndsj/2012/indexch.htm).

[170] International Monetary Fund, '5. Report for Selected Countries and Subjects', in 'World Economic Outlook Database, October 2014', available on line at: www.imf.org/external/pubs/ft/weo/2014/02/weodata/index.aspx; Ben Carter, 'Is China's Economy Really the Largest in the World?' *BBC News Magazine*, 16th December 2014, available on line at: www.bbc.co.uk/news/magazine-30483762.

[171] China's National Bureau of Statistics, '3-5 Gediqu Renkoude Chengxiang Guocheng He Chushenglü, Siwanglü, Ziran Zengzhanglü (2011)' (Regional Urban–Rural Population Structure, Birth, Mortality and Growth Rates, 2011) (China's National Bureau of Statistics website: www.stats.gov.cn/tjsj/ndsj/2012/indexch.htm). Post-Mao rapid urbanisation in China has been achieved by city-bound migration of 400 million rural people within one generation; see, Cai Li, *Zhongguo Jingji Xi Changtai* (*The New Norm of the Chinese Economy*) (Beijing: Xihua Press, 2014), p. 146.

Table 73.   China's New Economic Structure, 1980 to 2010 (% in Total).

	Primary sector	Secondary sector	Services
1980 GDP*	30.2	48.2	21.6
Employment	68.7	18.2	13.1
GDP/labour ratio	0.44	2.65	1.65
1990 GDP*	27.1	41.4	31.5
Employment	60.1	21.4	18.5
GDP/labour ratio	0.45	1.93	1.70
2000 GDP*	15.1	45.9	39.0
Employment	50.0	22.5	27.5
GDP/labour ratio	0.30	2.04	1.42
2010 GDP*	10.1	46.7	43.2
Employment	36.6	28.7	35.7
GDP/labour ratio	0.28	1.63	1.21

Source: China's National Bureau of Statistics, '2-2 Guonei Shengchan Zongzhi Guocheng' (Structure of GDP) (China's National Bureau of Statistics website, available on line at www.stats.gov.cn/tjsj/ndsj/2012/indexch.htm).
Note: * Current prices.

employed in the primary sector (mainly farming) declined by a massive 47 percent: the secondary and services sectors increased by 58 percent and 273 percent, respectively. The GDP ratio between the primary and non-primary sectors changed from 30:70 to 10:90. But GDP per worker ratio declined the fastest (38 percent) in the secondary sector and appeared to be the slowest in the services sector (27 percent) (Table 73), showing that the latter is China's next growth platform.

It is important to know that internally the main driving force of China's new growth in the post-Mao Era has, so far, been that of the private sector. In 1990–9, the number of workers employed by the state sector and collective enterprises steadily dropped 2.1 percent and 7.8 percent a year, respectively. In contrast, the number of sole traders increased 12.8 percent a year; the number of workers hired by private firms, 28.1 percent a year; and the number of workers hired by foreign firms, 31.7 percent a year.[172] In another account, China's small and medium firms created 80 percent of all new jobs; foreign firms did 12 percent, leaving the rest of

[172] Lu, *Survey of Social Strata*, p. 237.

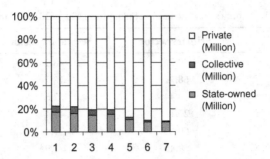

Figure 27.   Employment Pattern: State, Collective and Private Sectors, 1980–2010.

Source: China's National Bureau of Statistics, '4-2 An Chengxiang Fen Jiuye Renyuan Shu' (Employees with the Urban and Rural Divide) (China's National Bureau of Statistics website, available on line at www.stats.gov.cn/tjsj/ndsj/2012/indexch.htm).
Note: 1 = 1980; 2 = 1985; 3 = 1990; 4 = 1995; 5 = 2000; 6 = 2005; 7 = 2010.

8 percent to China's large firms (2012).[173] Compared with 1995, the state sector lost 42 percent of its workforce in 2010 and was no longer a net job provider in the economy.[174] China's job market was thus systematically privatised and passed the point of no return (see Figure 27).

The capitalist economy also allowed the failing Maoist economy to die with dignity without massive unemployment: From 1980 to 2000, China's unemployment rate was a modest 2.7 percent on average.[175] After the 2008 global financial meltdown, China's unemployment rate was still 4.1–4.3 percent.[176] This was remarkable compared with appalling unemployment records in most ex-Soviet Bloc countries in their market reforms.

Undeniably, ordinary people's material life improved since 1980. In the 1980s the number of citizens under the official poverty line was

[173] Gu *et al.*, *Annual Report on China's Economic Security*, pp. 28–9.
[174] China's National Bureau of Statistics, '4-2 An Chengxiang Fen Jiuye Renyuan Shu' (Employees with the Urban and Rural Divide) (China's National Bureau of Statistics website, available on line at: www.stats.gov.cn/tjsj/ndsj/2012/indexch.htm).
[175] Ministry of Finance, *Zhongguo Caizheng Nianjian, 2004* (*China's Financial Year Book, 2004*) (Beijing: China's Finance Magazine Press, 2004), p. 411.
[176] China's National Bureau of Statistics, '4-2 An Chengxiang Fen Jiuye Renyuan Shu' (Employees with the Urban and Rural Divide) (China's National Bureau of Statistics website: www.stats.gov.cn/tjsj/ndsj/2012/indexch.htm).

Table 74. Population Poverty Levels, 1978–1988.

	1978	1982	1988
Poverty, China-wide	49.3	30.8	15.9
Index	100	62	32
Rural poverty	65.1	32.7	15.7
Index	100	50	24

Source: Chen, *Income Differentiation, Poverty and Unemployment*, pp. 132–3.
Note: % in China's total population.

drastically reduced by about 70 percent (Table 74). By the end of 2000, only three percent of China's population still remained under the official poverty line.[177]

Regarding people's living standards, China's Engel Coefficient declined 33–37 percent: from 0.618 (rural) and 0.569 (urban) in 1980 to 0.411 (rural) and 0.357 (urban) in 2010.[178] People's consumption increased 400 percent from 1980 to 2000 (352 percent for the rural sector).[179] The illiteracy rate dropped to 5.2 percent (2011) compared Mao's 34 percent.[180] Life expectancies increased from 54 years under Mao to 68.5 in 1990 (a 27 percent gain) and 74.8 in 2010 (a 39 percent gain).[181]

[177] Based on the rural percentage; see Li Qiang, *Shehui Fenceng Yu Pinfu Chabie* (*Social Stratification and Income Inequality*) (Xiamen: Lujiang, 2000), p. 345.
[178] China's National Bureau of Statistics, '10-2 Chengxiang Junren Jiating Renjun Shouru Ji Enge-er Xishu' (Urban and Rural per Capita Income and Engel Coefficient) (China's National Bureau of Statistics website, available on line at: www.stats.gov.cn/tjsj/ndsj/2012/indexch.htm).
[179] National Bureau of Statistics, *Statistical Year Book, 2003*, p. 72.
[180] National Bureau of Statistics, *Zhongguo Nongcun Zhuhu Diancha Nianjian, 2002* (*China's Rural Households Survey Year Books 2002*) (Beijing: China's Statistics Press, 2002), p. 11; National Bureau of Statistics, *Statistical Year Book, 2003*, p. 99; China's National Bureau of Statistics, '3-14 Ge Diqu An Xingbie Fende 15 Sui Ji Yishang Wenwang Renkou (2011)' (Regional Data for 15 Years Old and Above Illiterate People, 2011) (China's National Bureau of Statistics website, available on line at www.stats.gov.cn/tjsj/ndsj/2012/indexch.htm).
[181] China's National Bureau of Statistics, '3-7 Ge Diqu Renkuo Pingjun Yuqi Shouming' (Regional Life Expectancies) (China's National Bureau of Statistics website, available on line at www.stats.gov.cn/tjsj/ndsj/2012/indexch.htm).

5. Problems and Challenges, 2010 to 2020 and beyond

Many problems and challenges resolved themselves in the process of growth. The best examples were high poverty and low urbanisation. Under Mao, economy-wide poverty and stagnation in urbanisation were both institutionalised by food control, scissors pricing, and *hukou* discrimination against the peasantry. De-collectivisation, privatisation, and marketisation reversed the trend within one generation.

The breath-taking speed, scale, and scope of China's industrialisation and modernisation have however left much to be desired. On the top of our list of challenges is the moribund state sector. The sheer scale and scope of the Maoist inefficiency and waste finally came to light in the 1980s when all the state-run firms were tested for their market fitness for the first time. At that time, about a third of state-owned enterprises chronically lost money; another third barely broke even; and only a third managed to stay in black.[182] The state sector fell behind as the economy as a whole became more efficient. In a survey of 50,000 state-owned firms conducted in 1992, 15 percent of them still held the value of their capital stock, 62 percent lost part of their capital value, and 23 percent only had negative equity.[183] One-third of all state workforces had to be laid out as the last resort (*xiagang*).[184] By 2000, after several rescue attempts, the state sector had remained the least efficient in the economy: It possessed half of China's fixed capital but produced less than a third of China's industrial GDP, 60 percent lower than the non-state sector.[185]

In an ideal world, the state sector should be subject to business euthanasia via market competition — especially in light of China's membership of the World Trade Organization. But the new policy of 'promoting the state sector at the expense of the growth of the private sector' (*guojin mintui*) in the 2000s has created a monster of monopoly in several

---

[182] He Qinglian, *Xiandaihuade Xianjin* (*Trap of Modernisation*) (Beijing: Today's China Press, 1998), pp. 84–5; Chen Zhengyun, Yang Wenshu and Sun Ming, *Zhongguo Guozi Liushi Zhuangkuang Diaocha* (*Investigation of Losses of State Assets in China*) (Beijing: Law Press, 2000), p. 82; also Ministry of Finance, *China's Financial Year Book, 1997*, p. 482.

[183] Chen *et al.*, *Losses of State Assets*, p. 25.

[184] He, *Praying*, p. 21.

[185] National Bureau of Statistics, *China's Statistical Year Book, 2003*, pp. 186, 461.

'key' markets (land wholesale, banking and insurance, iron and steel, energy, communication, and transport),[186] very much like the Western Han state-run salt, iron and wine businesses, in order to seek rent. The new approach came with a package of institutional assistance to these monopolists: There was easy and unlimited financial support, exclusive government procurement orders, and monopolistic pricing. This was the extension of the practice of 'dual track pricing' (*jiage shuangui zhi*), which allowed the state sector to arbitrage legally between the low 'government planned prices' (*jihua jiage*) and the high 'market prices' (*shichang jiage*) with guaranteed profits. This time the idea was to not only resuscitate the ailing state sector, but also make it 'bigger, stronger and expanding more to the outside world' (*zuo da, zuo qiang, zou chuqu*). Currently, most internationally listed Chinese conglomerates and most Chinese outgoing foreign direct investing corporations belong to this government-protected monopolistic group.

There have been several severe consequences. First, the reforms in the state sector have stalled. Second, the sector has become self-serving. The CEOs of the state-owned Bank of China, Sinopec, China Mobile and China Power and so forth are all paid salaries equal to their counterparts of the G7 (Group of Seven) countries.[187] In 2009, state-owned companies also became the main beneficiaries of the government's RMB four trillion *yuan* stimulus package, which aimed to sustain the demand for China's outputs. This in effect elbowed the private sector out. Third, there has been a rapid concentration of wealth in the hands of a tiny minority in society who have now formed a formidable vested interest group. Deng Xiaoping's policy of 'allowing a few to become rich first' has worked;[188] but the policy did not address what should be done after 'a few' have become wealthy.

---

[186] Liu Jinhe, Li Muqun and Li Meng, 'Zhongguo Guoqi Gaige Zhengce Yu Guojin Mintui' (Policy of State-owned Enterprises' Reform and Promoting the State Sector at the Expense of the Growth of the Private Sector), *SERI China Review*, 10/2 (2010), pp. 1–9; Leng Zhaosong, 'Guojin Mintui Zhuyao Fenqi Zongshu' (Review of the Debate on 'Promoting the State Sector at the Expense of the Growth of the Private Sector'), 11/1/2013, available on line at: cpecc.cnpc.com.cn/.../1df0a7f552794ee8bf72749485d1508f.shtml.

[187] The Group of Seven (G7) is a governmental forum of leading advanced economies in the world. They refer to Canada, France, Germany, Italy, Japan, the United Kingdom and the United States.

[188] Zhang, 'Effect of 'Allowing a Few to Become Rich First', p. 41.

It has been commonly cited that 2,932 children of high-ranking officials are among 3,220 business tycoons, each worth over 100 million *yuan* (US$ 14.6 million).[189] Mao's nationalisation and collectivisation campaigns resulted in no private 'old money' in the economy, hence the wealth of the 'few' had to come from some part of the public economy. As a result, China's Gini Coefficient has increased very quickly within a few decades: From 0.28 (in 1983) to 0.48 (in 2000),[190] and then to alarming 0.73 (in 2012). This means that the top one percent of families possesses over a third of China's assets while the bottom 25 percent posses only one percent of those assets.[191] A 'Kuznets Curve' does not seem to work in China. Rather, China has become the least equal society on this planet, which jeopardises social tranquillity. Fourth, the lack of universally adequate social welfare (i.e., work accident insurance, health care, unemployment benefits, and old-age pensions) has made the current income inequality utterly unjustifiable. On the socioeconomic front, ordinary workers' rights have often been ignored and violated, which sometimes have had explosive social consequences. Social unrest has become common recurrence, typically the 'Shanghai Rebellion against Maglev extension' in 2008, the 'Wukan Incidence' in Guangdong Province in 2011, the 'Protests against PX (Xylene) projects' in Xiamen City (Fujian) in 2007, in Dalian (Liaoning) in 2011, and in Maoming City (Guangdong) in 2014, and the mass demonstration in Wanfeng District of Chongqing City in 2014, name but a few, not to mention ethnic unrest in Xinjiang and Tibet.

In addition, rent-seeking behaviour has become rampant. The crony relationship between the government and the state-owned companies, and the monopolistic power of both, have created a fertile breeding ground for corruption. The vast majority of corruption cases since 1978 have been associated with the state sector: From 1978 to 1998, 2.4 million communist party members were found guilty of corruption of various

---

[189] C. A. Holz, 'Have China Scholars All Been Bought?' *Far Eastern Economic Review*, 170/3 (April 2007), p. 38.

[190] Lu, *Survey of Social Strata*, p. 41. The Work Bank rates China's Gini coefficients at 0.403 and 0.447 for 1998 and 2001, respectively, similar to many Latin American countries such as Bolivia, Costa Rica, Dominican Republic, Ecuador, and Guatemala; see World Bank, *Development Report 2000/2001*, p. 282; World Bank, *Development Report 2005*, p. 258.

[191] Anon., 'Ruhe Kandai Beida Baogao Cheng Zhongguo Caifu Jini Xishu 0.73' (How to Understand China's Gini Coefficient at 0.73 Cited in the Report by Peking University), 7th August, 2014, available on line at: http://economics.cenet.org.cn/show-1545-36886-1.html.

types; over 70 percent cases were related to officials in charge of state-owned enterprises.[192] From 1978 to 2000, the number of corruption cases increased 22 percent a year, faster than China's GDP growth rate; and China has been ranked one of the top 20 most corrupt countries in the world.[193] It has been estimated that from 1978 to 2000 a total of 15,037 billion *yuan* was embezzled, equivalent to China's GDP of 1998 and 1999 put together.[194] The annual total corruption revenue amounted to 650–800 billion *yuan* (as of the 1990s).[195] By 2004, a total of 4,000 officials managed to take refuge in the West with an aggregate of US$ 50 billion of illicit money.[196] The problem is that there is no sign for corruption to slow down. According to the recent '2014 Blue Paper on Anti-Corruption and Promoting Honesty' (2014 *Fanfu Changlian Lanpishu*), in 2013, there were 172,532 corruption cases with 182,038 people found guilty, including 53 ranking officials at the ministerial level. The report also indicates new and disturbing trends of astronomical amount of illicit moneys discovered (up to RMB 200 million *yuan* coming from one official) and proliferation of severe corruption at the lowest level of government (*xiaoguan jutan*).[197] There was also annual money laundering of 200 billion *yuan*.[198] It has been argued that unless China curbs the autocratic state power, over 10 percent of GDP per year goes to official corruption indefinitely.[199] Under the new anti-corruption initiatives of Xi Jingping, these figures seem to be

---

[192] Ma and Li, *Wen Jiabao*, p. 200.

[193] He, *New Path to Combat Corruption*, pp. 2, 50.

[194] Zong, *Conversations with Zhao Ziyang*, p. 225; National Bureau of Statistics, *Statistical Year Book, 2002*, p. 51.

[195] The breakdown is as follows: RMB 400 billion *yuan* illegally collected as fees and dues; RMB 200–300 billion *yuan* extracted from state-private sectoral arbitrage; and RMB 50 to 100 billion *yuan* embezzled from state-owned enterprises; see He, *Combat Corruption*, pp. 37, 109–10, 161, 232.

[196] See He, *Combat Corruption*, pp. 1–2, 113; see Li Youjun and Liu Xiaolin, 'Zhongguo Zhuji Tanguan Waitao' (China Stops Corrupt Officials from Escaping), *Renmin Ribao* (*People's Daily*), 10th September 2004, p. 7.

[197] Li Qiufang and Zhang Yingwei, '2014 *Fanfu Changlian Lanpishu*' ('2014 Blue Paper on Combating Corruption and Promoting Honesty'), available on line at: http://book.sohu.com/20141217/n407030606.shtml.

[198] Ma and Li, *Wen Jiabao*, p. 198.

[199] Zong, *Conversations with Zhao Ziyang*, p. 244. A higher estimate is 17 percent of the GDP; see Ma and Li, *Wen Jiabao*, p. 192. Hu Angang, 'Fubai: Zhongguo Zuidade Shehui Wuran' (Corruption: China's Largest Social Pollution', *Beijing Guncha* (*Beijing Observation*), 6 (2001), pp. 6–9.

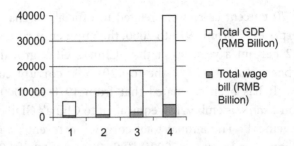

Figure 28. China's Total Wage Bill in Total GDP, 1995 to 2010.

Source: China's National Bureau of Statistics, '2-1 Guonei Shangchan Zongzhi' (Total GDP and GNP), and '6-3 Huowu Jinchukou Zong-e' (Aggregate Imports and Exports of Goods) and '4-10 Chengzhen Danwei Jiuye Renyuan Gongzi Zong-e He Zhishu' (Total Wage Bill and Growth Index of Urban Workforce) (China's National Bureau of Statistics website, available on line at www.stats.gov.cn/tjsj/ndsj/2012/indexch.htm).

Note: 1 = 1995; 2 = 2000; 3 = 2005; 4 = 2010.

merely the tip of the iceberg. Even so, any political reform seems to be remote: The public outcry for declaration of official properties and assets has met with stiff and persistent resistance from officials, and so has been the public outcry for transparency and democratisation of the Chinese political system. So far, corruption has been treated as a problem of some loose ends of China's system, and not the system itself.

The second type of problems and challenges comes from China's low labour cost production mode. The country's total wage bill accounts for pathetically 11–13 percent of China's total GDP in the past two decades (see Figures 28). Cheap labour is a double-edged sword. It attracts capital investment and exports but leaves at the same time a huge margin within which other resources can be generously employed and wasted.

As shown in Table 73, China's GDP per worker ratio declined steadily over the last three decades. China's high-speed growth has not been fuelled by an increase in labour productivity but by an 'extensive growth model': High in capital investment, high in material inputs, and high in pollutant emissions (three 'highs'). For example, in 2006, to produce US$ 1 worth of GDP, China used three times more energy than the global average and four times more than that of the United States.[200] This is because China's energy inefficiency could easily be overcompensated by China's cheap labour which

---

[200] Jane A. Leggett, 'China's Greenhouse Gas Emissions and Mitigation Policies', *Congressional Research Service*, R41919, July 18, 2011, that is available on line: http://fpc.state.gov/documents/organization/169172.pdf.

cost one-tenth of that in Europe and the United States.[201] Currently, China is the largest polluter in the world and faces a crisis of water, air and soil pollution across its territory. Regular smog in China's major cities has become a health hazard for the general public as well as a political eyesore to Beijing.

The third challenge is asymmetric market information. China's recent high-speed growth has created an illusion that the market offers unlimited demand for what China is able to produce. Figure 25 shows that China's exports have declined since 2009 and that the market faces the danger of over-supply. Indeed, during the 2000s, five lines of industrial production in China suffered from serious overcapacity: Mineral ores, metals, chemicals, synthetic fibre, and paper. They had about 30–50 percent of spare capacity and about 30 percent of their outputs going straight into inventory. Solar panels had the worst overcapacity: 95 percent.[202] But 'blind investment' (*mangmu touzi*), often by the state, has still been made in these industries ever since in order to boost GDP.[203]

Earlier, there were non-performing loans and bad debts in the banking sector. In 1991, the national aggregate debt to capital asset ratio in all state-owned enterprises was 0.6. It quickly increased to 0.8 in 1997.[204] A third of the state-owned enterprises had a debt-to-capital asset ratio of 0.9 that year.[205] It was documented that:

> The current average debt to capital asset ratio in China's state-owned enterprises is 0.83. The source of debts is almost exclusively state-owned banks. Most such debts have no prospect to be repaid in future.[206]

---

[201] Clyde Prestowitz, *Three Billion New Capitalists: The Great Shift of Wealth and Power to the East* (New York: Basic Books, 2003), p. 76. In nominal terms, in 2005 the wage level of China was about five percent of that of the United States and Japan, six percent of South Korea and 42 percent of Mexico; see International Labour Office, *Yearbook of Labour Statistics* (Geneva: International Labour Organisation, 2006), pp. 763–838.

[202] Cao, *New Norm*, p. 225.

[203] Han Guogai, Gao Tiemei, Wang Liguo, Qi Yingfei and Wang Xiaozhu, 'Zhongguo Zhizaoye Channeng Guoshengde Cedu, Bodong Jiqi Chengyin Yanjiu' (Measuring Overcapacity, Its Pattern and Causes in China's Manufacturing Sector) *Jingji Yanjiu* (*Economic Study*), 12 (2011), pp. 18–31.

[204] Ministry of Finance, *Financial Year Book, 1997*, pp. 499–501, 505–7; Ministry of Finance, *Zhongguo Caizheng Nianjian, 1998* (*China's Financial Year Book, 1998*) (Beijing: China's Finance Magazine Press, 1998), pp. 498–501.

[205] Chen *et al.*, *Losses of State Assets*, pp. 5–6, 88, 91.

[206] He, *Trap of Modernisation*, pp. 96–7.

Nationally, the loan repayment rate for the state-owned enterprises was merely 3.3 percent.[207] So, the prospect of any sizeable repayment of these debts is slim. It has been estimated that the total bad debts in 2002 were equivalent to about 40 percent of China's GDP.[208] Similarly since 2008, a crisis of domestic debts has loomed large. In mid-2014, China's debt-to-GDP ratio reached 216 percent, a massive increase of 76 percent from the 2008 level. Such a level is close to what was in many countries during recent financial crises.[209] Apart from local governments that borrowed heavily in the post-2008 period to uplift local GDP, China's overpriced housing market has played a major role in domestic debt accumulation. In terms of the ratio of the housing property price to the annual household's income, in 2011, Chongqing's housing costs were on par with New York; Guangzhou with London; Tianjin with Tokyo. In Shanghai and Beijing, it took 15–20 years of household pre-consumption income to buy a family home; this was two to three times the cost in New York or London.[210] A bubble is therefore not a question of 'whether', but 'when'.

The root cause of the property over-pricing is institutional. Land sales by local governments have become an import source of revenue since 1980 when local government revenues and expenditures moved in opposite directions (see Figures 29 and 30). High land sale prices have been systematically shifted to ordinary house buyers. Beijing squeezes local governments; local governments squeeze consumers.

6. What Does the Future Hold for China?

Nowadays, Beijing talks about 'China's dream' (*zhongguo meng*) on the one hand and 'China's new norm' (*xin changtai*), 're-structuring of the economy' (*tiaozheng jingji jieguo*) and 'deep water for reforms' (*gaige*

---

[207] *Ibid.*, pp. 98–9.
[208] Ma and Li, *Wen Jiabao*, p. 222.
[209] Gabriel Wildau, 'China to Cap Local Government Debt', *Finance Times*, 2nd October, 2014, available on line at: www.ft.com/cms/s/0/a2fb9fec-4a18-11e4-8de3-00144feab7de.html#axzz3N1QNwLth.
[210] Jamil Anderlini, 'Property Bubble Is 'Major Risk to China', *Finance Times*, 25th August 2014, available on line at: www.ft.com/cms/s/2/42ed2476-1648-11e4-93ec-00144feabdc0.html#axzz3N1QNwLth.

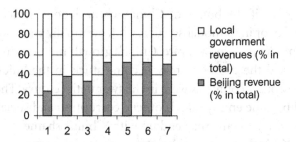

Figure 29. Trend of Central and Local Government Revenues, 1980 to 2010.

Source: China's National Bureau of Statistics, '8-3 Zhongyang He Difang Caizheng Zhichu Ji Bili' (Expenditures of Central Government and Local Governments and Their Weights) (China's National Bureau of Statistics website, available on line at: www.stats.gov.cn/tjsj/ndsj/2012/indexch.htm). *Note*: 1 = 1980; 2 = 1985; 3 = 1990; 4 = 1995; 5 = 2000; 6 = 2005; 7 = 2010.

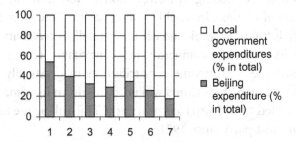

Figure 30. Trend of Central and Local Government Expenditures, 1980 to 2010.

Source: China's National Bureau of Statistics, '8-2 Zhongyang He Difang Caizheng Shouru Ji Bili' (Revenues of Central Government and Local Governments and Their Weights) (China's National Bureau of Statistics website, available on line at: www.stats.gov.cn/tjsj/ndsj/2012/indexch.htm). *Note*: 1 = 1980; 2 = 1985; 3 = 1990; 4 = 1995; 5 = 2000; 6 = 2005; 7 = 2010.

shenshuiqu) on the other.[211] These ideas mean that China wants to become a superpower (hence the dream) with the allegedly unique growth model formulated by Deng Xiaoping; but China has, in reality, been facing a slowdown in its growth after the 2008 global financial crisis. In 2009, China's exports declined by 16 percent, and in the following years a total of 25 million blue-collar workers lost their city jobs and returned to the rural sector to make a living.[212]

---

[211] Cao, *New Norm*.

[212] Gu *et al.*, *Annual Report on China's Economic Security*, p. 34; Cao, *New Norm*, p. 135.

Realistically, if the bonus of China's cheap labour, which so far has made Deng Xiaoping's model so successful, eventually runs out, the 'shelf life' of the model may soon expire. China's growth momentum may eventually stall, and the economy may become stuck in the 'middle-income trap' as many other countries were in the twentieth century. Then, 'China's dream' will become empty talk. If official corruption and social inequality continue, 'China's dream' may end up with 'China's shame'.

In fact, 'China's new norm', 're-structuring of the economy', and 'deep water for reforms' all question the suitability of Deng's model during this century in terms of growth speed (8–12 percent GDP increase per year), growth sources (cheap labour, cheap infrastructure, and cheap exports) and growth target (efficiency at the expense of equality). All these indicate two factors that are missing in Deng's model: New technology and new redistribution of income. Inevitably, China has to allow its citizens, especially its intellectuals, to think and act freely to allow creativity to flourish to enhance its economic competitiveness. Inevitably, China also has to perform much delayed income redistribution to drastically narrow its alarming income gap. If so, China will need to reform its aging party-state that was exported from Russia a century ago. This will be the toughest test to the communist party since 1921.

Chapter Eight

Concluding Remarks

This book aims to take the reader through China's remarkably long and colourful saga of growth and development, full of ups, downs, twists and turns from 221 BC to 2020, thanks to China's exceptionally rich historical records.

Operationally speaking, China's economy had two internal and one external models. Figure 31 represents an output maximisation model. The upper part of the diagram represents China's product output and its input (here labour as a proxy for all factor inputs) as well as how big the population the economy is able to sustain. The lower part shows where the labour input and product output stop. The three curves from the top downwards are (1) the 'Total Output Curve' (TP) to depict growth (A–C) and stagnation (C–D) of the product output and its corresponding labour input in the economy. (2) The second is the 'Marginal Product of Labour Curve' (MT), only valid in a capitalist economy, to decide where product output and labour input stop in relation to business profit. (3) The third curve is the 'Average Output Curve' (AP), relevant to China's traditional private household farming and the Maoist planned autarky in which the total product output is shared relatively evenly amongst the labourers/population.

If one talks about China's traditional economy, the labour input will stop at Point d where the average product output along the double bar is at the minimum to support the population. The interval between Point c and Point d represents the extra leeway for population to grow, *ceteris paribus*, which explains why during Qing China became the 'Nursary of

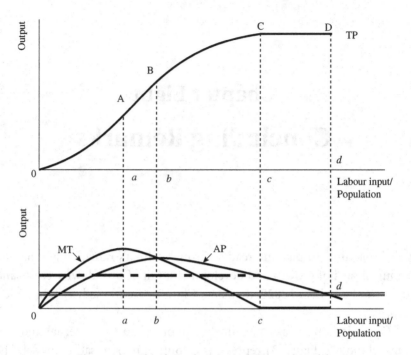

Figure 31.   China's Product Output-Oriented Model.
Source: Author's own research.

the World' in terms of producing more babies. In other words, the Qing economy was able to effectively convert output to population. If it is the Maoist centrally planned economy, the product output and labour input stop at Point *c* (or any arbitrary point) where the broken bar is, indicating the amount of product output extracted forcefully by the state for reinvestment at the expenses of people's livelihood (see Figure 31).

After Deng Xiaoping, capitalism and the market economy were injected into China's dysfunctional communist economy. The 'Marginal Product of Labour Curve' (MT), which measures profitability, begins to play a dominate role in determining product output and labour input in the economy. Because profitability drives the economy (see Figure 32), the 'Average Output Curve' (AP) loses its appeal. The ideal point for product output and labour input to stop is after Point *a* where the marginal product of labour reaches its peak. The economy intentionally maximises profit but not product output or population.

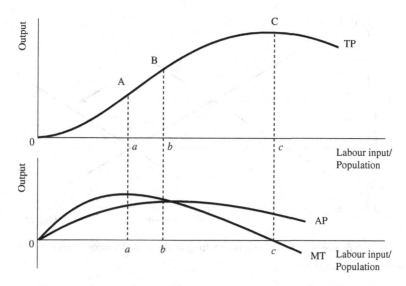

Figure 32.   Post-Deng Xiaoping Profit-Oriented Model.

Source: Author's own research.

Moreover, with China's opening up, an external model began to function after China was successfully transformed from an administratively controlled autarky to an open, excessively to some extent, economy to the global market. The sheer size of the economy, now the 'Workshop of the World', alters the global supply of products. In Figure 33, China's ever-growing export pushes the global aggregate supply curve from S_1 to S_2. The aggregate goods traded increase from q to q', but wages and profits of Chinese producers slow down due to a drop in product prices from p to p'. Now, the total revenue area thrinks from the original 0 p a q to the new 0 p' b q'. The efficiency of the post-Deng profit-oriented model only makes this situation worse. This is simply because the capacity of the global market is limited at any given time. China is on its way to become a victim of its own success.

To combat the slowing down, new technology is often viewed as a quick fix. With it, the supply curve shifts from S–S_1 to S–S_2. But new technology necessarily makes per unit of products cheaper. Then, price elasticity kicks in; the demand curve shifts spontaneously from D–D_1 to D–D_2 to accomodate cheaper goods. The shaded area represents a loss of the total

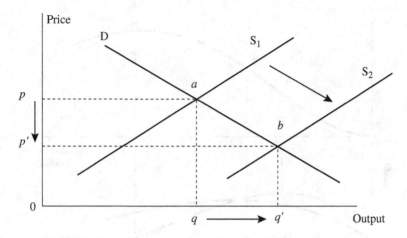

Figure 33.   China and the Shifting of the Global Supply Curve.
Source: Author's own research.

revenue for the supplier (see Figure 34). So, new technology is not the panacea. The remedy can only be short-lived.

China's way out of its excessive exports is to find a new market where products made in China can be supported by new demand. After the 2008 global economic crisis, such a new market is now inside China, no less.

Morover, it becomes clear that China's 'rise', either as a premodern power in East Asia or as an emerging power in the temporary world, has neither been linear nor trouble-free. Its growth trajectory over the past two millennia has been chaotic and unpredictable. It has been a miracle that, as a civilisation, China has been able to survive continuously for so long. It has also been a puzzle that China's potentials have not been fully realised most of the time.

This is because both historical contingencies (such as civil wars, invasions, and climate changes) and ideologies (including Legalism, Confucianism, Social Darwinism, nationalism, and Marxism–Leninism–Stalinism) played equal parts in producing endless possibilities for China's growth path. The main agency — power-holders and decision-makers — that has translated these possibilities into choices of institutions and policies has always been a tiny minority of the population who have disproportionately gained more control over China's growth and

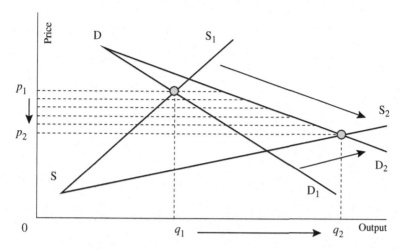

Figure 34. Shifting of the Global Supply Curve with New Technology and Price Elasticity. *Source*: Author's own research.

development than the rest of society. The common illusion that economic growth and development should automatically be beneficial to the general public is now seriously questioned.

China's long-term experience confirms two fundamentals in growth and development: efficiency and equality. It has therefore raised the question: 'For whom' growth and development should ever be generated and sustained? If growth and development becomes a means for an end of heavy taxation and wealth concentration, it may not be worth having. On the other hand, a high living standard among the ordinary folks may well become self-maintained without rapid commercialisation, urbanisation, or industrialisation — as long as the state does not endlessly squeeze producers for surpluses.

The lesson that one can learn from China's long history is that distributing incomes (equality) is as important as producing them (efficiency). By the same token, to secure growth and development, government and governance are as critical in determining growth and development as resource endowments, technology, and market exchanges. This applied to China's past, and will inevitably apply to China's future.

Bibliography

Ai, Na, the Lay Buddhist, *Doupeng Xianhua* (*Gossip from a Bean Shed*) (N.d. Reprint. Shanghai: Shanghai Classics Press, 1983).

Anderlini, Jamil, 'Property Bubble Is 'Major Risk to China', *Finance Times*, 25th August 2014, available online at: www.ft.com/cms/s/2/42ed2476-1648-11e4-93ec-00144feabdc0.html#axzz3N1QNwLth.

Anon., 'Ruhe Kandai Beida Baogao Cheng Zhongguo Caifu Jini Xishu 0.73' (How to Understand China's Gini Coefficient at 0.73 Cited in the Report by Peking University), 7th August 2014, available on line at: http://economics. cenet.org.cn/show-1545-36886-1.html.

Anon., *Beiyang Haijun Zhangcheng* (*Regulations of the Northern Sea Fleet*) (Originally published in 1890. Reprint. Taipei: Wenhai Press, 1968).

Anon., *Jiaqing 25 Nian Qinding Libu Zeli* (*The 1820 Regulations of Ministry of Personnel, Made by Imperial Order*) (Originally published in 1820. Reprint. Taipei: Chengwen Press, 1966).

Anon., *Mao Zedong Sixiang Wansui* (*Long Live Mao Zedong's Thought*) (Beijing: Peking University, August 1969, SOAS Library Copy).

Anon., *Qing Gaozong Shilu* (*Veritable Records of Emperor Gaozong of the Qing Dynasty*) (Originally published in 1799. Reprint. Taipei: Hualian Press, 1964).

Arrighi, Giovanni, Takeshi Hamashita and Mark Selden, *The Resurgence of East Asia: 500, 150 and 50 Year Perspectives* (London and New York: Routledge, 2003).

Attman, Arthur, *American Bullion in the European World Trade 1600–1800*, translated by Eva and Allan Green (Göteborg: Kungl, 1986).

Ban, Gu, *Han Shu* (*History of the Han Dynasty*) (Originally published in 82 AD. Reprint), in *Er-shi-wu Shi* (*Twenty-Five Official Histories*) (Shanghai: Shanghai Classics Press, 1986).

Bao, Weimin, *Songdai Difang Caizhengshi Yanjiu (A History of Local Finance during the Song Period)* (Shanghai: Shanghai Classic Press, 2001).

Bergere, Marie-Claire, *The Golden Age of the Chinese Bourgeoisie, 1911–1937* (Cambridge: Cambridge University Press, 1982).

Bernhardt, Kathryn and P. C. C. Huang (eds.), *Civil Law in Qing and Republican China* (Stanford: Stanford University Press, 1994).

Bodde, Derk, and Clarence Morris, *Law in Imperial China* (Philadelphia: University of Pennsylvania Press, 1967).

Booth, Martin, *Opium: A History* (New York: St. Martin's Press, 1996).

Boxer, C. R., *South China in the Sixteenth Century* (London: Robert Maclehose, 1953).

Bramall, Chris, *Sources of Chinese Economic Growth, 1978–1996* (New York: Oxford University Press, 2000).

Brook, Timothy and B. T. Wakabayashi (eds.), *Opium Regimes: China, Britain, and Japan, 1839–1952* (Berkeley: University of California Press, 2000).

Broomhall, Marshall, *Martyred Missionaries of China Inland Mission* (London: Morgan & Scott and CIM, 1901).

Buck, J. L., *Land Utilization in China: Atlas* (London: Oxford University Press, 1937).

Buck, J. L., *Land Utilization in China: Statistics* (London: Oxford University Press, 1937).

Bureau of Social Affairs of Shanghai, *The Cost of Living Index Numbers of Laborers, Great Shanghai, January 1926–December 1931* (Shanghai: Bureau of Social Affairs of Shanghai, 1932).

Cao, Keping, 'Jiangxi Wannian Xianrendong Yicun Zaiyanjiu Ji Zhongguo Daozuo Nongye Qiyuan Xin Renshi' (Re-examination of Remains of the 10,000 Year Old Cave of Immortals in Jiangxi and the New Insight into the Origin of Rice Farming in China), *Dongnan Wenhua (South-eastern Culture)*, 3 (1998), pp. 25–31.

Cao, Shui, *Zhongguo Renkoushi (A Demographic History of China)* (Shanghai: Fudan University Press, 2001), Vol. 4, pp. 828–9.

Cao, Shuji, 'He Pu Jiaoshi' (Annotated Thesaurus of Rice), *Zhongguo Nongshi (Agricultural History of China)*, 3 (1985), pp. 74–84.

Cao, Shuji, *Zhongguo Renkou Shi (A Demographic History of China)* (Shanghai: Fudan University Press, 2001).

Chang, Chung-li, *The Chinese Gentry: Studies on Their Role in Nineteenth-Century Chinese Society* (Seattle: University of Washington Press, 1955).

Chang, Chung-li, *The Income of the Chinese Gentry* (Seattle: University of Washington Press, 1962).

Chang, J. K., *Industrial Development in Pre-Communist China, A Quantitative Analysis* (Edinburg: University of Edinburg Press, 1969).

Chao, Kang, *Man and Land in Chinese History: An Economic Analysis* (Stanford: Stanford University Press, 1986).

Carter, Ben, 'Is China's Economy Really the Largest in the World?' *BBC News Magazine*, 16th December 2014, available on line at: www.bbc.co.uk/news/magazine-30483762

Chaudhuri, K. N., *The Trading World of Asia and the English East India Company* (Cambridge: Cambridge University Press, 1978).

Chen, Chun and Zheng Jianming, 'Daozuo Qiyuande Kaogu Tansuo' (Archaeological Discoveries of the Origin of Rice Cultivation), *Fudan Xuebao* (*Research Bulletin of Fudan University*), 4 (2005), pp. 126–31.

Chen, Chunsheng and Liu Zhiwei, 'Gongfu Shichang Yu Wuzhi Shenghuo — Shilun Shiba Shiji Meizhou Baiyin Shuru Yu Zhongguo Shehui Bianqianzhi Guanxi' (Tributary Market and Material Life — The Relationship between Silver Imports from the Americas from the Eighteenth Century and Changes in Chinese Society) *Qinghua Daxue Xuebao* (*Bulletin of Tsinghua University*), 25/5 (2010), pp. 65–81.

Chen, Ciyu, 'Yi Zhong Yin Ying Sanjiao Maoyi Wei Jizhou Tantao Shijiu Shiji Zhongguode Duiwai Maoyi' (Study of Nineteenth Century Sino-foreign Trade Based on the Trade Triangle of China, India, and Britain), in Zhongguo Haiyang Fazhanshi Lunwenji Bianji Weiyuanhui (Editing Committee for *Maritime History of China*) (ed.), *Zhongguo Haiyang Fazhanshi Lunwenji* (*Selected Essays on the Maritime History of China*) (Taipei: Academia Sinica, 1984), Vol. 1, pp. 131–73.

Chen, Dunyi and Hu Jishan, *Zhongguo Jingji Dili* (*Economic Geography of China*), Beijing: China's Perspective Press, 1983).

Chen, Fu, *Chenfu Nongshu* (*Chen Fu's Treatise on Agriculture*) (Originally published in 1149 AD. Reprint. Beijing: Agricultural Press, 1956).

Chen, Gaohua and Wu Tai, *Songyuan Shiqide Haiwai Maoyi* (*China's Maritime Trade during the Song and Yuan Periods*) (Tianjin: Tianjin People's Press, 1981).

Chen, Gaoyong, *Zhongguo Lidai Tianzai Renhuo Biao* (*Chronological Tables of Chinese Natural and Man-made Disasters*) (Shanghai: Jinan University Press, 1937).

Chen, Guodong, 'Pan Youdu (Pan Qiguan Ershi): Yiwei Chenggongde Yanghang Shangren' (Pan Youdu, Pan Qiguan, the Second: A Successful Chartered Foreign Trade Dealer), in Zhang Bincun and Liu Shiji (eds.), *Zhongguo Haiyang Fazhanshi Lunwenji* (*Selected Essays on the Maritime History of China*) (Taipei: *Academia Sinica*, 1993), Vol. 5, pp. 245–300.

Chen, Hua, *Qingdai Quyu Shehui Jingji Yanjiu* (*Regional Socio-Economic Conditions during the Qing Period*) (Beijing: People's University Press, 1996).

Chen, Mingguang, *Qianzhuang Shi* (*A History of Native Banks*) (Shanghai: Shanghai Arts Press, 1997).

Chen, Mingyuan, *Zhishifenzi Yu Renminbi Shidai* (*Intellectuals and the Age of People's Currency*) (Shanghai: Wenhui Press, 2006).

Chen, Zhengping, 'Shixi 1895–1930 Nian Zhongguo Jinchukou Shangpin Jieguode Bianhua' (A Structural Change in China's Imports and Exports in 1895–1930), *Zhongguo Jingjishi Yanjiu* (*Research into Chinese Economic History*), 3 (1997), pp. 42–53.

Chen, Zhengyun, Yang Wenshu and Sun Ming, *Zhongguo Guozi Liushi Zhuangkuang Diaocha* (*Investigation of Losses of State Assets in China*) (Beijing: Law Press, 2000).

Chen, Zongsheng, *Shouru Chabie Pinkun Ji Shiye* (*Income Differentiation, Poverty and Unemployment* (Tianjin: Nankai University Press, 2000).

Chen, Zugui, *Dao* (*Rice*) (Beijing: Zhonghua Books, 1958).

Chen, Fu-mei C. and R. H. Myers, 'Customary Law and the Economic Growth of China during the Ch'ing Period', *Ch'ing-shih Wen-t'i*, 3/5 (1976), pp. 1–32, and 3/10 (1978), pp. 4–27.

Chen, Huan-chang, *The Economic Principles of Confucius and His School* (New York: Columbia University Press, 1911).

Cheng, Hao and Cheng Yi, *Ercheng Ji* (*Collected Works by Cheng Hao and Cheng Yi*) (Beijing: Zhonghua Books, 1981).

Cheng, Minsheng, *Songdai Diyu Jingji* (*Regional Economies during the Song Period*) (Zhengzhou: Henan University Press, 1992).

Cheng, Minsheng, *Songdai Wujia Yanjiu* (*Research into Song Commodity Prices*) (Beijing: People's Press, 2009).

Chiang, Kai-shek, *China's Destiny and Chinese Economic Theory*, translated by Philip Jaffe (New York: Roy Publishers, 1947).

China's National Bureau of Statistics, available on line at: www.stats.gov.cn/tjsj/ndsj/2012/indexch.htm.

Chinese Academy of Agricultural Sciences, *Zhongguo Nongxue Shi* (*History of Chinese Agronomy*) (Beijing: Sciences Press, 1984).

Chinese Communist Party Central Committee, *1956 Nian Dao 1957 Nian Quanguao Nongye Fazhan Gangyao* (*The 1956 to 1957 Guideline for National Agricultural Development*) (Nanjing: Jiangsu People's Press, 1956).

Chinese Historical Society (ed.), *Taiping Tianguo* (*Heavenly Kingdom of Great Peace*) (Shanghai: Shenzhou Guoguang Press, 1952).

Chow, Kai-Wing, K. M. Doak, and Poshek Fu, *Constructing Nationhood in Modern East Asia* (Ann Arbor: University of Michigan Press, 2001).

Coble, P. M., *The Shanghai Capitalists and the Nationalist Government* (Cambridge [MA]: Harvard University Press, 1980).

Cohen, J. A., R. R. Edwards, and F. C. Chen, *Essays on China's Legal Tradition* (Princeton: Princeton University Press, 1980).

Cohen, M. L., 'Family Management and Family Division in Contemporary China', *The China Quarterly*, 130/2 (1992), pp. 357–77.

Cohen, M. L., *House United, House Divided: The Chinese Family in Taiwan* (New York: Columbia University Press, 1976).

Contemporary Agricultural History Study Group, Rural Economy Institute, Ministry of Agriculture (ed.), *Dangdai Zhongguo Nongye Biange Yu Fazhan Yanjiu* (*A Study of Agricultural Reforms and Development in Contemporary China*) (Beijing: China's Agriculture Press, 1998).

Cribb, Joe, *Money in the Bank, An Illustrated Introduction to the Money Collection of the Hongkong and Shanghai Banking Corporation* (London: Spink & Son Ltd, 1987).

Croll, Elisabeth, *The Family Rice Bowl, Food and the Domestic Economy in China* (Geneva: UNRISD, 1983).

Cui, Xiaoli, 'Tongguo Tongxiao Yu Gongye Jilei' (Government Monopsonic Procurement and Monopolistic Sale and Industrial Capital Accumulation), *Zhongguo Jingjishi Yanjiu* (*Research into Chinese Economic History*), 4 (1988), pp. 120–46.

Cui, Xiaoli, 'Xinzhongguo Chengxiang Guanxide Jingji Jichu Yu Chengshihua Xianxiang' (The Economic Basis of the Urban–Rural Relationship and Urbanisation in New China), *Zhongguo Jingjishi Yanjiu* (*Study of Chinese Economic History*), 4 (1997), pp. 1–22.

Dai Yi (ed.), *Er-shi-liu Shi Da Zidian* (*Encyclopaedia of the Twenty-Six Official Histories*) (Changchun: Jilin People's Press, 1993).

Dang, Jiangzhou, *Zhongguo Songshi Wenhua* (*The Shysters' Culture in Traditional China*) (Beijing: Peking University Press, 2005).

Deng, Ciyu, *Zhongguo Kaoshi Zhidu Shi* (*History of the Chinese Imperial Examination System*) (Taipei: Xuesheng Books, 1967).

Deng, Guangming and Qi Xia, 'Songdai Guanzhi' (Bureaucracy of the Song Dynasty), *Baike Zhishi* (*Encyclopaedia Knowledge*), 5 (1987), pp. 29–31.

Deng, Xiaoping, *Deng Xiaoping Wenxuan* (*Selected Works of Deng Xiaoping*) (Beijing: People's Press, 1994).

Deng, Zhixing and Tien Shang, 'Shilun Dujiangyan Jingjiubushuaide Yuanyin' (The Reasons for the Endurance of Dujiangyan Irrigation System), *Zhongguoshi Yanjiu* (*Research in Chinese History*), 3 (1986), pp. 101–10.

Deng, Gang, *Chinese Maritime Activities and Socio-economic Consequences, c. 2100 B.C.–1900 A.D.* (New York and London: Greenwood Press, 1997).

Deng, Gang, *Development versus Stagnation: Technological Continuity and Agricultural Progress in Premodern China* (New York and London, 1993).

Deng, Gang, *The Premodern Chinese Economy — Structural Equilibrium and Capitalist Sterility* (London, Routledge Press, 1999).

Deng, Kent G., 'Unveiling China's True Population Statistics for the Pre-Modern Era with Official Census Data', *Population Review*, 43/2 (2004), pp. 1–28.

Deng, Kent G., 'Miracle or Mirage? Foreign Silver, China's Economy and Globalisation of the Sixteenth to Nineteenth Centuries', *Pacific Economic Review*, 13/3 (2008), pp. 320–57.

Deng, Kent G., *China's Political Economy in Modern Times* (London: Routledge, 2011).

Dikötter, Frank, *Mao's Great Famine* (London: Bloomsbury, 2010).

Ding, Shiyuan, *Meileng Zhangjing Biji* (*Witness Account of the 1911 Revolution*) (Originally published in 1942. Reprint. Beijing: Zhonghua Books, 2007).

Dobson, R. B., *The Peasants' Revolts of 1381* (London: MacMillan, 1983).

Dong, Lun, *Ming Taizu Shilu* (*Veritable Records of Emperor Taizu of the Ming Dynasty*) (Originally published in c. 1399. Reprint. Taipei: Academia Sinica, 1966).

Dupre, Huntley, 'Review of Robert W. Barnett's *Economic Shanghai: Hostage to Politics, 1937–1941*', *Journal of Farm Economics*, 24/4 (1942), p. 919.

Durand, J. D., 'The Population Statistics of China, A.D. 2–1953', *Population Studies*, 13 (1960), pp. 209–57.

Ebrey, Patricia B., Anne Walthall, and James Palais, *East Asia: A Cultural, Social, and Political History* (Boston: Houghton Mifflin Company, 2006).

Ebrey, Patricia B., *The Cambridge Illustrated History of China* (Cambridge: Cambridge University Press, 1999).

E-Ertai, *Shoushi Tongkao* (*Compendium of Works and Days*) (Originally published in 1742. Reprint. Beijing: Zhonghua Books, 1956).

Elvin, Mark, *The Pattern of the Chinese Past* (Stanford: Stanford University Press, 1973).

Fairbank, J. K. (ed.), *Chinese Thought and Institutions* (Chicago: University of Chicago Press, 1957).

Fairbank, J. K. (ed.), *The Cambridge History of China, Late Ch'ing, 1800–1911, Part I* (Cambridge: Cambridge University Press, 1978).

Fairbank, J. K. and Kwang-ching Liu (eds.), *The Cambridge History of China, Late Ch'ing, 1800–1911* (Cambridge: Cambridge University Press, 1980).

Fairbank, J. K., *The United States and China* (Cambridge [MA]: Harvard University Press, 1965).

Fan, Jinmin, *Guoji Minsheng — Mingqing Shehui Jingji Yanjiu* (*The National Economy and People's Life — Selected Essays on Socio-Economic Issues of the Ming-Qing Period*) (Fuzhou: Fujian People's Press, 2008).

Fan, Jinmin, *Mingqing Jiangnan Shangyede Fazhan* (*Commercial Development in the Jiangnan Region during the Ming-Qing Period*) (Nanjing: Nanjing University Press, 1998).

Fan, Wenlan, *Zhongguo Tongshi Jian Bian* (*A Brief Panorama of Chinese History*) (Beijing: People's Press, 1964-5).

Fan, Yuzhou, 'Jiangnan Diqude Shiqian Nongye' (Pre-historical Farming in the Lower Yangzi Region), *Zhongguo Nongshi* (*Agricultural History of China*), 2 (1995), pp. 1-8.

Fei, Xiaotong, *Fei Xiaotong Lun Xiaochengzhen Jianshe* (*Fei Xiaotong on Development of Small Cities and Towns*) (Beijing: Qunyan Press, 2000).

Fei, Xiaotong, *Xiangtu Zhongguo* (*Rural Life in China*) (Beijing: Beijing Press, 2004).

Fei, Hsiao–t'ung, *Peasant Life in China; A Field Study of Country Life in the Yangtze Valley* (London: Paul, Trench, Trubner, 1939).

Feng, Chengjun, *Zhongguo Nanyang Jiaotong Shi* (*A History of Communication between China and Southeast Asia*) (Hong Kong: Pacific Books, 1963).

Feng, Er-kang, *Zhongguo Zongzu Shehui* (*Clans in China*) (Hangzhou: Zhejiang People's Press, 1994).

Feng, Xianliang, *Mingqing Jiangnan Diqude Huanjing Biandong Yu Shehui Kongzhi* (*Environmental Changes and Social Control in the Jiangnan Region during the Ming-Qing Period*) (Shanghai: Shanghai People's Press, 2002).

Feuerwerker, Albert, 'The State and the Economy in Late Imperial China', *Theory and Society*, 13/3 (1984), pp. 297-326.

Feuerwerker, Albert, *State and Society in Eighteenth-Century China: The Ch'ing Empire in Its Glory* (Ann Arbor: Center for Chinese Studies of the University of Michigan, 1976).

Feuerwerker, Albert, *The Chinese Economy, 1870–1949* (Ann Arbor: Center for Chinese Studies of the University of Michigan, 1995).

Flohn, Hermann (ed.), *World Survey of Climatology, Vol. 2, General Climatology* (New York, 1969).

Flynn, D. O. and Arturo Giraldez (eds.), *Metals and Monies in an Emerging Global Economy, an Expanding World: The European Impact on World History, 1450–1800* (Aldershor: Variorum, 1997).

Flynn, D. O. and Arturo Giráldez, 'China and the Spanish Empire', *Revista de Historia Econimica* (*Journal of Economic History*), 14/2 (1996), pp. 309-38.

Flynn, D. O. and Giráldez, Arturo, 'Cycles of Silver: Global Economic Unity through the Mid-Eighteenth Century', *Journal of World History*, 2 (2002), pp. 391–427.

Flynn, D. O., Arturo Giráldez and Richard von Glahn (eds.), *Global Connections and Monetary History, 1470–1800* (Aldershot: Ashgate, 2003).

Fogel, J. A. and P. G. Zarrow, *Imaging the People, Chinese Intellectuals and the Concept of Citizenship, 1890–1902* (Armonk: M. E. Sharpe, 1997).

Forsyth, R. C., *The China Martyrs of 1900* (London: Publishers unknown, 1904).

Francks, Penelope, *Japanese Economic Development, Theory and Practice* (London: Routledge, 1992).

Frank, A. G., *ReOrient: Global Economy in the Asian Age* (Berkeley: University of California Press, 1998).

Fu, Zhongxia, Tian Zhaolin, Zhang Xing, Yang Boshi, *Zhongguo Junshi Shi* (*A Military History of China*) (Beijing: PLA Press, 1985).

Gamble, S. D., 'Daily Wages of Unskilled Chinese Laborers, 1807–1902', *The Far Eastern Quarterly*, 3/1 (1943), pp. 41–73.

Gamble, S. D., *North China Villages, Social Political, and Economic Activities before 1933* (Berkeley: University of California Press, 1963).

Gao, Shulin, 'Jinchao Hukou Wenti Chutan' (Inquiry into the Census of the Jin Dynasty), *Zhongguoshi Yanjiu* (*Research in Chinese History*), 2 (1986), pp. 31–9.

Gao, Wangling, 'Zhongguo Chuantong Jingjide Fazhan Xulie' (Developmental Sequence in China's Traditional Economy), *Shixue Lilun Yanjiu* (*Study of Historiography*), 3 (1994), pp. 69–80.

Ge, Jianxiong, *Zhongguo Renkou Shi — Qing Shiqi* (*A Demographic History of China — The Qing Period*), Vol. 5 (Shanghai: Fudan University Press, 2000).

Ge, Jianxiong (ed.), *Zhongguo Yimin Shi* (*A History of Migration in China*) (Fuzhou: Fujian People's Press, 1997).

Ge, Jinfang and Gu Rong, 'Songdai Jiangnan Diqude Liangshi Muchan Jiqi Gusuan Fangfa Bianxi' (Estimation and Evidence of Yield Level in the Lower Yangzi Region during the Song Period), *Hubei Daxue Xuebao* (*Bulletin of the University of Hubei*), 3 (2000), pp. 78–83.

Ge, Jingfang, *Song Liao Xia Jin Jingji Yanxi* (*Analysis of the Song, Liao, Xia, Jin Economies*) (Wuhan: Wuhan Press, 1991).

Gipouloux, Francois, *The Asian Mediterranean, Port Cities and Trading Networks in China, Japan and Southeast Asia, 13th–21st Century* (Cheltenham: Edward Elgar, 2011).

Glosser, S. L., *Chinese Visions of Family and State, 1915–1953* (Berkley: University of California Press, 2003).

Gong, Yingyan, *Yapiande Chuanbo Yu Duihua Yapian Maoyi* (*Spread of Opium Consumption and Opium Imports by China*) (Beijing: East Press, 1999).

Gong, Zhen, *Xiyang Fanguo Zhi* (*Journeys to Foreign Countries in the Indian Ocean*) (Originally published in the Ming Period. Reprint. Beijing: Zhonghua Books, 1961).

Gu, Haibing, Sun Ting and Chen Fangfang, *Zhongguo Jingji Anquan Niandu Baogao 2014: Jiance Yujing* (*Annual Report on China's Economic Security: Monitoring and Early Warning, 2014* (Beijing: China's People's University Press, 2014).

Gu, Shutang, *Shehuizhuyi Shichang Jingji Lilun Yanjiu* (*A Model for Socialist Market Economy*) (Beijing: China's Audit Press, 2001).

Gu, Xin, 'Danwei Fuli Shehui Zhuyi Yu Zhongguode Zhiduxing Shiye' (Enterprise-based Welfare Socialism and China's Structural Unemployment), *Xinhua Wenzhai* (*Xinhua Compilation*), 11 (1998), p. 61.

Guo, Dongxu, 'Songchaode Wujia Biandong Yu Jizang Lunzui', *Zhongguo Jingjishi Yanjiu*, 1 (2004), pp. 69–75.

Guo, Hong and Jin Runcheng, *Zhongguo Xingzheng Quhua Tongshi, Ming* (*A General History of Administrative Division in China, the Ming Period*) (Shanghai: Fudan University Press, 2007).

Guo, Wentao, *Zhongguo Nongye Keji Fazhan Shilue* (*A Brief History of Development of Agricultural Science and Technology in China*) (Beijing: Chinese Science and Technology Press, 1988).

Guo, Zhengzhong, *Liansong Chengxiang Shangpin Huobi Jingji Kaolue* (*The Commercial and Cash Economy of the Northern and Southern Song Periods*) (Beijing: Economics and Management Press, 1997).

Guo, Zhengzhong, *Zhongguo Yanye Shi* (*A History of the Salt Sector in China*) (Beijing: People's Press, 1997).

Hall, D. L. and R. T. Ames, *Thinking through Confucius* (Albany: State University of New York, 1987).

Hamilton, E. J., *American Treasure and the Price Revolution in Spain, 1501–1650* (Cambridge [MA]: Harvard University Press, 1934).

Han, Guogai, Gao Tiemei, Wang Liguo, Qi Yingfei and Wang Xiaozhu, 'Zhongguo Zhizaoye Channeng Guoshengde Cedu, Bodong Jiqi Chengyin Yanjiu' (Measuring Overcapacity, Its Pattern and Cause in China's Manufacturing Sector) *Jingji Yanjiu* (*Economic Study*), 12 (2011), pp. 18–31.

Han, Rulin, *Yuanchao Shi* (*A History of the Yuan Dynasty*) (Beijing: People's Press, 1986).

Hane, Mikiso, *Modern Japan: A Historical Survey* (New York: Westview Press, 2001).

Hanley, S. B., *Everyday Things in Premodern Japan* (Berkeley: University of California Press, 1997).

Hao, Peiyun, *Zhongguo Haijun Shi* (*A Naval History of Modern China*) (Beiping: Xuewu Books, 1929).

Hao, Yen-p'ing, *The Commercial Revolution in Nineteenth-Century China* (Berkeley: University of California Press, 1986).

Hao, Yen-P'ing, *The Comprador in Nineteenth-Century China: Bridge between East and West* (Cambridge [MA]: Harvard University Press, 1970).

Harrison, Henrietta, *China* (London: Arnold, 2001).

Hartwell, R. M., 'A Cycle of Economic Change in Imperial China', *Journal of the Economic and Social History of the Orient*, 10/1 (1967), pp. 102–59.

Hartwell, R. M., 'A Revolution in the Chinese Iron and Coal Industries during the Northern Sung, 960–1126 A.D.', *Journal of Asian Studies*, 21/1 (1962), pp. 153–62.

Hartwell, R. M., 'Markets, Technology, and the Structure of Enterprise', *Journal of Economic History*, 26/1 (1966), pp. 29–58.

Hartwell, R. M., *Iron and Early Industrialism in Eleventh-Century China* (Chicago: University of Chicago Press, 1963).

He, Bochuan, '2000 Nian Zhongguo Mubiao Xitongde 20 Ge Cuiruodian' (Twenty Weak Points in China's Targets for the Year 2000), *Xinhua Wenzhai* (*Xinhua Compilation*), 5 (1994), pp. 8–9.

He, Changling and Wei Yuan (eds.), *Huangchao Jingshi Wenbian* (*Collection of Documents of the Qing Administration*) (N.d. Reprint. Beijing: Zhonghua Books, 1992).

He, Qinglian, *Women Rengzai Yangwang Xingkong* (*We Are Still Praying*) (Guilin: Lijiang Press, 2001).

He, Qinglian, *Xiandaihuade Xianjin* (*Trap of Modernisation*) (Beijing: Today's China Press, 1998).

He, Zengke, *Fanfu Xinlu* (*New Path to Combat Corruption*) (Beijing: Central Translation Services Press, 2002).

Head, J. W. and Yanping Wang, *Law Codes in Dynastic China* (Durham: Carolina Academic Press, 2005).

History Society of China, *Yapian Zhanzheng* (*The Opium War*) (Shanghai: Shenzhou Guoguang Press, 1954).

Ho, Ping-ti, 'Early-Ripening Rice in Chinese History', *Economic History Review*, 9/2 (1956), pp. 200–18.

Ho, Ping-ti, *The Ladder of Success in Imperial China; Aspects of Social Mobility, 1368–1911* (New York: Columbia University Press, 1962).

Holz, C. A., 'Have China Scholars All Been Bought?' *Far Eastern Economic Review*, 170/3 (April 2007), pp. 36–40.

Hou, Wailu (ed.), *Zhongguo Dabaike Quanshu Zhongguo Lishi* (*Encyclopaedia of Chinese History*) (Beijing and Shanghai: China's Encyclopaedia Publisher, 1992).

Hou, Yangfang, *Zhongguo Renkoushi* (Shanghai: Fudan Press, 2001).

Hu, Angang, 'Fubai: Zhongguo Zuidade Shehui Wuran' (Corruption: China's Largest Social Pollution), *Beijing Guncha* (*Beijing Observation*), 6 (2001), pp. 6–9.

Hu, Daojing, *Nongshu Nongshi Lunji* (*Selected Works on Agricultural Books and Agronomic History*) (Beijing: Agriculture Press, 1985).

Hu, Jintao, *Gaoju Zhongguo Tese Shehuizhuyi Weida Qizhi Wai Duoqu Quanmian Xiaokang Shehui Xin Shengli Er Fendou* (*Upholding the Great Banner of Socialism with China's Characteristics and Striving for a New Victory in Building a Comprehensive Well-off Society*) (Beijing: People's Press, 2007).

Hu, Qili, 'Zhonggong Zhongyang Guanyu Jiaoyu Tizhi Gaigede Jueding Chutai Qianhou' (How Was Educational Reform Decided by the Chinese Communist Party Central Committee), *Yanhuang Chunqiu* (*History of Chinese*), 12 (2008), pp. 1–6.

Hu, Xiaopeng, *Zhongguo Shougongye Jingji Tongshi, Song Yuan Juan* (*A General History of Handicraft Industry in China, the Song and Yuan Periods*) (Fuzhou: Fujian People's Press, 2004).

Hua, Guofeng, 'Tuanjie Qilai, Wei Jianshe Shehuizhuyide Xiandaihua Qianguo Er Fendou' (United to Build a Socialist Modern Power), *Renmin Ribao* (*People's Daily*), 27 February, 1978, p. 1.

Hua, Shan, *Songshi Lunji* (*Collected Essays on Song History*) (Jinan: Qilu Press, 1982).

Huang, Jianhui, 'Qingchu Shangyong Huipiao Yu Shangpin Jingjide Fazhan' (Commercialisation and the Rise of Bank Drafts during the Early Qing), *Wenxian* (*Literature*), 1 (1987), pp. 3–15.

Huang, Miantang, *Zhongguo Lidai Wujia Wenti Kaoshu* (*Study of Prices in China's History over the Long Term*) (Jinan: Qilu Books, 2007).

Huang Qichen, 'Mingqing Guangdong Shangbang' (The Guangdong Merchant Group during the Ming-Qing Period), *Zhongguo Shehui Jingjishi Yanjiu* (*Study of Chinese Socio-Economic History*), 4 (1992), pp. 31–8.

Huang Yousong and Liang Enze, *Xinjuan Yinjing Fami* (*Unveiling the Secret of Silver, New Edition*) (c. 1821).

Huang, Jikun and Scott Rozelle, 'Technological Change: Rediscovering the Engine of Productivity Growth in China's Rural Economy', *Journal of Development Economics*, 49/2 (1996), pp. 337–69.

Huang, P. C. C., 'Civil Adjudication in China, Past and Present', *Modern China*, 32/2 (2006), pp. 135–80.

Huang, P. C. C., *Civil Justice in China: Representation and Practice in the Qing* (Stanford: Stanford University Press, 1996).

Huang, P. C. C., *The Peasant Economy and Social Change in North China* (Stanford: Stanford University Press, 1985).

Institute of Documents of the Chinese Communist Party Central Committee (ed.), *Mao Zedong Wenxuan* (*Collected Works of Mao Zedong*) (Beijing: People's Press, 1999).

Institute of Modern History of the Chinese Academy of Social Sciences (ed.), *Wusi Yundong Huiyilu* (*Memoirs of the May Fourth Movement*) (Beijing: China's Social Sciences Press, 1979).

Institute of Modern History, *Academia Sinica* (Taiwan) (ed.) *Haifang Dang* (*Archival Materials on Naval Defence*) (Taipei: Yiwen Press, 1957).

International Labour Office, *Yearbook of Labour Statistics* (Geneva: International Labour Organisation, 2006).

International Monetary Fund, '5. Report for Selected Countries and Subjects', in 'World Economic Outlook Database, October 2014, available on line at: www. imf.org/external/pubs/ft/weo/2014/02/weodata/index.aspx.

Jerome, Bourgon, 'Uncivil Dialogue: Law and Custom Did Not Merge into Civil Law under the Qing', *Late Imperial China*, 23/1 (2002), pp. 50–90.

Ji Liuqi, *Mingji Beilue* (*A Short History of North China*) (1671 AD).

Jiang Tao, *Lishi Yu Renkou — Zhongguo Chuantong Renkou Jieguo Yanjiu* (*History and Demography — China's Traditional Demographic Pattern*) (Beijing: People's Press, 1998).

Jiang Tao, *Renko Yu Lishi, Zhongguo Chuantong Renko Jiego Yanjiu* (*Population and History, a Study of Chinese Traditional Demographic Structure*) (Beijing: People's Press, 1998).

Jiang Yuanming, *Wangshi 1966 Xiezhen* (*Memory of 1966*) (Tianjin: Hundred-Flower Art Press, 1998).

Jiang Zemin, *Lun Senge Daibiao* (*Three Represents*) (Beijing: Central Documents Press, 2001).

Joint Committee of Congress of the United States, *China's Economic Dilemma in the 1990s* (New York: M. E. Sharp, 1993).

Jörg, C. J. A., *Porcelain and the Dutch China Trade* (Lange: Martinus Nijhoff, 1982).

Kaoru, Sugihara, 'Intra-Asian Trade and East Asia's Industrialisation, 1919–1939', *Working Papers in Economic History*, 44 (1998), London School of Economics and Political Sciences.

Katz, Milton (ed.), *Government under Law and the Individual* (Washington D.C.: American Council of Learned Societies, 1957).

Kennedy, Paul, *The Rise and Fall of the Great Powers* (New York: Random House, 1987).

Kong, Qingfeng, 'Jianlun Zhongtang Yilai Chuantong Nongyede Yaosu Shengchanlü' (Factor Productivities of Traditional Agriculture since the Mid-Tang Period), *Wen Shi Zhe* (*Literature, History and Philosophy*), 6 (2006), pp. 100–107.

Kong, Qiu (Confucius), *Lunyu* (*The Analects*) (*c.* 479 BC), in Wu Genyou (ed.), *Sishu Wujing* (*Four Books and Five Classics*) (Beijing: China's Friendship Press, 1993), pp. 9–35.

Kong, Xiangxian, 'Jiangnan Geshengde Shuangjidao Shizai Kangxi Houqi Kaishi Tuiguangde' (Promotion of Double-Cropping Rice in the Late Years of the Kangxi Reign), *Nongye Kaogu* (*Agricultural Archaeology*), 1 (1983), pp. 33–8.

Kuang, Haolin, *Jianming Zhongguo Jindai Jingjishi* (*A Brief Economic History of Early Modern China*) (Beijing: Central National University Press, 1989).

Kuroda, Akinobu, 'Copper Coins Chosen and Silver Differentiated: Another Aspect of the 'Silver Century' in East Asia', *Acta Asiatica* (Tokyo), 88 (2005), pp. 65–86.

Lau, D. C. (trans.), *Mencius* (Hong Kong: The Chinese University Press, 1984).

Laurenceson, James and Kam Ki Tang, 'The FDI-Income Growth Nexus: A Review of the Chinese Experience', *Discussion Paper No. 9* (March 2007), School of Economics, The University of Queensland.

Lee, En-han, *China's Quest for Railway Autonomy, 1904–1911* (Singapore: Singapore University Press, 1977).

Lee, Hongyung, *From Revolutionary Cadres to Party Technocrats in Socialist China* (Berkeley: University of California Press, 1991).

Lee, James and Wang Feng, 'Malthusian Models and Chinese Realities: The Chinese Demographic System 1700-2000', *Population and Development Review*, 25/1 (1999), pp. 33–65.

Lee, James and Wang Feng, *One Quarter of Humanity: Malthusian Mythology and Chinese Realities, 1700–2000* (Cambridge: Harvard University Press, 1999).

Lee, James, 'Population Growth in Southwest China, 1250–1850', *Journal of Asian Studies*, 41/4 (1982), pp. 711–46.

Lee, M. P., *The Economic History of China, with Special Reference to Agriculture* (New York: AMS Press, 1969).

Leggett, Jane A., 'China's Greenhouse Gas Emissions and Mitigation Policies', *Congressional Research Service*, R41919, July 18, 2011, available on line at: http://fpc.state.gov/documents/organization/169172.pdf.

Leng, Zhaosong, 'Guojin Mintui Zhuyao Fenqi Zongshu' (Review of the Debate on 'Promoting the State Sector at the Expense of the Growth of the Private Sector'), 11/1/2013, available on line at: cpecc.cnpc.com.cn/.../1df0a7f552794 ee8bf72749485d1508f.shtml.

Leonard, Jane Kate and John Robertson Watt, *To Achieve Security and Wealth* (Ithaca: Cornell University Press, 1992).

Lewis, A. W., 'Economic Development with Unlimited Supplies of Labour', *Manchester School,* 22/2 (1954), pp. 139–91.

Li, Bozhong, 'Songmo Zhi Mingchu Jiangnan Nongmin Jingyingde Bianhua' (Changes in Peasant Production Pattern in the Lower Yangzi Region from Late Song to Early Ming Times), *Zhongguo Nongshi* (*Agricultural History of China*), 2 (1998), pp. 30–9.

Li, Bozhong, *Duoshijiao Kan Jiangnan Jingjishi, 1250–1850* (*Multiple Aspects of Economic History of the Lower Yangzi, 1250–1850*) (Beijing: Sanlian Books, 2003).

Li, Bozhong, *Tangdai Jiangnan Nongyede Fazhan* (*Development of Jiangnan Agriculture during the Tang Period*) (Beijing: Peking University Press, 1990).

Li, Changfu, *Zhongguo Zhimin Shi* (*A History of Chinese Settlement*) (Shanghai: Shanghai Books, 1984).

Li, Genpan, 'Changjiang Xiayou Daomai Fuzhongzhide Xingcheng He Fazhang' (Formation and Development of the Rice-Wheat Multi-cropping System in the Low Yangzi Reaches), *Lishi Yanjiu,* 5 (2002), pp. 3–28.

Li, Guangbi, Qian Junye and Lai Xinxia, *Zhongguo Nongmin Qiyi Lunji* (*Chinese Peasant Rebellions*) (Beijing: Sanlian Books, 1958).

Li Honglin, 'Wode Lilun Gongzuozhe Jingli' (My Experience as a Party Theorist), *Yanhuang Chunqiu* (*History of Chinese*), 11 (2008), p. 21.

Li, Jiannong, *Song Yuan Ming Jingjishi* (*An Economic History of the Song, Yuan and Ming Periods*) (Beijing: Sanlian Books, 1957).

Li, Jiannong, *Xianqin Lianghan Jingjishi Gao* (*An Economic History of the Period from Pre-Qin to the Western and Eastern Han Dynasties*) (Beijing: Zhonghua Books, 1962).

Li, Jie, *Wenwu Beiyang* (*Achievements of the 'Northern Modern' Elite*) (Nanning: Guangxi Normal University Press, 2004).

Li, Jingde (ed.), *Zhuzi Yulei* (*Analects of Master Zhu Xi*) (Beijing: Zhonghua Books, 1986).

Li, Li-an and Zheng Keyang (eds.), *Deng Xiaoping Yu Gaige Kaifang Shisi Nian* (*Deng Xiaoping and Fourteen Years of Reforms and Opening Up*) (Beijing: Beijing Normal University Press, 1993).

Li, Longsheng, 'Qingdai (1644–1911) Meinian Liuru Zhongguo Baiyin Shulangde Chubu Guji' (Preliminary Estimates of Annual Silver Inflow to China during the Qing Period (1644–1911), *Journal of Humanities and Social Sciences* (Taiwan), 5/2 (2009), pp. 31–58.

Li, Peilin, Li Qiang and Sun Liping, *Zhongguo Shehui Fenceng* (*Social Stratification in Contemporary China*) (Beijing: Social Science Literature Press, 2004).

Li, Qiang, *Shehui Fenceng Yu Pinfu Chabie* (*Social Stratification and Income Inequality*) (Xiamen: Lujiang, 2000).

Li, Qiufang and Zhang Yingwei, '2014 *Fanfu Changlian Lanpishu*' ('2014 Blue Paper on Combating Corruption and Promoting Honesty', available on line at: http://book.sohu.com/20141217/n407030606.shtml).

Li, Shimin, *Di Fan* (*How to Become a Model Emperor*) (648 AD).

Li, Wei, *Nongye Shengyu Yu Gongyehua Ziben Jilei* (*Agricultural Surpluses and Capital Accumulation for Industrialisation*) (Kunming: Yunnan People's Press, 1993).

Li, Wenhai, Xia Mingfang and Huang Xingtao (eds.), *Minguo Shiqi Shehui Diaocha Congbian, Chengshi Laogong Shenghuojuan* (*Selected Social Surveys of the Republican Period, Volume on Urban Workers*) (Fuzhou: Fujian Education Press, 2005).

Li, Wenzhi, 'Lun Mingqing Shidai Nongmin Jingji Shangpinlü' (Marketing Rates of Peasant Products in Ming–Qing Times), *Zhongguo Jingjishi Yanjiu* (*Study of Chinese Economic History*), 1 (1993), pp. 21–42.

Li, Xiao, *Songchao Zhengfu Goumai Zhidu Yanjiu* (*Government Procurement Systems during the Song Period*) (Shanghai: Shanghai People's Press, 2007).

Li, Xinchuan, *Jianyan Yilai Xinian Yaolu* (*Annuals of Important Events since 1128*) (Originally published in 1202. Reprint. Beijing: Zhonghua Books, 1956).

Li, Yanshou, *Beishi* (*History of Northern Kingdoms*) (Originally published in 659 AD. Reprint), in *Er-shi-wu Shi* (*Twenty-Five Official Histories*) (Shanghai: Shanghai Classics Press, 1986).

Li, Youjun and Liu Xiaolin, 'Zhongguo Zhuji Tanguan Waitao' (China Stops Corrupt Officials from Escaping), *Renmin Ribao* (*People's Daily*), 10th September, 2004, p. 7.

Li, L. M., 'Silk by Sea: Trade, Technology, and Enterprise in China and Japan', *Business History Review*, 2 (1982), pp. 192–217.

Li, Yi, *The Structure and Evolution of Chinese Social Stratification* (Lanham [Maryland]: University Press of America, 2005).

Liang, Fangzhong, *Liang Fangzhong Jingjishi Lunwen Ji* (*Collected Works by Liang Fangzhong in Economic History*) (Beijing: Zhonghua Books, 1989).

Liang, Fangzhong, *Zhongguo Lidai Hukou Tiandi Tianfu Tongji* (*Dynastic Data for China's Households, Cultivated Land and Land Taxation*) (Shanghai: Shanghai People's Press).

Liang, Gengyao, *Nansongde Nongcun Jingji* (*The Rural Economy in the Southern Song Period*) (Beijing: New Star Press, 2006).

Liang, Qichao, *Yinbingshi Heji* (*Readings for Ice Drinkers' Hut*) (Originally published in 1896. Reprint. Beijing: Zhonghua Books, 1989).

Liang, Zhiping, *Qingdai Xiguanfa: Shehui Yu Guojia* (*Customary Law during the Qing Period: Society and the State*) (Beijing: Chinese University of Law and Politics Press, 1996).

Lieu, D. K. and Ta Cheun Liu, *China's Economic Stabilization and Reconstruction* (New Brunswick: Rutgers University Press, 1948).

Lin, Chengkun, 'Changjiang Qiantanjiang Zhongxiayou Diqu Xinshiqi Shidai Dili Yu Daozuode Qiyuan He Fenbu' (The Origin and Geographic Distribution of Rice Cultivation during the Neolithic Period in the Middle and Lower Reaches of the Yangzi and Qiantang Rivers), *Nongye Kaogu* (*Agricultural Archaeology*), 1 (1987), pp. 283–91.

Lin, Manhong, 'Jia-Dao Qianjian Xianxiang Chansheng Yuanyin Qianduo Qianlie Zhi Shangque' (On 'Over-Supply of Inferior Currency' as the Causes of Devaluation of Money in China during 1808–50), in Zhang Bincun and Liu Shiji (eds.), *Zhongguo Haiyang Fanzhanshi Lunwen Ji* (*Selected Essays on the Maritime History of China*) (Taipei: *Academia Sinica*, 1993), Vol. 5, pp. 357–426.

Lin, Renchuan, *Fujian Duiwai Maoyi Yu Haiguan Shi* (*A History of Fujian's Foreign Trade and Customs*) (Xiamen: Lujiang Press, 1991).

Lin, Renchuan, *Mingmo Qingchu Siren Haishang Maoyi* (*Private Maritime Trade during the Late Ming and Early Qing Periods*) (Shanghai: East China Normal University Press, 1987).

Lin, Shixuan, *Qingji Dongbei Yimin Shibian Zhengcezhi Yanjiu* (*Qing Policy of Manchurian-bound Migration to Strengthen Frontiers*) (Taipei: National Cheng-Chi University, 2001).

Lin, J. Y., 'Rural Reforms and Agricultural Growth in China', *The American Economic Review*, 82/1 (1992), pp. 34–51.

Lin, Yueh-hwa, *The Golden Wing: A Sociological Study of Chinese Familism* (London: Kegan Paul, 1947).

Lindley, A. F., *Ti-Ping Tien-Kwoh: the History of the Ti-ping Revolution* (London: Day and Son, 1866).

Ling, Mengchu, *Chuke Pai-an Jingqi* (*Table-Slapping Stories*) (1632. Reprint. Beijing: People's Press, 1991).

Ling, Zhijun, *Lishi Buzi Paihuai* (*History, No More Hesitation*) (Beijing: People's Press, 1997).

Lippit, V. D., *The Economic Development of China* (Armonk, New York and New York: M. E. Sharpe, 1987).

Liu, Bima, 'Xiandai Zhongguoren Tizhi Tezheng Yanjiude Xishouhuo' (New Achievements in the Study of Modern Chinese Physical Characteristics), *Keji Ribao* (*Science and Technology Daily*), October 6 (1987), p. 4.

Liu, Foding and Wang Yuru, *Zhongguo Jindaide Shichang Fayu Yu Jingji Zengzhang* (*Market Development and Economic Growth in Early Modern China*) (Beijing: Tertiary Education Press, 1996).

Liu, Foding, Wang Yuru and Zhao Jin, *Zhongguo Jindai Jingji Fazhan Shi* (*A History of Economic Development in Early Modern China*) (Beijing: Tertiary Education Press, 1999).

Liu, Jiansheng, Liu Pengsheng, Liang Sibao, Yan Hongzhong, Wang Ruifen and Fan Jiangchun, *Jinshang Yanjiu* (*Shanxi Merchants*) (Taiyuan: Shanxi People's Press, 2005).

Liu, Jingzhong, *Huabei Riwei Zhengquan Yanjiu* (*The Japanese Puppet Regime in North China*) (Beijing: People's Press, 2007).

Liu, Jinhe, Li Muqun and Li Meng, 'Zhongguo Guoqi Gaige Zhengce Yu Guojin Mintui' (Policy of State-owned Enterprises' Reform and Promoting the State Sector at the Expense of the Growth of the Private Sector), *SERI China Review*, 10/2 (2010), pp. 1–9.

Liu, Qiugen, *Mingqing Gaolidai Ziben* (*Usury Capital during the Ming-Qing Period*) (Beijing: Social Science Literature Press, 2000).

Liu, Ti, '1600–1840 Nian Zhongguo Guonei Shengchan Zongzhide Gusuan' (Estimation of China's GDP between 1600 and 1840), *Jingji Yanjiu* (*Economic Study*), 10 (2009), pp. 144–55.

Liu, Ts'ui-Jung and J. C. H. Fei, 'An Analysis of the Land Tax Burden in China, 1650–1865', *The Journal of Economic History*, 43/3 (1977), pp. 358–81.

Liu, Xin and Liu Gang, *Zhongguo Jingjixue Sanshinian* (*Economics in China in the Past Thirty Years*) (Beijing: China's Finance and Economy Press, 2008).

Liu, Xu, *Jiu Tangshu* (*Old History of the Tang Dynasty*) (946 AD. Reprint. Beijing: Zhonghua Books, 1975).

Liu, Zehua, Yang Zhijiu, Wang Yuzhe, Yang Yixiang, Feng Erkang, Nan Bingwen, Tang Gang, Zheng Kesheng and Sun Liqun, *Zhongguo Gudaishi* (*History of Pre-modern China*) (Beijing: People's Press, 1979).

Liu, Kwang-Ching and Richard Shek, *Heterodoxy in Late Imperial China* (Honolulu: University of Hawaii Press, 2004).

Liu, Ta-chung and Kung-chia Yeh, *The Economy of the Chinese Mainland: National Income and Economic Development, 1933–1959* (Princeton: Princeton University Press, 1965).

Loehle, Craig, 'A 2000-Year Global Temperature Reconstruction Based on Non-Tree-Ring Proxies', *Energy and Environment*, 7–8/18 (2007), pp. 1048–58.

Lu, Xiqi, 'Zhongguo Jindai Nongmin Litu Xianxiang Qianxi' (Causes for Rural Emigration in Early Modern China), *Zhongguo Jingjishi Yanjiu* (*Research into Chinese Economic History*), 3 (1995), pp. 91–101.

Lu, Xueyi, *Dangdai Zhongguo Shehui Jiecen Yanjiu Baogao* (*Survey of Social Strata in Contemporary China*) (Beijing: Social Science Literature Press, 2002).

Luan, Chengxian, 'Mingmuo Dianye Huishang Yili: Chongzhen Ernian Xiuning Cheng Xuyu Li Fenshu Yanjiu' (A Case Study of *Family Property Division Document by Cheng Xuyu of Xiuning County in 1629*), *Huizhou Shehui Kexue* (*Social Sciences in Anhui*), 3 (1996), pp. 30–40.

Luo, Ergang, 'Yushushu Chuanru Zhongguo' (How Maize Was Introduced to China), *Lishi Yanjiu* (*Study of History*), 3 (1956), p. 70.

Luo, Ergang, *Zhongwang Li Xiucheng Zizhuan Yuangao Jianzheng* (*Annotated Confession of Li Xiucheng*) (Beijing: Zhonghua Books, 1957).

Ma, Hong (ed.), *2000 Niande Zhongguo Kexue Jishu* (*China's Science and Technology in 2000*) (Beijing: Social Sciences Press, 1988).

Ma, Huan, *Yingya Shenglan* (*Tours to Great Sites Overseas*) (Originally published in 1451. Reprint. Beijing: Zhonghua Books, 1955).

Ma, Licheng, *Jiaofeng Sanshi Nian* (*Thirty Years of Confrontation*) (Nanjing: Jiangsu People's Press, 2008).

Ma, Ling and Li Ming, *Wen Jiabao Xinzhuan* (*New Biography of Wen Jiabao*), 8th edition (Hong Kong: Mingpao Press, 2003).

Maddison, Angus, *Chinese Economic Performance in the Long Run* (Paris: OECD, 1998).

Mann, Michael, *The Sources of Social Power, The Rise of Classes and Nation States, 1760–1914*) (Cambridge: Cambridge University Press, 1993).

Mann, Susan, *Local Merchants and the Chinese Bureaucracy, 1750–1950* (Stanford: Stanford University Press, 1987).

Mao Hanwen, 'Zhonghua Minzude Liang Da Fayandi' (Two Major Geographic Origins of the Chinese), *Xinhua Wenzhai* (*New China Readers' Digest*), 1 (1987), pp. 199–200.

Marsh, R. M., *The Mandarin: The Circulation of Elite in China, 1600–1900* (London: The Free Press, 1980).

McEvedy, Colin and Richard Jones (eds.), *Atlas of World Population History* (Harmondsworth: Penguin Books, 1978).

McMillan, John, John Whalley and Lijing Zhu, 'The Impact of China's Economic Reforms on Agricultural Productivity Growth', *The Journal of Political Economy* 97/4 (1989), pp. 781–807.

Mencius, *Mengzi* (*Master Meng's Book*) (Warring States Period: 475–221 BC).

Metzger, T. A., *The Internal Organization of Ch'ing Bureaucracy: Legal, Normative, and Communication Aspects* (Cambridge [MA]: Harvard University Press, 1973).

Michael, F. H. (ed.), *The Taiping Rebellion, History and Documents* (Seattle: University of Washington Press, 1966–71).

Ministry of Finance, *Zhongguo Caizheng Nianjian, 1997* (*China's Financial Year Book, 1997*) (Beijing: China's Finance Magazine Press, 1997).

Ministry of Finance, *Zhongguo Caizheng Nianjian, 1998* (*China's Financial Year Book, 1998*) (Beijing: China's Finance Magazine Press, 1998).

Ministry of Finance, *Zhongguo Caizheng Nianjian, 2004* (*China's Financial Year Book, 2004*) (Beijing: China's Finance Magazine Press, 2004).

Mokyr, Joel, *The Lever of Riches* (Oxford: Oxford University Press, 1990).

Moloughney, Brian and Xia Weizhong, 'Silver and the Fall of the Ming: A Reassessment', *Papers on Far Eastern History*, 40 (1989), pp. 51–78.

Morse, H. B., *The Chronicles of the East India Company Trading to China, 1635–1834* (Oxford: Oxford University Press, 1926–9).

Mousnier, Roland, *Peasant Uprisings in Seventeenth-Century France, Russia and China* (London: George AU, 1971).

National Bureau of Statistics, *Zhongguo Jingji Nianjian, 2002* (*China Statistical Year Book, 2002*) (Beijing: China Statistics Press, 2002).

National Bureau of Statistics, *Zhongguo Keji Tongji Nianjian, 1991* (*China's Statistical Year Book of Science and Technology, 1991*) (Beijing: China's Statistics Press, 1992).

National Bureau of Statistics, *Zhongguo Laodong Tongji Nianjian, 1998* (*China's Labour Statistical Year Book, 1998*) (Beijing: China's Statistics Press, 1998).

National Bureau of Statistics, *Zhongguo Laodong Tongji Nianjian, 2004* (*China's Labour Statistical Year Book, 2004*) (Beijing: China's Statistics Press, 2004).

National Bureau of Statistics, *Zhongguo Nongcun Zhuhu Diancha Nianjian, 2002* (*China's Rural Households Survey Year Book, 2002*) (Beijing: China's Statistics Press, 2002).

National Bureau of Statistics, *Zhongguo Nongcun Zhuhu Diaocha Nianjian, 2000* (*Yearbook of National Survey of Rural Households, 2000*) (Beijing: China's Statistics Press, 2000).

National Bureau of Statistics, *Zhongguo Shichang Tongji Nianjian, 2001* (*China's Market Statistical Year Book, 2001*) (Beijing: China's Statistics Press, 2001).

National Bureau of Statistics, *Zhongguo Tongji Nianjian, 1981* (*China's Statistical Year Book, 1981*) (Beijing: China's Statistics Press, 1981).

National Bureau of Statistics, *Zhongguo Tongji Nianjian, 1987* (*China's Statistical Year Book, 1987*) (Beijing: China's Statistics Press, 1987).

National Bureau of Statistics, *Zhongguo Tongji Nianjian, 2002* (*China's Statistical Year Book, 2002*) (Beijing: China's Statistics Press, 2002).

National Bureau of Statistics, *Zhongguo Tongji Nianjian, 2003* (*China's Statistical Year Book, 2003*) (Beijing: China's Statistics Press, 2003).

National Statistical Bureau, *Zhongguo Renkou He Jiuye Tongji Nianjian, 2013* (*China's Statistical Yearbook of Population and Employment*) (Beijing: China's Statistical Press, 2013).

Naval Institute of Ocean Cartography and Department of Maritime History, and Dalian Sea Transportation Institute (eds.), *Xinbian Zhenghe Hanghai Tuji* (*A New Compilation of the Navigation Chart of Zheng He's Voyages*) (Beijing: People's Communication Press, 1988).

Needham, Joseph, *Science and Civilisation in China* (Cambridge: Cambridge University Press, 1954–2008).

Neue, Heinz-Ulrich, 'Methane Emission from Rice Fields', *BioScience*, 43/7 (1993), pp. 466–73.

Nie, Bochun and Han Pinzheng, *Taiping Tianguo Tianjing Tushuo Ji* (*Illustrated Maps of the Capital City of the Heavenly Kingdom of Great Peace*) (Nanjing: Jiangsu Classics Press, 1985).

Niu, Guanjie, 'Cong Shouwang Xiangzhu Dao Lizhi Yingyi Tuanlian Weixian: You Tuanlian Zuzhide Fazhan Yanbian Kan Guojia Zhengquan Yu Jiceng Shehuide Hudong Guanxi' (From Vigilante to Local Order: the Interplay between the State and Grassroots Society), *Zhongguo Nongshi* (*Agricultural History of China*), 23/1 (2004), pp. 73–80.

Niu, Renliang, 'Lun Zai Jiuye' (Re-Employment), *Xinhua Wenzhai* (*Xinhua Compilation*), 2 (1998), p. 56.

Norman, E. H., *Japan's Emergence as a Modern State* (Westport: Greenwood Press, 1973).

North, D. C., and R. P. Thomas, *The Rise of the Western World: A New Economic History* (Cambridge: Cambridge University Press, 1973).

North, D. C., *Institutions, Institutional Change and Economic Performance* (Cambridge: Cambridge University Press, 1990).

North, D. C., *Structure and Change in Economic History* (New York: W.W. Norton, 1981).

Office of Management and Budget, the US Government, 'Historical Tables', Table 1.1 and Tables 2–5, available on line at: www.whitehouse.gov/omb/budget/Historicals.

Oi, J. C., *Rural China Takes Off: Institutional Foundations of Economic Reform* (Berkeley: University of California Press, 1999).

Ong, Aihwa and Donald Nonini, *Ungrounded Empires: The Cultural Politics of Modern Chinese Transnationalism* (New York and London: Routledge, 1997).

Ostler, Nicholas, *Empires of the World* (London, HarperCollins, 2005).

Peng Xinwei, *Zhongguo Huobi Shi* (*A History of Currencies in China*) (Shanghai: Shanghai People's Press, 1965).

Peng, Zeyi, *Shijiu Shiji Houbanqide Zhongguo Caizheng Yu Jingji* (*China's Finance and Economy during the Second Half of the Nineteenth Century*) (Beijing: Chinese Finance Press, 1990).

Peng, Zeyi, *Zhongguo Gongshang Hanghui Shiliao Ji* (*Historical Materials of China's Industrial and Commercial Guilds*) (Beijing: Zhonghua Books, 1995).

Peng, Zeyi, *Zhongguo Jindai Shougongyeshi Ziliao* (*Historical Materials of Handicraft Industry in Early Modern China*) (Beijing: Sanlian Books, 1957).

Perkins, D. H., *Agricultural Development in China, 1368–1968* (Edinburgh: Edinburgh University Press, 1969).

Perkins, D. H., 'Reforming China's Economic System', *Journal of Economic Literature*, 26/2 (1988), pp. 601–45.

Peterson, W. J. (ed.), *The Cambridge History of China* (Cambridge: Cambridge University Press, 2002).

Pomeranz, Kenneth, *The Great Divergence, Europe, China and the Making of the Modern World Economy* (Princeton: Princeton University Press, 2000).

Pomfret, John, *Chinese Lessons* (New York: Henry Holt, 2007).

Preston, Diana, *The Boxer Rebellion; The Dramatic Story of China's War on Foreigners that Shook the World in the Summer of 1900* (New York: Walker & Company, 2000).

Prestowitz, Clyde, *Three Billion New Capitalists: The Great Shift of Wealth and Power to the East* (New York: Basic Books, 2003).

Pritchard, E. H., *Anglo-Chinese Relations during the Seventeenth and Eighteenth Centuries* (Urbana: The University of Illinois Press, 1929).

Pritchard, E. H., *The Crucial Years of Early Anglo-Chinese Relations, 1750–1800* (Washington: Pullman, 1936).

Pryor, F. L., 'The Asian Mode of Production as an Economic System', *Journal of Comparative Economics*, 4/4 (1980), pp. 420–42.

Pusey, J. R., *China and Charles Darwin* (Cambridge [MA]: Harvard University Press, 1983).

Qi, Sihe, *Yapian Zhanzheng* (*The Opium War*) (Shanghai: Shanghai People's Press, 2000).

Qi, Xia, 'Songdai Shehui Shengchanlide Fazhan Jiqizai Zhongguo Gudai Jingji Fazhan Guochengzhongde Diwei' (Productivity Increase in Song Times and Its Importance in China's Premodern Economic Growth), *Zhongguo Jingjishi Yanjiu* (*Research into Chinese Economic History*), 1 (1986), pp. 29–52.

Qi, Xia, *Songdai Jingjishi* (*An Economic History of the Song*) (Beijing: Zhonghua Books, 2009).

Qi, Zhaonan, *Qingchao Wenxian Tongkao* (*Comprehensive Study of Qing Records*) (1787).

Qiao, Shuzhi, 'Pufan Tianguanqi Kao' (A Study of the Bronze Container of the Agricultural Administrator in the Pufan Region), *Lishi Yanjiu* (*Research in History*), 4 (1987), pp. 67–70.

Qu, Tongzu, *Zhongguo Falü He Zhongguo Shehui* (*Chinese Law and Chinese Society*) (Beijing: Zhonghua Books, 1981).

Qu, Yanbin, *Diandang Shi* (*Pawning, A Journey through Time*) (Taipei: Huacheng Books, 2004).

Quan, Hansheng, 'Tang Song Zhengfu Suiru Yu Hubi Jingjide Guanxi' (Relationship between Government Revenues and the Cash Economy), in *Academia Sinica* (ed.), *Guoli Zhongyang Yanjiuyuan Lishi Yuyan Yanjiusuo Jikan* (*Bulletin of the Institute of History and Linguistics, Academia Sinica*), 20 (1948), pp. 189–220.

Rawlinson, J. L., *China's Struggle for Naval Development* (Cambridge: Harvard University Press, 1967).

Rawski, E. S., *Education and Popular Literacy in Ch'ing China* (Ann Arbor: The University of Michigan Press, 1979).

Rawski, E. S., *The Last Emperors: A Social History of Qing Imperial Institutions* (Berkeley: University of California Press, 1998).

Rawski, T. G. and L. M. Li (eds.), *Chinese History in Economic Perspective* (Berkeley: University of California Press, 1992).

Rawski, T. G., *Economic Growth in Prewar China* (Berkeley: University of California Press, 1989).

Research Centre of History of Railways in China (ed.), *Zhongguo Tielu Dashiji, 1876–1995* (*Main Events in the History of Chinese Railways, 1876–1995*) (Beijing: China's Railway Press, 1996).

Richards, J. F. (ed.), *Precious Metals in the Late Medieval and Early Modern Worlds* (Durham [NC]: Carolina Academic Press, 1983).

Rickett, W. A. (trans.), *Guanzi: Political, Economic, and Philosophical Essays from Early China* (Princeton: Princeton University Press, 1985).

Rona-Tas, Akos, 'The First Shall Be Last? Entrepreneurship and Communist Cadres in the Transition from Socialism', *American Journal of Sociology*, 100/1 (1994), pp. 40–69.

Saith, Ashwani, 'From Collectives to Markets: Restructured Agriculture-Industry Linkages in Rural China: Some Micro-Level Evidence', *Journal of Peasant Studies*, 22/2 (1995), pp. 201–60.

Schneider, S. H. and Clifford Mass, 'Volcanic Dust, Sunspots, and Temperature Trends', *Science*, 190/4216 (1975), pp. 741–6.

Selden, Mark and Patti Eggleston (eds.), *The People's Republic of China: A Documentary History of Revolutionary Change* (New York: Monthly Review Press, 1979).

Shanxi Finance and Economics College and Shanxi Branch of the People's Bank (eds.), *Shanxi Piaohao Shi* (*Materials on Shanxi Native Banks*) (Taiyuan: Shanxi People's Press, 1990).

Shanxi School of Finance and Economics and Shanxi Office of People's Bank of China (eds.), *Shanxi Piaohao Shiliao* (*Materials of Shanxi Native Banks*) (Taiyuan: Shanxi People's Press, 1990).

Shen, Fuwei, 'Zhenghe Baochuanduide Dongfei Hangcheng' (Zheng He's Treasure Fleet and Its Voyages to the Eastern African Coast), in Institute of Maritime History of China (ed.), *Zhenghe Xia Xiyang Lunwen Ji* (*Selected Works on Zheng He's Voyages in the Indian Ocean*) (Beijing: People's Communication Press, 1985), pp. 166–83.

Shen, Zhihua, 'Guanyu 20 Shiji 50 Niandai Sulian Yuanhua Daikuande Lishi Kaocha' (Soviet Loans to China in the 1950s), *Zhongguo Jingjishi Yanjiu* (*Research into Chinese Economic History*), 3 (2002), pp. 83–93.

Shi, Tanjin, *Laodong Fa* (*Labour Law*) (Beijing: Economic Sciences Press, 1990).

Shiba, Yoshinobu, *Commerce and Society in Sung China* (Ann Arbor: University Michigan Press, 1970).

Shiga, Shūzō, 'Family Property and the Law of Inheritance in Traditional China', in D. C. Buxbaum (ed.), *Chinese Family Law and Social Change in Historical and Comparative Perspective* (Seattle: University of Washington Press, 1979), pp. 109–50.

Sibo, Yixin (Shiba, Yoshinobu), *Songdai Jiangnan Jingjishi Yanjiu* (*An Economic History of the Lower Yangzi Region during the Song Period*), translated by Fang Jian and He Zhongli (Nanjing: Jiangsu People's Press, 2001).

Sima, Qian, *Shi Ji* (*The Book of History*) (Originally published in 91 BC. Reprint), in *Er-shi-wu Shi* (*Twenty-Five Official Histories*) (Shanghai: Shanghai Classics Press, 1986).

Skinner, G. W., 'Chinese Peasants and Closed Community: An Open and Shut Case', *Comparative Studies in Society and History* 13/3 (1971), pp. 270–81.

Skinner, G. W., 'Marketing and Social Structure in Rural China', *The Journal of Asian Studies*, 24/1 (1964), pp. 3–44; 24/2 (1965), pp. 195–228; 24/3 (1965), pp. 363–400.

Song, Lian, *Yuan Shi* (*History of the Yuan Dynasty*) (Originally published in 1370. Reprint. Beijing: Zhonghua Books, 1976).

Song, Zhenghai, Gao Jianguo, Sun Guanlong, and Zhang Binglun, *Zhongguo Gudai Ziran Zaiyi Dongtao Fenxi* (*Dynamic Analysis of Natural Disasters in Premodern China*) (Hefei: Anhui Educational Press, 2002).

Spence, J. D., *The Search for Modern China* (New York: W. W. Norton, 1990).

Su, Fuyuan, *Xinzeng Yin Lun (On Silver, Enlarged)* (1874).

Su, Hua, *Songci Jianshang Zidian (Annotated Song Poems)* (Shanghai: Shanghai Books, 1987).

Sun, Guangqi, *Zhongguo Gudai Hanghaishi (A Nautical History of Premodern China)* (Beijing: Maritime Press, 1989).

Sun, Xiugang, *Jianming Zhongguo Caizhengshi (A Concise History of Government Finance)* (Beijing: China's Finance and Economics Press, 1988).

Sun, Yutang, *Zhongguo Jindai Gongyeshi Ziliao (Materials of Early Modern Industries in China)* (Beijing: Sciences Press, 1957).

Sun, Zhongshan (Yat-sen), *Sun Zhongshan Quanji (Complete Selection of Works by Sun Zhongshan)* (Beijing: Zhonghua Books, 1981).

Tan, Qixiang, *Jianming Zhongguo Lishi Dituji (Concise Maps of Chinese History)* (Beijing: China's Map Press, 1991).

Tan, C. C., *The Boxer Catastrophe* (New York: Columbia University Press, 1955).

Tang, Degang, *Wanqing Qishinian, Yihetuan Yu Baguo Lianjun (The Last Seventy Years of the Qing, the Boxer Riot and the Eight-Nation Alliance)* (Taipei: Yuanliu Press, 1998).

Tang, Jing and Zheng Chuanshui, *Zhongguo Guojia Jigoushi (A History of Administrative Structures in China)* (Shenyang: Liaoning People's Press, 1993).

Tang, Xianglong, *Zhongguo Jindai Haiguan Shuishou He Fenpei Tongji (Statistics of Customs Revenue and its Distribution in Modern China)* (Beijing: Zhonghua Books, 1992).

Taylor, R. L., *The Cultivation of Sagehood as a Religious Goal in Neo-Confucianism* (Missoula [Mont]: Scholars Press, 1978).

Teng, Ssu-yü, *The Taiping Rebellion and the Western Powers* (Oxford: Clarendon, 1971).

Tian, Fang and Chen Yijun, *Zhongguo Yimin Shilue (Brief History of Migration in China)* (Beijing: Knowledge Press, 1986).

Ting, Ying, 'Zhongguo Zaipei Daozhongde Qiyuan Jiqi Yanbian' (The Origin and Differentiation of Cultivated Rice in China), *Nongye Xuebao (Acta Agriculturae Sinica)*, 8/3 (1957), pp. 243–60.

Tong, Zhuchen, 'Zhongguo Xinshiqi Shidai Wenhuade Duozhong Xi Fazhan Lu He Fazhan Bu Pingheng Lun' (On the Multi-centre Nature and Heterogeneity of the Chinese Neolithic Age), *Wenwu (Cultural Relics)*, 2 (1986), pp. 16–39.

Tuotuo, *Jin Shi (History of the Jin Dynasty)* (Originally published in 1344 AD. Reprint), in *Er-shi-wu Shi (Twenty-Five Official Histories)* (Shanghai: Shanghai Classics Press, 1986).

Tuotuo, *Song Shi* (*History of the Song Dynasty*) (Originally published in 1345 AD. Reprint), in *Er-shi-wu Shi* (*Twenty-Five Official Histories*) (Shanghai: Shanghai Classics Press, 1986).

Twitchett, Denis and P. J. Smith (eds.), *The Cambridge History of China, Vol. 5, Part One* (Cambridge: Cambridge University Press, 2009).

Twitchett, Denis, 'Merchant, Trade and Government in Late T'ang', *Asia Major*, 14/1 (1968), pp. 63–95.

United Nations' Population Division, *World Population Prospects: The 2006 Revision*, available on line at: http://www.un.org/esa/population/publications/wpp2006/wpp2006.htm.

Van Dyke, P. A., *The Canton Trade, Life and Enterprise on the China Coast, 1700–1845* (Hong Kong: Hong Kong University Press, 2005).

Vladimirov, Peter, *The Vladimirov Diaries, Yenan, China: 1942–1945* (New York: Doubleday, 1975).

Von Glahn, Richard, *Fountain of Fortune, Money and Monetary Policy in China, 1000–1700* (Berkeley: University of California Press, 1996).

Voskressenski, A. D., *Russia and China: A Theory of Inter-State Relations* (London: Routledge Curzon, 2003).

Wagner, Donald B., 'The Administration of the Iron Industry in Eleventh-Century China', *Journal of the Economic and Social History of the Orient*, 44/2 (2001), pp. 175–97.

Walder, Andrew, 'Local Government as Industrial Firm: An Organizational Analysis of China's Transitional Economy', *American Journal of Sociology*, 101/2 (1995), pp. 263–301.

Walder, A. G., J. W. Esherick, and P. G. Pickowicz (eds.), *China's Cultural Revolution as History* (Stanford: Stanford University Press, 2006).

Wan, Guoding, 'Han E *Sishi Zuanyao*' (Han E and *Important Rules for the Four Seasons*), *Zhongguo Nongbao* (*Chinese Agricultural Journal*), 11 (1962), p. 33.

Wang, Dezhao, *Qingdai Keju Zhidu Yanjiu* (*A Study of the Civil Examinations of the Qing Dynasty*) (Hong Kong: The Chinese University Press, 1982).

Wang, Gengjin and Zhang Xuansan, *Woguo Nongye Xiandaihua Yu Jilei Wenti Yanjiu* (*Agricultural Modernisation and Capital Accumulation*) (Taiyuan: Shanxi Economy Press, 1993).

Wang, Hao, *Guang Qunfangpu* (*Complete Thesaurus of Botany, Enlarged*) (Originally published in 1708. Reprint. Shanghai: Commercial Press, 1936).

Wang, Jingyu, *Zhongguo Jindai Gongyeshi Ziliao* (*Historical Materials of Early Modern Industries in China*) (Beijing: Sciences Press, 1957).

Wang, Jingyu, *Zhongguo Jindai Jingjishi, 1895–1927* (*An Economic History of Early Modern China, 1895–1927*) (Beijing: People's Press, 2000).

Wang, Jinke and Chen Meijian, 'Zongjie Woguo Gudai Mianhua Zhongzhi Jishu Jingyande Yishu Zhenpin, Mianhuatu Kao' (The Essence of Technology for Cotton Production in Premodern China), *Nongye Kaoku* (*Agricultural Archaeology*), 2 (1982), pp. 157–66.

Wang, Lihua, *Zhongguo Jiating Shi, Diyi Juan* (*A History of Families in China, Vol. 1*) (Guangzhou: Guangdong People's Press, 2007).

Wang, Pu, *Tang Huiyao* (*Complete Record of the Tang Dynasty*) (961 AD).

Wang, Qi, *Xu Wenxian Tongkao* (*Continued Comprehensive Study of Historical Records*) (1586).

Wang, Shengduo, *Liangsong Caizheng Shi* (*A Fiscal History of the Northern and Southern Songs*) (Beijing: Zhonghua Books, 1995).

Wang, Yangming, *Chuanxi Lu* (*Analects for Propagating and Learning Knowledge*) (N.d. Reprint. Zhengzhou: Henan Classics Press, 2008).

Wang, Yejian, *The Database of Grain Prices in the Qing Dynasty* (Institute of Modern History, *Academia Sinica*, 2013), available on line at http://ccts.ascc. net/integration.php?lang=en.

Wang, Yuhu, *Zhongguo Nongxue Shulu* (*Bibliography of Chinese Classical Agronomy*) (Beijing: Agriculture Press, 1964).

Wang, Zhuo, *Tangshuang Pu* (*Treatise on Sugar-making*) (1154 AD).

Wang, Kewen, *Modern China, An Encyclopedia of History, Culture and Nationalism* (New York: Garland Press, 1998).

Wang, Yeh-chien, 'Evolution of the Chinese Monetary System, 1644–1850', in Hou Chi-ming (ed.), *Modern Chinese Economic History* (Taipei: The Institute of Economics, *Academia* Sinica, 1979), pp. 425–56.

Wang, Yeh-chien, *Late Taxation in Imperial China, 1750–1911* (Cambridge [MA]: Harvard University Press, 1973).

Watt, J. R., *The District Magistrate in Late Imperial China* (New York: Columbia University Press, 1972).

Wei, Qingyuan, *Mingqingshi Bianxi* (*Scrutiny of the Ming-Qing History*) (Beijing: China's Social Sciences Press, 1989).

Wei, Shou, *Wei Shu* (*History of the Wei Kingdom*) (Originally published in 554 AD. Reprint. Beijing: Zhonghua Books, 1974).

Wei, Tian-an, *Songdai Guanying Jingji Shi* (*A History of State-owned Sector during the Song Period*) (Beijing: People's Press, 2011).

Wei, C. X. G. and Xiaoyuan Liu, *Exploring Nationalisms of China: Themes and Conflicts* (London and West Port: Greenwood Press, 2002).

Wen, Tiejun, *Zhongguo Nongcun Jiben Jingji Zhidu Yanjiu* (*Basic Institutions in Rural China*) (Beijing: China's Economy Press, 2000).

Whalley, John and Xian Xin, 'China's FDI and Non-FDI Economies and the Sustainability of Future High Chinese Growth', *Working Paper No. 12249* (Cambridge [MA]: National Bureau of Economic Research, 2006).

Wildau, Gabriel, 'China to Cap Local Government Debt', *Finance Times*, 2nd October, 2014, available on line at: www.ft.com/cms/s/0/a2fb9fec-4a18-11e4-8de3-00144feab7de.html#axzz3N1QNwLth.

Will, Pierre-Etienne and R. B. Wong, *Nourish the People: The State Civilian Granary System in China, 1650–1850* (Ann Arbor: University of Michigan Center for Chinese Studies, 1991).

Will, Pierre-Etienne, *Bureaucracy and Famine in Eighteenth-Century China* (Stanford: Stanford University Press, 1990).

Williams, P. F. and Yenna Wu, *The Great Wall of Confinement: The Chinese Prison Camp through Contemporary Fiction and Reportage* (Berkeley: University of California Press, 2004).

Wittfogel, K. A., *Oriental Despotism — A Comparative Study of Total Power* (New Haven: Yale University Press, 1957).

Wong, R. B., *China Transformed, Historical Change and the Limits of European Experience* (Ithaca and London: Cornell University Press, 1997).

Wood, Frances, *Did Marco Polo Go to China?* (London: Secker & Warburg, 1995).

World Bank, *China, Socialist Economic Development* (Washington, D.C.: World Bank, 1983).

World Bank, *World Development Report 2000/2001* (New York: Oxford University Press, 2001).

World Health Organization, *World Health Statistics 2006* (Geneva: WHO, 2006).

Wright, M. C., *The Last Stand of Chinese Conservatism* (Stanford: Stanford University Press, 1957).

Wright, Tim (ed.), *The Chinese Economy in the Early Twentieth Century* (New York: St Martin's Press, 1992).

Wu, Baosan, *Zhongguo Guomin Suode, 1933* (*China's National Income, 1933*) (Shanghai: Zhonghua Books, 1947).

Wu, Chengming, *Zhongguode Xiandaihua: Shichang Yu Shehui* (*China's Modernization: Market and Society*) (Beijing: Sanlian Books, 2001).

Wu, Genyou (ed.), *Sishu Wujing* (*Four Books and Five Classics*) (Beijing: China's Friendship Press, 1993).

Wu, Hui, *Zhongguo Jingjishi Rugan Wentide Jiliang Yanjiu* (*Quantitative Studies of Chinese Economic History*) (Fuzhou: Fujian People's Press, 2009).

Wu, Li, '1949–1978 Nian Zhongguo Jiandaocha Cha-e Bianzheng' (Assessment of the Gain from Scissors Pricing in 1949–1978), *Zhongguo Jingjishi Yanjiu* (*Research into Chinese Economic History*), 4 (2001), pp. 3–12.

Wu, Songdi, *Zhongguo Renkoushi, Disan Juan, Liao, Song, Jin, Yuan Shiqi* (*Demographic History of China: Vol. III, the Liao, Song, Jin and Yuan Periods*) (Shanghai: Fudan University Press, 2000).

Wu, Yumin, *Wuxingde Wangluo* (*The Invisible Network — China's Traditional Culture from the Angle of Communication*) (Beijing: International Culture Press, 1988).

Wu, Silas, *Communication and Imperial Control in China: The Evolution of the Palace Memorial System, 1693–1735* (Cambridge: Harvard University Press, 1970).

Xia, Dongyuan, *Yangwu Yundong Shi* (*A History of the Westernisation Movement*) (Shanghai: East China Normal University Press, 1992).

Xia, Zhengnong (ed.), *Cihai* (*Encyclopaedia*) (Shanghai: Encyclopaedia Publisher, 1989).

Xiao, Xiaoqin and Li Liangzhi, *Zhongguo Geming Shi* (*A History of Revolutions in China*) (Beijing: Red Flag Press, 1983).

Xie, Hui and Chen Jinduo, *Minjian Fa* (*Customary Law*) (Jinan: Shandong People's Press, 2002).

Xing, Tie, *Zhongguo Jiating Shi, Disi Juan* (*A History of Families in China, Vol. 4*) (Guangzhou: Guangdong People's Press, 2007).

Xu, Dixin and Wu Chengming (eds.), *Zhongguo Ziben Zhuyide Mengya* (*Sprouting Capitalism in China*) (Beijing: People's Press, 1985).

Xu, Guangqi's *Nongzheng Quanshu* (*Complete Treatise on Agricultural Administration* (Originally published in 1628. Reprint. Shanghai: Shanghai Classics Press, 1979).

Xu, Jie and Zhang Juzheng, *Ming Shizong Shilu* (*Veritable Records of Emperor Shizong of the Ming*) (Originally published in *c.* 1567. Reprint. Taipei: *Academia Sinica*, 1961).

Xu, Song, *Song Huiyao Jigao* (*Edited Administrative Statutes of the Song Dynasty*) (Originally published in 1809. Reprint. Taipei: Xinwenfeng Press, 1976).

Xu, Tailai, *Yangwu Yundong Xinlun* (Re-examination of the Westernisation Movement) (Changsha: Hunan People's Press, 1986).

Xu, Xinwu, *Jiangnan Tubu Shi* (*A History of Homemade Cotton Cloth in the Lower Yangzi Delta*) (Shanghai: Shanghai Academy of Social Sciences Press, 1989).

Xu, Xuejun, *Shanghai Jindai Shehui Jingji Fazhan Gaikuang, 1882–1931* (*A Survey of Shanghai's Socio-economic Development in Early Modern Times, 1882–1931*) (Shanghai: Shanghai Social Sciences Press, 1985).

Xue, Muqiao, *Xue Muqiao Huiyilu* (*Memoir of Xue Muqiao*) (Tianjin: Tianjin People's Press, 1996).

Xue, Yaling, 'Zhongguo Lishishang Tong Xi Kuangye Fenbude Bianqian' (Distribution of Copper and Tin Mines and its Changes in China's History), *Zhongguo Jingjishi Yanjiu* (*Research in Chinese Economic History*), 4 (2001), pp. 102–6.

Yan, Wenming, 'Zhongguo Daozuo Nongyede Qiyuan' (The Origin of Rice Cultivation in China), *Nongye Kaogu* (*Agricultural Archaeology*), 1 (1982), pp. 19–31.

Yan, Zhongping, 'Shilun Zhongguo Maiban Zichanjiejide Fasheng' (Emergence of the Comprador Class in China), *Zhongguo Jingjishi Yanjiu* (*Research into Chinese Economic History*), 1 (1986), pp. 85–93.

Yan, Zhongping, 'Shilun Zhongguo Maiban Zichanjiejide Fasheng' (Emergence of the Comprador Class in China), *Zhongguo Jingjishi Yanjiu* (*Research into Chinese Economic History*), 1 (1986), pp. 81–98.

Yan, Zhongping, *Zhongguo Jindai Jingjishi Ziliao Xuanji* (*Selected Statistical Materials of Economic History of Early Modern China*) (Beijing: Sciences Press, 1955).

Yang, Jisheng, *Mubei — Zhongguo Liushi Niandai Dajihuang Jishi* (*Gravestone for the Great Leap Famine Victims, Evidence from History*) (Hong Kong: Tiandi, 2008).

Yang, Ling, *Songdai Chuban Wenhua* (*Printing Culture of the Song Period*) (Beijing: Cultural Relics Press, 2012).

Yang, Qing, *Yin Lun* (*On Silver*) (1865).

Yang, Shiqi, *Ming Chengzu Shilu* (*Veritable Records of Emperor Chengzu of the Ming Dynasty*) (Originally published in *c.* 1425. Reprint. Taipei: *Academia Sinica*, 1966).

Yang, Yong, 'Jingdai Jiangnan Diandangyede Shehui Zhuanxing' (Transition of the Pawning Sector in Early Modern Jiangnan), *Shixue Yuekan* (*Study of History Monthly*), 5 (2005), pp. 102–8.

Yang, Yonggang, *Zhongguo Jindai Tielu Shi* (*A History of Railways in Early Modern China*) (Shanghai: Shanghai Books, 1997).

Yang, Zhimei, *Zhongguo Gudai Guanzhi Jiangzuo* (*Bureaucracy of Premodern China*) (Beijing: Zhonghua Books, 1992).

Yang, Zihui (ed.), *Zhongguo Lidai Renkou Tongji Ziliao Yanjiu* (*China's Historical Population Statistics in the Long Run*) (Beijing: Reforms Press, 1996).

Yao, Hanyuan, *Zhongguo Shuili Fazhanshi* (*Development in Water Control in China*) (Shanghai: Shanghai People's Press, 2005).

Ye, Tan, 'Songdai Gongshangye Fazhangde Lishi Tezheng' (Features of Development in Handicrafts and Commerce during the Song Period), *Shanghai Shehui Kexueyuan Xueshu Jikan* (*Academic Quarterly of the Shanghai Academy of Social Sciences*), 2 (1991), pp. 103–11.

Yinhang Zhoubao (*Baking Weekly*) (Shanghai).

Yoshihara, Kunio, *Japanese Economic Development: A Short Introduction* (Tokyo: Oxford University Press, 1979).

Yu, Dechang, *Nonghu Jingji Xingwei Ji Laodong Shijian Liyong Tiaocha Ziliaoji* (*Survey Data for Rural Households' Economic Behaviour and Labour Input Patterns*) (Beijing: China's Statistical Press, 1992).

Yu, Guangyuan (ed.), *China's Socialist Modernization* (Beijing: Foreign Language Press, 1984).

Yu, Xinzhong, *Zhongguo Jiating Shi, Disi Juan* (*A History of Families in China, Vol. 4*) (Guangzhou: Guangdong People's Press, 2007).

Yu, Yaohua, *Zhongguo Jiage Shi* (*A History of Prices in China*) (Beijing: China's Prices Press, 2000).

Yuan, Gang, *Zhongguo Gudai Zhengfu Jigou Shezhi Yange* (*Evolution of the State Apparatus in Premodern China*) (Harbin: Heilongjiang People's Press, 2003).

Yuan, Yida and Zhang Cheng, *Zhongguo Xingshi: Qunti Yichuan He Renko Fenbu* (*Chinese Surnames: Group Genetics and Demographic Distribution*) (Shanghai: East China Normal University Press, 2002).

Zelin, Madeleine, 'The Rights of Tenants in Mid-Qing Sichuan: A Study of Land-Related Lawsuits in the Baxian Archives', *Journal of Asian Studies*, 45/3 (1986), pp. 499–526.

Zeng, Guofan, *Zeng Wenzhenggong Quanji, Wenji* (*Complete Collection of Master Zeng Guofan's Works, Essays*) (N.d. Reprint. Taipei: Wenhai Press, 1966–83).

Zeng, Xiongsheng, 'Songdaide Shuangji Dao' (Double-cropping of Rice in the Song Period), *Ziran Kexueshi Yanjiu* (*Study of History of Natural Sciences*), 21/3 (2002), pp. 255–68.

Zhang, Bincun, 'Shiliu Shiji Zhoushan Qundaode Zousi Maoyi' (Illegal Trade Activities from Zhoushan Archipelago during the Sixteenth Century), in Editing Committee for *Maritime History of China* (ed.), *Zhongguo Haiyang Fazhanshi Lunwenji* (*Selected Essays on the Maritime History of China*) (Taipei: *Academia* Sinica, 1984), Vol. 1, pp. 71–95.

Zhang, Daoge, 'Bufen Xianfude Gaige Xiaoying' (Effect of 'Allowing a Few to Become Rich First'), *Xinhua Wenzhai* (*Xinhua Compilation*), 4 (1994), p. 41.

Zhang, Dechang, 'Qingdai Yapian Zhanzheng Qianzhi Zhongxi Yanhai Tongshang' (Sino-Western Maritime Trade in Qing Times Prior to the Opium Wars), *Qinghua Xuebao* (*Bulletin of Qinghua University*), 10/1 (1935), pp. 97–145.

Zhang, Deze, *Qingdai Guojia Jiguan Kaolue* (*The State Apparatus of the Qing Period*) (Beijing: Xueyuan, 2001).

Zhang, Donggang, 'Shipin Jiegou He Yingyang Jiegou: 20 Shiji Er-sanshi Niandai Yige Zhongguo Guomin Shehui Shenghuode Shizheng Fenxi' (Dietary Structure and Nutrition Structure: Analysis of Social Life in China in the 1920s and 30s), *Zhongguo Jingjishi Yanjiu* (*Research into Chinese Economic History*), 4 (2007), pp. 13–22.

Zhang, Donggang, *Zhongguo Jiating Shi, Dier Juan* (*A History of Families in China, Vol. 2*) (Guangzhou: Guangdong People's Press, 2007).

Zhang, Doqing, *Zhongguo Jingjishi Cidian* (*Encyclopaedia of Chinese Economic History*) (Wuhan: Hubei Books, 1990).

Zhang, Guogang, *Zhongguo Jiating Shi, Dier Juan* (*A History of Families in China, Vol. 2*) (Guangzhou: Guangdong People's Press, 2007).

Zhang, Haiying, *Mingqing Jiangnan Shangpin Liutong Yu Shichang Tixi* (*Commodity Flows and Market Structure in the Jiangnan Region during the Ming-Qing Period*) (Shanghai: East China Normal University Press, 2001).

Zhang, Hua and Su Caiqing (eds.), *Huizhou Wedge, Zhongguo Simian Wedge Benxi Yu Fans* (*Recollection of the Decade of Cultural Revolution, Analyses and Soul-Researching*) (Beijing: Chinese Communist Party History Press, 2000).

Zhang, Huixin, 'Yinliangde Pingse Ji Mingcheng' (Qualities and Names of Silver), *Gugong Wenwu Yuekan* (*Palace Museum Cultural Relics Monthly*) (Taipei), 52 (1987), p. 130.

Zhang, Jiacheng, *Qihou Yu Renlei* (*Climate and Humankind*) (Zhengzhou: Henan Science and Technology Press, 1988).

Zhang, Jiayan, 'Mingqing Jianghan Pingyuande Nongye Kaifa Dui Shangren Huodong He Shizhen Fazhande Yingxiang' (Impact of Agricultural Development in the Yangzi-Han Plain on Commercial Activities and Urbanization during the Ming–Qing Period), *Zhongguo Nongshi* (*Agricultural History of China*), 4 (1995), pp. 40–6.

Zhang, Limin, 'Chuang Guandong Yiminchao Jianxi' (Advancing to Manchuria), *Zhongguo Shehui Jingjishi Yanjiu* (*Study of Chinese Socio-Economic History*), 2 (1998), pp. 57–64.

Zhang, Renshan, *Li, Fa, Shehui* (*Rights, Laws and Society*) (Tianjin: Tianjin Classics Press, 2002).

Zhang, Shaoliang and Zheng Xianjin, *Zhongguo Nongmin Geming Douzhengshi* (*A History of Revolutionary Struggle of the Chinese Peasantry*) (Beijing: Qiushi Press, 1983).

Zhang, Tingyu, *Ming Shi* (*History of the Ming Dynasty*) (Originally published in 1735. Reprint. Beijing: Zhonghua Books, 1974).

Zhang, Wei (ed.), *Shengtong Shi* (*The Song Prodigy's Poem on Schooling*) (Beijing: Zhonghua Books, 2013).

Zhang, Xiangshu, Zhou Wenbin, and Zhou Wenbiao, *Zhongguo Nongye Jubian Yu Zhanlue Xuanze* (*Huge Changes in and Strategic Choices for China's Agriculture*) (Beijing: China's Price Press, 1993).

Zhang, Xie, *Dongxiyang Kao* (*A Comprehensive Maritime History*) (Originally published in 1616. Reprint. Beijing: Zhonghua Books, 1981).

Zhang, Yufa, *Qingjide Lixian Tuanti* (*Societies for Constitutional Changes during the Qing*) (Taipei: Academia Sinica, 1971).

Zhang, K. H., 'Foreign Direct Investment and Economic Growth in China: A Panel Data Study for 1992–2004', A Paper for 'WTO, China and Asian Economies Conference', the University of International Business and Economies, Beijing, June, 2006.

Zhao, Deqin, 'Zhongguo Jingji Wushinian Fazhande Lujing Jieduan Yu Jiben Jingyan' (Path, Stages and Main Lessons from the 50-Year Long Growth of the Chinese Economy), *Zhongguo Jingjishi Yanjiu* (*Study of Chinese Economic History*), 1 (2000), pp. 73–86.

Zhao, Dexin, *Zhongguo Jingjishi Cidian* (*Dictionary of Chinese Economic History*) (Wuhan: Hubei Dictionary Press, 1990).

Zhao, Erxun, *Qingshi Gao* (*Draft of the History of the Qing Dynasty*) (Originally published in 1927. Reprint. Beijing: Zhonghua Books, 1977).

Zhao Gang and Chen Zhongyi, *Zhongguo Tudi Zhidu Shi* (*A History of Land Ownership in China*) (Beijing: New Star Press, 2006).

Zhao, Gesheng, Lai Laizhan and Zheng Jingui, *Zhongguo Tezhong Dao* (*Sorted Rice Types in China*) (Shanghai, 1995).

Zhao, Hongjun and Yin Bocheng, 'Gongyuan 11 Shijihoude Qihou Bianleng Dui Songyihou Jingji Fazhande Dongtai Yingxiang' (Dynamic Impact of Cooling Down in Climate after the Eleventh Century on Economic Development in Post-Song China), *Shehui Kexue* (*Social Sciences*), 4 (2011), pp. 68–78.

Zhao, Lianfa, *Zhongguo Diandangshi Shuping* (*Survey of the Pawning Sector in China*) (Taipei: Stone House Press, 1978).

Zhao, Rukuo (Zhao Rushi), *Zhufan Zhi* (*Records of Foreign Peoples*) (Originally published in 1225. Reprint. Beijing: Zhonghua Books, 1956).

Zhao, Tongmao, 'Zhonghua Minzu Qiyuandide Xin Tansuo' ('A New Inquiry into the Original Regions of the Chinese'), *Dazong Yixue* (*Popular Medical Science*), 3 (1986), pp. 5–6.

Zhao, Xiukun, Tian Shaolin, Heshaoheng, Cai Zhipu, He Shouquan, Wei Zhenfu and Zhang Jiyin, *Zhongguo Junshi Shi* (*A Military History of China*) (Beijing: PLA Press, 1987).

Zhao, Xiukun, Tian Zhaolin, Kang Ning, Tao Wenhuan, Shi Shibi, Chen Yangping, Zhu Ansheng, Xu Fei, Zhang Chunyi and Zhang Shufang, *Zhongguo Junshishi* (*A Military History of China*) (Beijing: PLA Press, 1991).

Zhao, Xuezhang (ed.), *Yong Baozhi Xie Lishi, Jiefanghou* (*History Seen on Newspapers, pre-1949*) (Taipei: Seadove Publishing Co., 2007).

Zhao, Yi, *Gaiyu Congkao* (*Reading Notes While Looking after Parents*) (Originally published in 1772. Reprint. Beijing: Zhonghua Books, 1963).

Zhao, Yun, 'Jishu Wucha, Zhemu Jiqi Juli Shuaijian Guilü Yanjiu' (Technical Errors: Land Unit Conversion and the Law of Diminishing Distance), *Zhongguo Shehui Jingjishi Yanjiu* (*Research in Chinese Social and Economic History*), 3 (2007), pp. 1–13.

Zheng, Quanhong, *Zhongguo Jiating Shi, Diwu Juan* (*A History of Families in China, Vol. 5*) (Guangzhou: Guangdong People's Press, 2007).

Zheng, Xuemeng, Jiang Zhaocheng and Zhang Wenqi, *Jianming Zhongguo Jingji Tongshi* (*A Brief Panorama of Chinese Economic History*) (Harbin: Heilongjiang People's Press, 1984).

Zheng, Xuemeng, *Zhongguo Gudai Jingji Zhongxin Nanyi He Tangsong Jiangnan Jingji Yanjiu* (Southward Shift of China's Economic Centre of Gravity and the Economy of the Lower Yangzi Delta during the Tang and Song Periods) (Changsha: Yuelu Books, 1996).

Zheng, Yukui, *Zhongguo Duiwai Maoyi He Gongye Fazhan* (*Growth in China's Foreign Trade and Industry*) (Shanghai: Shanghai Social Sciences Press, 1984).

Zheng, Zhaojing, *Zhongguo Shuili Shi* (*History of Water Control in China*) (Taipei: Taiwan Commercial Press, 1970).

Zheng, Ziming, *Zhongguo Lidaide Xianzheng* (*County Administration in Premodern China*) (Shanghai: Cangjie Publishing Co, 1938).

Zhong, Dajun, *Guomin Daiyu Bupingdeng Shenshi* (*Assessment of Unequal Entitlement amongst Citizens*) (Beijing: China's Workers' Press, 2002).

Zhong, Xiangcai, 'Zhongguo Gudai Nongye Guanli Sixiang Shulun' (On the Thought of the Agricultural Administration in Ancient China), *Zhongguo Nongshi* (*Chinese Agricultural History*), 4 (1985), pp. 1–10.

Zhongguo Wenhua Yanjiusuo (The Institute for the Advanced Chinese Studies) (ed.), *Zhongwen Dacidian* (*An Encyclopaedic Dictionary of the Chinese Language*) (Taipei: Institute of Chinese Culture, 1962–8).

Zhou, Bodi, *Zhongguo Caizheng Shi* (*A History of State Finance in China*) (Shanghai: Shanghai People's Press, 1981).

Zhou, Hui, *Jinling Suoshi Shenglu* (*More on Everyday Life in Nanjing*) (Originally published in 1610. Reprint. Beijing: Literature and Classics Press, 1955).

Zhou, Qufei, *Lingwai Daida* (*Knowledge about South China and Beyond*), in Ji Jun (ed.), *Wenyuange Siku Quanshu* (*The Qing Imperial Complete Collection of Books in the Wenyuan Library*) (Originally published in 1178. Reprint. Taipei: Taiwan Commercial Press, 1983).

Zhu, Delan, 'Qingchu Qianjieling Shi Zhongguo Chuan Haishang Maoyizhi Yanjiu' (On Trade Activities of Chinese Ships under the Qing Law of Anti-maritime Immigration from the Coastal Region), in Editing Committee for *Maritime History of China* (ed.), *Zhongguo Haiyang Fazhanshi Lunwenji* (*Selected Essays on the Maritime History of China*) (Taipei: Academia Sinica, 1986), pp. 110–35.

Zhu, Jiefan, *Zhongguo Nongyan* (*Traditional Chinese Farmers' Proverbs*) (Originally published in 1941. Reprint. Taipei: Tianyi Press, 1974).

Zhu, Kezhen, 'Woguo Jinwuqiannianlai Qihou Bianqiande Chubu Yanjiu' (Preliminary Analysis of Climatic Changes in China in the Past 5,000 Years), *Kaogu Xuebao* (*Bulletin of Archaeology*), 1 (1972), pp. 15–38.

Zhu, Xi, *Yu Lei* (*Philosophical Analects*) (Publisher unknown, 1200 AD).

Zong, Fengming, *Zhao Ziyang Ruanjinzhongde Tanhua* (*Conversations with Zhao Ziyang under House Arrest*) (Hong Kong: Open Press, 2007).

Index